¡SOME PEOPLE!

ROBERT LIMA

¡SOME PEOPLE!

Anecdotes, Images and Letters of Persons of Interest

O

THE **ORLANDO** PRESS

ISBN 978-0-940804-05-0

THE ORLANDO PRESS
485 Orlando Avenue
State College, PA 16803-3477
USA

¡SOME PEOPLE!

ACKNOWLEDGEMENTS

The following anecdotes first appeared as indicated:

"Nicanor Parra" in *Latin American Literary Review* (Pittsburgh. PA), Spring 1973.

"(Dylan Thomas) The Bard of Laugharne" in *The Centre Daily Times* (State College, PA), October 19, 2014.

"Antonio Buero Vallejo" in *Estreno* (Lubbock, TX), Spring 2015.

"José Martín Recuerda" in *Estreno* (Lubbock, TX), Spring 2015.

"William Carlos Williams. A Loss of Words." In *Poetry Bay* (Long Island, NY), Fall 2012.

Covers Designed by Keith Lima

ENCOUNTERS IN NEW YORK

I have been fortunate in my life as poet, critic, speaker, professor, and traveler to meet numerous interesting, even fascinating, people, in the fields of writing, art, music, theatre, religion, sport, and publishing. These encounters began in New York City, my home for twenty years.

I came to The City for the first time in 1945, shortly before the end of World War II. It was at night and, from the Lincoln Tunnel ramp in New Jersey, New York City was the most fabulous sight this nine-year-old Cuban immigrant had ever seen. "Baghdad on the Hudson," I would learn, was O. Henry's awed name for that spectacle of steel, masonry and glass aglow with endless lights. This was the place that nurtured me and opened my eyes to the American Experience. The City taught me "street smarts" and stick ball on 98th Street off Amsterdam Avenue, made me an addict of the Sabrett Frankfurters sold from pushcarts in midtown Manhattan, and imparted the ecumenical lesson that "You don't have to be Jewish to love Levy's," especially when the rye bread accompanied a deli's hot pastrami at The Stage Deli midtown or Katz's Deli on the Lower East Side.

I loved New York long before the slogan was invented and it was my "Big Apple" in the early 1960s when I returned there fresh out of military service at Fort Dix, New Jersey and became a regular on the poetry scene–coffeehouses, lofts, galleries, church halls–in Greenwich Village and its environs, what came to be known as the East Village. It was there I sought to fulfill a dream that had its inception during school days, through college, and that had been rekindled during my days of active duty in the Army.

Before heading back to New York City on different days after completing our military commitment, Allen Planz, Don Katzman and I agreed to meet in Greenwich Village the following week, there to plan our establishing a beachhead on the poetry front. It was an exciting prospect that the three of us relished even more in the headiness of our new-found freedom from military cares. For me, it would be the opportunity to empower my intent of pursuing a life in poetry, kindled by Marvin Bell in 1959 when he published "Chant," the first poem I had submitted to a poetry journal, in *statements*. The place of my military service in the larger scheme of things suddenly made sense.

Allen took us to Café (also Caffè) Cino. It was the spring of 1960. Founded in 1958 by Joe Cino (d. 1967), Café Cino was a diminutive Greenwich Village place just off Sixth Avenue at 31 Cornelia Street. Because of its location and atmosphere, the coffeehouse was a showcase for poetry and early improvised theatre events called "happenings." Café Cino was also the birthplace of "café theatre" and its intimate productions, including the original "Dames at Sea," even had an influence in Europe. A young Sam Shepherd got his start as a playwright at Café Cino in the early 1960s, as did Lanford Wilson with "Balm in Gilead," and Al Pacino made his acting debut there in 1963 in William Saroyan's "Hello Out There," directed by Charles Laughton.

We also sought to make our debuts at Café Cino. The impressive collage wall behind the espresso machine provided the proper setting for three fledgling poets to ease into the poetry-reading scene. Actually, for Allen, it was a return rather than an initiation since he had been there before his stint in the Army.

We brought poetry to read but soon found that we were spectators rather than participants. The coffeehouse, it turned out, was already committed to a coterie of somewhat established poets–Robert Kelly, Armand Schwerner, George Economou, Rochelle Owens, David Antin, Jerome Rothenberg, among others–and there was a reluctance to permit readings by anyone outside the group. Each of us did manage occasional appearances on the stage of the Cino, but these were, at best, tokens to placate our gnat-like persistence.

There were other reasons for our continued attendance at the Café Cino. We met any number of poets and other writers there, some, like ourselves, with the same need for public expression: others, unlike us, already well along in their creative writing careers ("upwardly-mobile," to borrow the later phrase). Among the latter were Denise Levertov (1923-1997) and David Ignatow (1914-1997).

No matter the level of accomplishment or lack thereof, we were all in need of a stage that could be ours whenever we wanted it. The Café Cino did not provide that outlet and so we resorted to pick-up readings wherever we could, even while walking along the street with a friend. Soon, there would be a new venue for our creative expression.

We found the right place in the fall of 1960. Mickey Ruskin and Ed Kaplan had just opened the Tenth Street Coffeehouse, located between Third and Fourth Avenues, and welcomed the idea of poetry readings that Howard Ant and Ree Dragonette had put to Mickey. Suddenly, we had our stage, and the readings were open to all comers. If a poet wanted to read, he or she went to Howard, who put the name on a schedule and acted unobtrusively as m.c. Subject only to a time limit and the number of poems that could be read, a poet was free to read, recite or perform whatever he or she wished. This procedure liberated the audience from the oppression of the endless poem, although at times we paid for our freedom by listening to trash of a different sort, as when Cassius Clay jabbed abominably with his doggerel. Still, most of what was read there was good. But Tenth Street Coffeehouse had its disadvantages, the principal one from our perspective being its size. Smaller than the Cino, or so it seemed because of its layout, it did not accommodate our growing group very well. It was particularly tight when someone the size of a Robert Kelly or with the oversize reputation and the Beat entourage of an Allen Ginsberg entered the premises; it was all Mickey could do to keep the walls of the café from exploding. There were many tight fits, along with the blend of smells from espresso machines, odorant bodies, and sidewalk-piled garbage that attacked the nasal passages relentlessly, especially on hot, humid New York nights when the door had to be kept open despite the intrusion of external smells. Something had to give.

The solution was not exactly around the corner but nearby. In June of 1961 Mickey Ruskin and Ed Kaplan, later joined by Bill Mackey, opened another coffeehouse, this time on East Seventh Street, not far from the fabled McSorley's Old Ale House, founded in 1854 and "home" to Max Bodenheim, "the last of the bohemians." The new place was named "Les Deux Mégots" in apparent homage to (or takeoff on) the old Parisian café "Les Deux Magots," even if a mispainted letter changed the meaning of our café's sign to "Two Cigarette Stubs." It was at this East Village coffeehouse that our group of writers found its real abode. Its entrance, a few steps down from the sidewalk, was flanked by plate glass windows behind each of which was a small table and two chairs for intimate encounters.

The open readings continued to be held on weekday evenings and the rules set up at Tenth Street continued to apply in the larger, more accommodating setting. Three or four steps below the sidewalk, we weren't exactly underground but sufficiently removed from street level to be more in our own milieu than ever before. The space was infinitely better, the air seemed more breathable, the poetry more appealing to the ear. Sometimes on Wednesdays, sometimes on Sundays, individual poets were invited to read, either singly or in a shared situation. Among the better-known who participated were Paul Blackburn, LeRoi Jones (only much later was he to become Amiri Baraka), Barbara Holland, Louis Zukofsky, Muriel Rukeyser and Denise Levertov, along with an occasional visitor to the city such as Robert Bly, then known largely as a publisher (*The Fifties*, *The Sixties*) and translator. In short course, "Les Deux Mégots" became the focus of the New York City poetry scene. Even the Café Cino poets began to read at the new coffeehouse. And the list grew on.

There were other venues in which I met interesting people. The first was in the world of publishing. At Las Américas, a publishing house cum bookstore founded by the genial and near-legendary Gaetano Massa, the worlds of writers, artists and academics came together. Every Hispanist in New York patronized the place and many Spanish and Spanish American writers visited when in the city. It was there that I met Robert O'Brien, with whom I collaborated on *Spanish Plays in English Translation* and projects for the magazine *La Voz*. With him I did a stint at T.Y. Crowell, where we worked for Gorton Carruth and Edward Tripp on such projects as the revisions of Benet's *The Reader's Encyclopedia of American Literature* and Roget's

International Thesaurus. I also did a stint at NYU Press, through the good graces of Robert Clements, selecting for publication, translating and editing A.M. Barrenechea's doctoral thesis, which I retitled *Borges the Labyrinth Maker*, the first critical study in English on the Argentine writer.

Then there was the film industry, where I learned the trade by splicing film, schlepping negatives to labs for processing, sitting-in on audio sessions, setting up lights, toting sound equipment, driving the crew to the sites... I worked at Pendulum Productions, on West 45th Street in the heart of Manhattan, learning how to produce documentaries and in-house films with the principals of the company, John Scudder Boyd, who, as word had it, had been tested for the role of Captain Kangaroo in a brief earlier avatar, and Gene Searchinger, whose claim to fame was that his wife was the literary agent Marian. The fact that in his absence I'd been hired as a writer by his partner bothered Searchinger, who wrote all the material and saw me as an intruder; we soon parted company at his behest.

My next life came about through the intervention of Pendulum's sales manager, who saw my plight at being without a job and contacted a friend at U.S.I.A. It was through his efforts that I was hired at the Voice of America in New York City, there to co-produce Spanish and Portuguese language programming under the guidance of Tony Jiménez and to record events at the United Nations, the New York Press Club and elsewhere for later broadcast. I met numerous diplomats, foreign correspondents and government officials in those venues.

Then, at the recommendation of my publisher Gaetano Massa, I began teaching at Hunter College of the City University of New York, at the time an exclusive women's college. I taught with the exiled Spanish jurist and critic Emilio González López, and began concurrent doctoral studies at New York University with three other noted Spanish exiles, the sociologist and novelist Francisco Ayala, the critic Joaquín Casalduero and the poet-critic Ernesto Guerra da Cal. It was at Hunter that I met Randall Jarrell and heard Robert Frost's last public reading.

New York City in the 1960s gave me the opportunity to meet many interesting and notable people, the writers of poetry and fiction, literary critics, publishers, academics, dramatists and actors, booksellers, musicians, painters, and composers who were a part of the cultural scene, especially in Greenwich Village and the adjacent East Side venue. Later, on leaving the city to teach at Penn State University in the center of the commonwealth, I encountered Paul West and other notables from all over the world, many of whom I hosted and introduced at university lectures and readings, among them Sir Walter Starkie, Jorge Luis Borges, Jorge Amado, Gregory Rabassa, Roberto González Echevarría, Gwendolyn Brooks, Willis Barnstone, William Empson, Raymond McNally, David Ignatow, Denise Levertov, John Barth... One of the most rewarding of these events was Surrealism–A Celebration, which I conceived and directed on the 50th anniversary of the revolutionary cultural movement, and which brought together David Hare, Marcel Jean, Julien Levy, Bernard Pfriem, Anna Balakian, and William Cply, among many, many other painters, writers, art historians, and literary critics. Of course, the spirit of André Breton hovered at all gatherings and art exhibits.

Travels in Africa and Asia proved fruitful in providing opportunities to meet prominent people in the cultural and political life of the nations visited. Numerous stays in Spain and Central and South America afforded occasions to encounter a diverse group of individuals: the Spanish playwrights Antonio Buero Vallejo, Lauro Olmo, José Martín Recuerda, José María Rodríguez Méndez, Francisco Nieva, and the critic José Monleón; the Brazilian novelist Jorge Amado and numerous practitioners of Candomble; the Peruvians, novelist Mario Vargas Llosa, poets Antonio Cisneros and Washington Delgado, as well as critic and APRA political leader Luis Alberto Sánchez. Many other names could be added to the list.

From such personal contacts over more than forty years, I have culled what follows, the anecdotes and correspondence that I feel are most representative of the variety of meaningful human encounters I've experienced, people whose interaction with me in person or through letters has proven to be instructive, uplifting, entertaining (or, in a few instances, negative). The individuals whose anecdotes and letters are presented here come largely from Latin America, the United States and Europe. These narratives are of varying length but, brief or long, they depict my recollection of individuals who have stayed in my memory and somehow shaped a moment in my life. Meeting them was fortunate for me. I see no need to exalt some of certain renown who have crossed my path but have proven less than worthy of attention; better to let them stew over their omission from these pages, should they come across this book. If not, perhaps some kind soul will inform them of their exclusion.

I trust that the reading of these anecdotes and letters will contribute to the knowledge of the individuals concerned and perhaps bring out elements in their lives not otherwise available to their biographers, present or future.

Robert Lima

I

ANECDOTES

II

CORRESPONDENCE

I
ANECDOTES

HAROLD ALTMAN

Etching of the Artist

While teaching at the Beaver Campus of The Pennsylvania State University, I came up with the idea of putting on an art show that would feature area artists and university art professors. The campus, which had opened in 1965 with an inaugural faculty of ten and one hundred students, needed some visibility in the environs of culture-rich Pittsburgh. The show was hung and became a reality on May 22, 1966.

The success of that first venture prompted me to reach higher the following year. Among the first artists I contacted was Harold Altman, who was at the University Park Campus of Penn State. I did not know him personally but I had heard of his reputation as an etcher and lithographer of fine prints whose works were in many private collections and museums. When I contacted him he had already had one-man exhibits in Paris, New York, Chicago, Mexico City, San Francisco, Santa Barbara, Los Angeles, and in group shows in Basel, Spoleto, New York, and Santiago de Chile, among many others.

Despite his stature in the field, Harold readily agreed to send some of his pieces for the exhibit. I was amazed when 24 of them arrived! He was also instrumental in getting his colleague George Zoretich to agree to participate. Thanks to him, I had a solid group of artists at the core of the exhibit. Soon, New York, New Jersey, Pittsburgh and Philadelphia area painters, sculptors and photographers joined the group, among the most distinguished being Mildred Dillon, Rose Graubart, Burton Wasserman and George Nama. The catalog bore Altman's "Five Figures" (1965) on its covers.

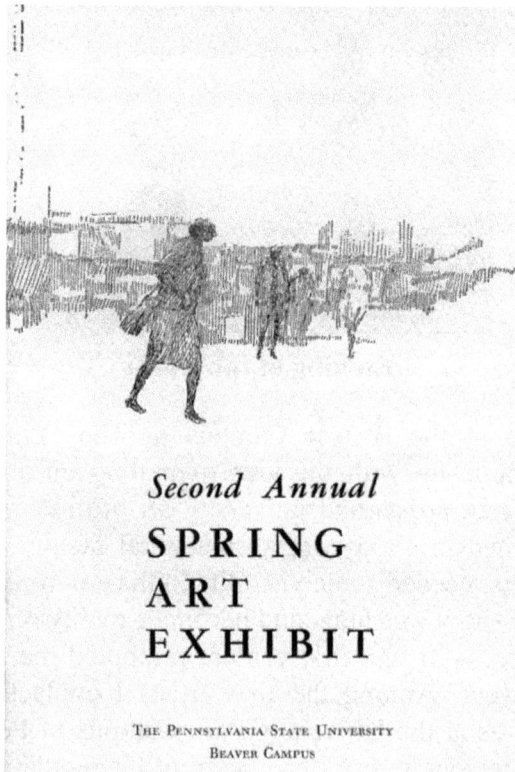

Second Annual

SPRING
ART
EXHIBIT

THE PENNSYLVANIA STATE UNIVERSITY
BEAVER CAMPUS

Although the exhibit area was less than ideal–a long hallway in the only building (a former TB sanatorium)–we hung the show and opened it to public view on April 8, 1967. The exhibit received excellent reviews in the local media.

When I transferred to University Park in 1967, I became friends with Harold. And in 1968, when I chaired the art, film and poetry events at The Central Pennsylvania Festival of the Arts, Harold and his colleagues were there to help me make a success of the show– by submitting their works to the Juried Art Exhibition and by participating in the Sidewalk Art Sale.

With such a talented cadre of artists, the two-week event was hugely successful. And, what's more, it was a very democratic event for alongside the likes of Harold Altman were exhibitors of lesser fame and talent.

In time, other hands took over the CPFA and worked it into a different mold, excluding many local artists. Although Harold was invited to exhibit by the later organizers, he was indignant at the exclusion of large numbers of painters, sculptors and crafts people in favor of those who traveled the "circuit" of art festivals throughout the US. I greatly missed his presence at his corner near the university gates and the conversations we had on those earlier occasions, albeit through interruptions whenever a comely lass passed by or stopped to view his works (and the bearded man with the welcoming eyes?). He had been the sage of the sidewalk exhibits.

When he retired from teaching in 1978, he was named Professor Emeritus by Penn State. But Harold did not sit on the proverbial laurels. He continued to work in the US and abroad, notably in France where his prints were "pulled" first at Atelier George LeBlance and later at Atelier Des Jobert, both in Paris. On one occasion when I encountered him on campus, he informed me with great amazement in his voice: "I've become a millionaire since I retired." He had always been concerned about money for he had three ex-wives and his children to support.

Now that Harold has passed (July 28, 2003), I regret not having spent more time in his company. During our first years of friendship, I had been in his studio in Pine Grove Mills and there listened as he explained his etching technique; later he had shown me his prints and I purchased two of them ("Table" and "Three Trees"). He had also visited my house, approving of the way I had his works matted, framed and displayed. On other occasions, I visited his studio in the nineteenth-century frame church in Lemont; this was the home of his Lemont Editions, which continues to be the sole distributor of his works under his son Toby.

The last time that I saw Harold was at the Lemont Post Office, near his studio home. Both of us bearded and grey-haired, we exchanged a few words only as we were both rushing off to do other errands. Harold seemed a tired old man (he was eleven years my senior) who was in need of social involvement. I suggested that we get together, and he agreed to meet for lunch in the very near future. That opportunity never came. Born in 1924, he died in 2003.

Harold is never very far, however. Walking the streets of State College, Pennsylvania I see his works on display in the several art galleries and stores. Sometimes, while visiting New York City, I happen on a window displaying his work. Then there are always the museums: New York's Museum of Modern Art, the Whitney and the Brooklyn each own over fifty of his pieces in their permanent collections. If in London, Amsterdam, Paris, Basel, or Copenhagen, I can find his works in the leading museums of those cities. And in my home.

JORGE AMADO

Oba of Candomble

In 1971 I had had occasion to review Jorge Amado's newest novel to appear in English, *Tent of Miracles*, translated by Barbara Shelby. The review appeared in *The Philadelphia Bulletin*, in the August 22, 1971 issue of the newspaper. And then, not long thereafter, the noted Brazilian novelist, creator of *Dona Flor and Her Two Husbands*, was in residence during the Fall Semester of 1971 as a Visiting Fellow of the Institute for the Arts and Humanistic Studies at Penn State University.

His visit had been arranged through my colleague Gerald Moser, who devoted himself to Brazilian and Portuguese studies. Jorge Amado was accompanied by his wife Zelia Gattai, who had a fine reputation as a photographer. A group of us from various disciplines interested in coordinating his visit met on September 16th. We planned a rather full program of activities for the Amados, including a reception on September 30th in the Rare Books Room of Pattee

Library, where his works and papers would be on display throughout his stay, several informal luncheons with faculty and students, and visits to classes in Spanish and Comparative Literature.

**THE AMADOS IN FRONT OF
IHLSENG COTTAGE, IAHS**

In my course, Comparative Literature 120, The Literature of the Occult, he addressed the subject of *Candomble*, the Brazilian religious tradition derived from the Yoruba beliefs in Nigeria and other areas of West Africa; although white, Amado was a practitioner and had become an *oba* or lay minister in Salvador de Bahia; he knew all the *terreiros* (temples) and *maes do santos* (priestesses). It was from that insider's perspective that he had written about the Afro-Brazilian belief system in many of his novels.

JORGE AMADO AT PATTEE LIBRARY

On November 10th, the Department of Spanish, Italian & Portuguese presented Än Evening with Jorge Amado." The Kern Graduate Auditorium was the site for Amado's selected readings in Portuguese from his novels, while seated next to Moser, and the readings of the same passages in English by Robert Lima, Jo C. Searles and Croy Pitzer standing at the podium. Moser served as translator for Jorge Amado's comments throughout the evening. Prior to the reading, I met with Amado at the Institute for the Arts and Humanistic Studies to go over the presentations.

THE REHEARSAL

THE READING

With Jorge Amado and Zelia life was always a party. Many of us held festive gatherings at our homes in their honor–sit-down dinners, buffets, cocktails. Alfred Schmidt, for one, held a memorable dance party that resulted in the floors of his house visibly vibrating as the enthusiasm of the revelers snaked through the premises to the samba beat. Sally and I hosted a dinner for Jorge and Zelia at our home and they came bearing gifts from Brazil: finely-sculpted figure of a Black man smoking a pipe, a piece from Goiana, state of Pernambuco, and two small clay figurines of seated Indian women of the Carajá (also Karajá) Indian tribe from the Bananal Island.

But while home visits were prime to getting to know Jorge and Zelia, the biggest party of all was Carnaval! Jo and Jack Searles, who had lived in Brazil, invited a party crowd of friends and Brazilian residents of State College to a pre-Carnaval celebration prior to the return of the Amados to Brazil. We arrived at their home in a vast and colorful array of costumes, with whistles and other noisemakers to accompany the samba rhythms. *Caipirinhas* were expertly prepared by Jack Searles, the floor was jammed with gyrating bodies and the entire house rocked. Oh, what a night it was! And Jorge and Zelia danced along with the rest of us.

For their part, the Amados invited a group of us to dine at The Tavern, the favorite and folksiest restaurant in town. The event took place on November 29th. It was their way of thanking us for hosting their visit but all of us felt that we had benefitted much more from their friendship.

There was a noticeable void in our lives when Jorge and Zelia returned to their Salvador de Bahia home. But not long thereafter the Brazilian magazine *Manchete* (January 15, 1972) had a special section featuring the Amados at Penn State and the photographs taken by Zelia and their photographer brought back many of the great moments we had spent together. For many years I corresponded with Jorge and Zelia, exchanging photographs, books and Christmas greetings, but despite an attempt to be with them during a trip to Salvador de Bahia in 1983, I was frustrated on learning that the couple was away from their home in Rio Vermelho. I would have liked sharing with him my many experiences at the "Second World Congress on Orisa Tradition and Culture" during the last two weeks of July, at which I had been privileged to participate in rituals at the very *terreiro* where Jorge was a celebrant of Candomble.

Jorge and Zelia have passed away, Jorge in 2001 and Zelia in 2008, both in Salvador de Bahia, their magical city.

FRANCISCO AYALA

The NYU Connection

Having accepted a teaching position at Hunter College, City University of New York, in 1962, at the beginning of my career in the field of Hispanic studies, I decided to do concurrent graduate work toward the Ph.D. Since I had been hired to teach five courses during the day, I could only pursue that goal at night. The prospect wasn't too appealing. And yet, despite misgivings, I matriculated at New York University in the Department of Romance Languages and Literatures, signing up for a program of five courses, one each evening, each three hours long. I was anxious to make significant headway through the 42-credit requirement of the degree.

During that first semester of the 1962-63 academic year there was, among the courses I signed up to take, an offering on the Latin American novel taught by one Francisco Ayala. The professor's name had no particular ring for me; I had come out of an English Literature B.A. and a Theatre-Drama M.A. background at Villanova University, my only real connection with Spanish literature being through research for *The Theatre of García Lorca*, a manuscript of mine that was about to be published in New York City. But when I discussed the course with my publisher, Gaetano Massa, and he learned that Francisco Ayala was to be the instructor, I was regaled with encomiums about the man, his work and his importance as a creative writer and sociologist. Enthusiastically, Massa showed me various of Ayala's books that he had on hand at Las Américas. I must admit that the imposing reputation represented by the books he held out frightened me somewhat in terms of the decision I had made. Nonetheless, heeding Massa's advice, as I had in accepting the position at Hunter, I pushed trepidation aside and decided to keep The Latin American Novel on my schedule.

The course meetings took place on Fridays in 803 Main, from six to nine. I came into the classroom on that first evening with lingering uneasiness: it was to be my first course ever in the Hispanic field and it was to be taught by a literary colossus. To my great relief, the distinguished, well-tailored professor who awaited us behind the desk, books at hand, looked down-to-earth, more normal than others I had seen. He wore a kindly smile as we straggled in from our different venues, some juggling books while devouring mustard-laden hot dogs from the counter of the nearby Chock-Full-O'Nuts, others, not having had time to eat at all, as in my case, were seemingly serene in our ascetic (deprived) state.

It was incongruous, I thought, that our first point of contact with the professor and each other as graduate students was in the context of food–envying those who had time for it, finding camaraderie with those who did not. Francisco Ayala, a traditional Spaniard, if only in his eating habits, was beyond these concerns since he was accustomed to a normal post-class *cena*. Ten o'clock was an early time for the evening meal of a Spaniard. Those of us who suffered the hunger imposed by the denial of the early dinner customary to the American way, awaited instead his food-for-thought to hold us until we could partake of our own repast after the session, provided, of course, that no other commitment beckoned (some had further courses to take, others lovers to meet in Washington Square Park or elsewhere).

Our classes always began with Ayala's extemporaneous discussion of the work-at-hand. From the very first, the pages of my notebook teemed with his brilliant annotations to works ranging from *El periquillo Sarniento* through *Amalia* and *María*, among many other novels. Then, too soon to my way of thinking, it would be our turn to assess the literary values of the piece. Some of my colleagues (no doubt the well fed) had not read or thought about the novel at all, relying on the dedication and sagacity of those who had completed the assignment (at the expense of eating) to pull the class through. Like a man-of-the-world who has seen much and lived through worse displays of inanity, Francisco Ayala was extremely patient with the naiveté of answers to some questions or the thud of silence that indolence dictated to others. But if irony and cynicism are often evident in his work, they were not present in his classroom; we were never subjected to snide comments regarding our inconsequent deductions, nor to tongue-lashings at our unpreparedness, nor to exasperating sighs over what at times must have seemed to him unconquerable ignorance. But there were moments when he could not mask his amusement (amazement?) at some outrageous statement emanating from our side of the room. It was all part of teaching, as I myself was learning daily uptown.

That was the first of four courses which I was to take under his able tutelage. The Spring Semester of 1963 was highlighted by a continuation of that initial course on the Latin American novel. I took two others in the Fall Semester of the following academic year: The Literature of Colonial Latin America and Spanish Baroque Theatre. It was in the first of these that I was encouraged by Francisco Ayala to translate some of Sor Juana's sonnets (he had seen poems and translations of mine in *La Voz*), receiving kudos from him for my efforts. That his reaction was not just academic forbearance became apparent some time later that semester when, over our regular after-class coffee, he asked if I would be interested in translating into English his *Muertes de perro* for publication by Scribner's. I was, and was flattered to have been asked. But it was not to be. The editor at the publishing house had made his own arrangements with another individual. Despite the author's efforts to have me replace the projected translator, the editor was steadfast in his desire not to rescind the contract. Nevertheless, I was honored to have been asked by Francisco Ayala to translate one of his most important, enduring works.

In the other course, Spanish Baroque Theatre, I read his 1961 essays on *El burlador de Sevilla* and *La vida es sueño* to gain insight into the professorial mind through the critic's stance. In "Burla, burlando..." I found an opening paragraph which addressed what his experience had taught him to be the student's perspective on Tirso's anti-hero: "los alumnos, que en su mayoría probablemente se enfrentan por vez primera con la obra de Tirso, lo hacen para este caso particular, no en aquel estado de total inocencia con que abordan otras piezas, del propio autor o de autores distintos, sino a través de una idea que se traen ya formada, y que ni siquiera han recogido del campo literario, sino más bien de la común experiencia, idea que se cifra en el nombre del protagonista: Don Juan." With the kind of pride that Aristotle justified, I excluded myself from those masses, seeing it as fortunate to have had earlier access to the play through one of my drama courses. But on reading further in the essay and later listening to Francisco Ayala's discussion of the play, I knew how much I had missed. There's little room for ego in the lifetime process of learning.

Just as I recall that first essay, to this day I have not forgotten "Porque no sepas que sé," the title taken from Segismundo's famous line when he expresses shame at having been overheard lamenting his *cuitas*. Years later, I received Ayala's latest book, *Las plumas del fénix. Estudios de literatura española*, and was pleased to find in its pages both favorite pieces. Re-reading them, I was back in that classroom at NYU listening to Ayala's incisive analysis of the plays and of their protagonists's troubled states. Having had access to his words, I could really count myself among the fortunate.

Upon completion of my coursework that semester, I prepared to take my oral comprehensives. There was no reading list; one simply had to know it all. In one of his films, Fellini captured the awed terror of a young student brought before a tribunal of priests over some offense, no doubt grave in their eyes; I was that student when I entered the fateful NYU classroom, 638 East, on Friday, May 22, 1964 for my oral examination and faced the five Inquisitors sitting on a platform at a level that seemed formidably high. Before me were Enesto Da Cal, James Stamm, Humberto Piñera (Cuban playwright Virgilio's brother), Robert Clements, and Francisco Ayala. I was directed to sit at the lowly, solitary student desk facing the panel of professors. And as I craned my neck, they proceeded to grill me on the whole range of Spanish and Latin American literatures. The only thing missing was a spotlight in my eyes; indeed, the room was as dim as my mind seemed to be under the circumstances. The thought kept racing across my ken that an earlier candidate had experienced a nervous breakdown under similar proceedings. But I survived the interrogation. Thereafter, I spent an eternity awaiting the decision on academic life or death. The meaning of the Inquisition was never clearer to me than during the long, agonizing star-chamber proceedings.

It was Francisco Ayala who came out of that sixth-floor torture chamber to bring me the good news of my having attained rebirth through the rite of academic passage. It was indeed Spring! I felt like Dionysus must have on overcoming dismemberment and death to be reborn yearly, but I was more fortunate: I did not have to go through the process again.

The three-hour ordeal over, Don Paco invited me for a *copa* to celebrate my status as a survivor and we repaired to a watering hole at the corner of University Place and Eighth Street. It was there that I asked him to be my thesis adviser. When he agreed, we discussed my plan to write on Valle-Inclán, whose novel *Tirano Banderas* he had interjected into the second Latin American novel class and whose works he felt should be made better known beyond the Hispanic world. He encouraged me to write the dissertation in English to that end and, the better to serve the author, required that it be in two volumes, the first on the life and works of Valle-Inclán, the second collecting bibliographical data on his publications and critical studies about him. To say that I was flabbergasted would not do justice to my feelings. But, caught up in his vision, I set out to fulfill Don Paco's plan and so began my trek through the reality and fantasy of Valle-

18

Inclán's life and writings. Despite the fact that my mentor abandoned me on taking a position at the University of Chicago, I pursued the quest as he had outlined it; that I was successful in its completion was attested by the awarding of New York University's Founders Day Award upon receipt of my Ph.D. in 1968. In time, these early efforts led to two publications in 1972: *Ramón del Valle-Inclán* in the prestigious Columbia Essays on Modern Writers Series, edited by William York Tindall, and the book-length *An Annotated Bibliography of Ramón del Valle-Inclán*. I continued to work on the vast panorama of the Spanish author's life and works, publishing numerous articles over my career. My translation of his *The Lamp of Marvels* came out in 1986 and *Valle-Inclán. The Theatre of His Life* in 1988; this biography was translated into Spanish, enhanced, and published in 1995 as *Valle-Inclán. El teatro de su vida*. 1993 saw the publication on my translation of *Savage Acts: Four Plays by Ramón del Valle-Inclán*. And in 1999 a new, wholly revised *Ramón del Valle-Inclán. An Annotated Bibliography: I. The Works* came out in England. More recently, my book *The Dramatic World of Valle-Inclán* appeared in 2003, also in England, and The International *Bibliography of Studies on the Life and Works of Ramón del Valle-Inclán*, in two volumes. These books acknowledge the influence of Francisco Ayala on my writings devoted to the great novelist, playwright and aesthetician that was Valle-Inclán.

Exchanges of letters, notes, and books... occasional encounters at professional meetings in the U.S. and in Spain... visits to his *piso* in Madrid... his visit to my home when he lectured at my invitation at the university where I taught... and, always, good memories, have kept me in touch from time to time with Francisco Ayala over the many years since NYU days. In 1990 I participated in a special issue of *Letras Peninsulares* devoted to him and Rosa Chacel.

I coincided with him in October 1999 in Granada when the university offered an *homenaje* in honor of the city's native son but I was myself involved in an event honoring the playwright José Martín Recuerda that same day and could not visit with Ayala. Thus, I have not seen him since he became an "Inmortal" of the Real Academia Española, of which, as a non-Spaniard, I was to become a

Corresponding Member in 1997, my ascension not through his sponsorship but by virtue of my election as an Academician in my own right by the Academia Norteamericana de la Lengua Española, a constituent body of the RAE.

Francisco Ayala's recognitions extended beyond the realm of professional institutions. He was further immortalized by the issuance by Spain of a postage stamp featuring his pensive pose.

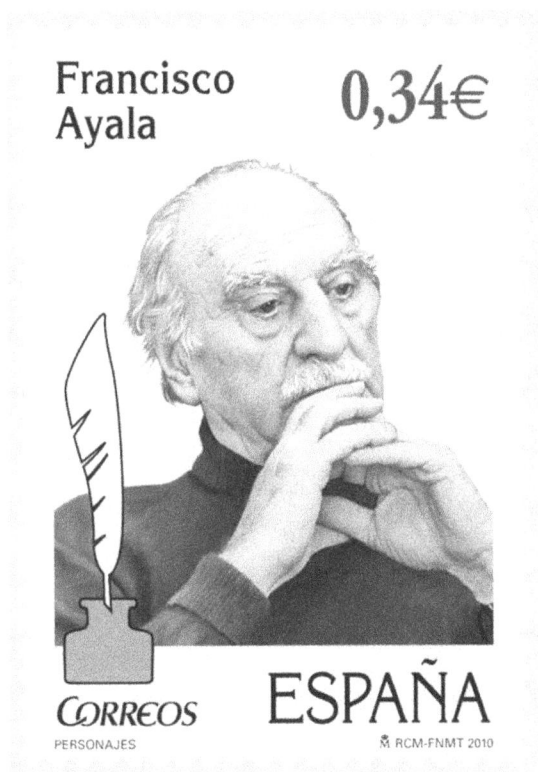

Francisco Ayala, who had lived to be 103, passed away in Madrid on November 3, 2009. He was cremated and his ashes are at the San Isidro cemetery in Madrid.

AMIRI BARAKA

Janus in Two Worlds

I first knew him in the 1960s as LeRoi Jones, an angry thirty-something, smallish Black poet and playwright who sometimes frequented the coffeehouses and other venues of New York's Greenwich Village where groups of poets read weekly. On occasion he would appear at Mickey Ruskin's Tenth Street Coffeehouse or later at the same owner's Les Deux Megots, also in the so-called East Village, more often than not to sit and listen rather than read. But when he chose to recite his poetry, it was to harangue one part of the establishment or another. His manner and voice were always strident, his poems diatribes. His plays had some success in the avant-garde theatres of New York City and extended his notoriety as an angry Black voice.

Many years later, in March of 1989, I attended the 15th Annual Meeting of the African Literature Conference, held in Dakar, Senegal. LeRoi Jones was also there, a special guest of the ALA as a representative of the Black Diaspora, but he had long before changed his name to reflect his African roots and was thereafter Amiri Baraka. New name, same identity. Amiri Baraka spoke words of derision that stung then as they had in his early New York years. He opened and closed doors, gates while facing in opposite directions. This is why I saw him with faces looking back and forward, like the ancient Roman deity.

JANUS

For Leroi Jones / Amiri Baraka

I

I remember you "back when,"

the Village as a setting for your shouts
of anger and disdain...
you being then among the loudest first
to cry out foul in voice and verse

the Sixties, in the *Fuck You* years,
before the anger metamorphosed
into guitar voice, and flower power
followed fists and clubs into the streets

You wore the name of king in that old time
but it didn't fit your rousing style,
the cause you battled to uphold
with words for actors and yourself

II

Today, you own a name with Africa inside.

And, in Dakar, I hear again your shouts,
your anger, your disdain and you are king,
as once before, but now it fits in this,
the continent where your ancestors live.

III

The old back home still use your early name.

To them you haven't changed, you said to me.
But you know that you've recomposed yourself–
become two poets now–looking, like the god,
in two directions, with two miens, at once
presiding over doors to old-time haunts
and gates that usher in the future wail.*

Having been born in 1934, Amiri Baraka died in 2014.

*The poem appeared in 1998 in *The Growth of African Literature*, the conference proceedings, edited by Edris Makward, Thelma Ravell-Pinto and Aliko Songolo, under the imprint of Africa World Press.

WILLIS BARNSTONE

Bard and Mystagogue

I met Willis Barnstone in New York City in the early 1960s at Las Américas Bookstore on East 23rd Street. We were introduced by the owner Gaetano Massa, who had featured both of us in *La Voz*, a literary magazine, and who published my book *The Theatre of García Lorca*. Willis and I have remained friends ever since, if separated by the distance between Indiana and Pennsylvania after we both moved in a westerly direction from the Atlantic coast.

Early on it became evident that we shared several interests. We were both poets (but I don't recall him reading in Greenwich Village as I did). We both worked on the writings of Jorge Luis Borges, were translators of Latin American and Spanish poetry, and shared a growing passion for the mystic lore of Gnosticism and the Kabbalah. He would go on to publish *Borges at Eighty* and compile *The Other Bible: Jewish Pseudepigrapha, Christian Aprocrypha, Gnostic Scriptures*, while I edited and translated *Borges the Labyrinth Maker*, edited *Borges and the Esoteric* (to which he contributed), wrote *Dark Prisms: Occultism in Hispanic Drama* and *Stages of Evil.*

We also had a friend in common, Mary Barnard Quiñones, my colleague in the Department of Spanish, Italian and Portuguese at The Pennsylvania State University. this connection kept me apprised of Willis and his activities. Together, Mary and I arranged for Willis to lecture at Penn State under the joint auspices of our department and Comparative Literature, along with Classics (due to his translations of Sappho), English (for his Pulitzer Prize niminated poetry books), and Religious Studies (*The Other Bible* is a standard source book).

Upon his arrival on Saturday March 28, 1987, my wife Sally and I hosted an intimate dinner at our home for Willis, with Mary present. It was an occasion to catch up on both our careers and for me to show Willis the books that Borges had autographed when he came to our home in 1968 and again in 1983.

In typical fashion, as with many an invited visitor, we really worked Willis hard the next few days. On Monday, March 30th, he spoke at the Comparative Literature Luncheon on "The Serpent as the Luminous Jesus and Eve as the Creator of Adam in Gnostic Scriptures," a topic that filled the room in the Kern Graduate Building and caused much pro and con discussion after the presentation. Later that afternoon we congregated at Pattee Library's Rare Books Room where he did a reading from several of his books of poetry (*From This White Island, China Poems*, and *5 a.m. in Beijing*) as well as from *My Voice Because of You*, his translation of Pedro Salinas's poems. We took him out for a well-deserved dinner at The Tavern Restaurant.

Mary and I ushered Willis around campus the following day. That night he presented the major lecture of his visit, "Poetry East and West: Aspects of Translation," under the auspices of the Department of Spanish, Italian and Portuguese, again in Kern Graduate Building. That night Sally and I held a reception at our home, which was attended by guests from many disciplines.

During his visit, Willis and I had ample time to reminisce about earlier interactions at conferences with Borges. At the University of Maine in Orono, the "Symposium (On) Borges and (With) Borges," organized by Carlos Cortínez and held from April 15 through 18,

1976, we had the opportunity to participate in a panel on translating Borges and in a poetical tribute to him, the latter with Alan Dugan, Robert Fitzgerald, Jorge Guillén, Oscar Hahn (whose poems I translated for the occasion), John Hollander, and Richard Howard, among others. Willis also had an exhibit of "Borges in Buenos Aires, 1975," a collection of his photographs. At the University of Oklahoma in Norman and later at Dickinson College, at Borges the Poet, also organized by Carlos Cortínez and held from April 6 through 8, 1983, we read papers in the same session.

Willis set out for Indiana the morning after his final talk at Penn State. During our drive to University Park Airport, we rued the death in 1986 of the man who had prompted so many opportunities to present our views of his writings before him, as well as read our translations of his poems, and also share his company as colleagues and friends.

In 1992 I invited Willis to contribute an article to *Borges and the Esoteric*, a collection of essays I was editing for a special issue of *Crítica Hispánica*. He sent me "Memoir about a Metaphysical and Mystical Poet," an intriguing assessment of the unisonal voice of Borges as man and writer derived from Barnstone's many conversations with him over nearly two decades. *Borges and the Esoteric* was published in Pittsburgh in 1993 by Duquesne University.

We have since exchanged books and correspondence. He now lives the fortunate life of the retired academic with greater time to write than ever before; he was one of the contributors to my *festschrift, A Confluence of Words. Essays in Honor of Robert Lima,* with an essay titled "Pedro Salinas, Poet in His Worlds," which opens the book.

JOHN BARTH

A Reclusive Visitor

John Barth based *Giles Goat Boy* on his experiences while teaching at The Pennsylvania State University from 1953 to 1965 and on Joseph Campbell's now classic study of myth *The Hero with a Thousand Faces*. The novel was published the year after Barth left the university to teach at the State University of New York at Buffalo. In that same year I came to Penn State, having taught for three years at Hunter College in New York City. Therefore, Barth and I did not meet. And, for better or for worse, I could not be included in the thinly-disguised cast of academics in the novel.

Barth may have left Penn State but the university still appealed to him in some ways. One of these was indicated by the fact that he had (probably still has) season tickets to Penn State home football games. I don't know how well, if at all, he knew Joe Paterno. Barth would arrive in town from Buffalo or, later, Baltimore when he taught at Johns Hopkins University, incognito. If he stayed overnight it was with former colleagues from the English Department. He did not wish his whereabouts known to the community at large and generally preferred to be reclusive. Although I too attended home football games, the ever-growing size of Beaver Stadium made it increasingly more difficult for us to have met. I heard of his visits after the fact from friends Bernard and Anne Oldsey, a couple with whom he sometimes stayed.

I finally met John Barth in 1991 when he agreed to be the guest speaker at a conference on Jorge Luis Borges. Barth always admired the Argentinian writer and continues to find inspiration in his labyrinthine tales of secret planets, libraries holding arcane texts, fictitious authors out of the past, cabbalistic intrigues... The event that brought him back was the Symposium: Borges Revisited, which was held from April 12 through 13 under the sponsorship of the Department of Spanish, Italian and Portuguese and organized by Martin S. Stabb. Because of my own work on Borges, I was one of the co-organizers.

That Friday morning we took Barth to the Rare Books Room at Pattee Library to view the exhibit of works by and about Jorge Luis Borges that Charles Mann, the curator and a former colleague of Barth's, had set up. The exhibit contained many autographed editions, signed by Borges on the occasions in 1968 and 1983 when I brought him to Penn State as a speaker and had him inscribe the books. A luncheon at The Nittany Lion Inn followed.

Barth presented the inaugural address, "Borges and I," at 1:45 on that Friday in 112 Kern Graduate Center, a building that did not exist when he had taught at Penn State. A slim, bespectacled and well-into-balding figure, Barth at once had a sophisticated look and the world-weary way of a prominent writer. And he spoke in a soft, unassuming voice. It was evident from the beginning of his talk (it wasn't an academic lecture) that the man and the writer had a deep admiration for and had bonded with the creator of such influential stories as "Tlön, Uqbar, Orbis Tertius," "The Garden of Forking Paths," "The Library of Babel," "The Approach to Al-Mutassim," "The Secret Miracle," and numerous other works of the Argentine's encyclopedic imagination. The talk and the chat that followed gave many insights into both writers. Years later, Barth was to express some of these ideas in "'The Parallels!' Italo Calvino and Jorge Luis Borges," published in the Dalkey Archive's on-line journal *Context*.

The symposium continued, with Barth in attendance at all the sessions. Unlike many speakers who leave after their performance, John Barth showed his true mettle in listening to the other participants. We heard from James Irby of Princeton and Daniel Balderston of Georgetown, both of whose sessions I moderated; on Saturday, the speakers were Edna Aizenberg of Marymount Manhattan, Jaime Alazraki of Columbia, Naomi Lindstrom of Texas, and Nicholas Shumway of Yale.

The evening of his lecture, we attended a cocktail party in honor of John Barth at the Centre Furnace Mansion, one of the region's historic sites that had been carefully restored. The event was hosted by the Department of English and attended by Symposium participants, local faculty and area writers. Borges was there, if only in spirit (he had died in 1986).

I and others bid John Barth farewell upon the closure of the symposium, grateful to have met the elusive author under circumstances that permitted chatting with him and seeing the man as a giving person. It would be five years and a month before I would meet him again.

That occasion came on May 12, 1996. Barth had been invited by the university to receive an honorary Doctor of Letters degree at Commencement exercises. That afternoon, Don and Sue Bialotosky held a reception at their College Heights home, not too distant from my house, to celebrate the special occasion. It was the kind of cozy, at-home affair in the company of friends that John Barth most enjoyed.

No doubt he continues his "anonymous" football weekend trips to State College, although the last several seasons have proven less than satisfactory and Paterno's past glories have faded in light of recent team failures and, more shockingly, with his dismissal in the context of the Sandusky scandal. No doubt longtime Penn State fan John Barth will be there to cheer on the squad and the new coach at Penn State. And no doubt he has his opinion on the firing of the beloved coach, JoePa. Will there be a sequel to *Giles Goat Boy* on the recent Penn State situation?

JORGE LUIS BORGES

Encounters in Reality

1968. The first call from Canada reached me at my house on February 6, 1968. The Argentine minister in Ottawa informed me that Jorge Luis Borges was en route to Pittsburgh at that moment via New York: I was expected to meet him at the airport that evening.

Since Borges was supposed to arrive at the air terminal serving State College, Pennsylvania on the following day and not at Pittsburgh on the 6th, I let out a slow groan which the minister echoed when I informed him of the real arrangements. Hurriedly, then, he excused himself to call the Argentine Consulate in New York in the hope that his counterpart there could intercept Borges during his flight's stopover at Kennedy International. Several calls later–from Canada and New York–I was relieved to learn that the contact had been made; Borges would be on the evening flight to Mid-State Airport in the wilds of Black Moshannon Park.

Accompanied by Gerald Moser, I drove out on the difficult road to the minute airport. Borges' flight arrived on time and we greeted the author with excitement. Borges too seemed elated at his arrival, perhaps overjoyed that the commuter flight was over.

I had first met the noted author at Columbia University's Casa Hispanica in 1962 when he lectured to a full house overflowing with enthusiasm and expectation; many in that audience had only recently "discovered" him through *Ficciones* and *Labyrinths*, two collections of his stories in translation recently published, which I myself had found by chance in the Post Library at Fort Dix, New Jersey while completing my military service. During that visit to the Casa Hispánica, Borges was accompanied by his mother, Doña Leonor, then in her mid-eighties. The Borges who disembarked now was a much older-looking man and he was now accompanied by Elsa, his bride of only a few months.

Moser and I helped the couple into the reception room, gathered their luggage and set out in the car. Despite their lengthy trip and the awkwardness of the arrangements that had been made for them, they were very enthused by their visit to central Pennsylvania, a region Borges had not set foot in before.

As the car lights cut through the crisp night, Borges sensed the beauty of the scenery around him, often asking us to verify his impressions. It was a jovial ride and its length was forgotten in the glow of our guest's wit and extroverted manner. Then, having made a brief stop at The Corner Room (The Borgeses had not yet eaten), we drove them to The Nittany Lion Inn for a well-deserved rest.

After breakfast the next morning, I accompanied Borges and his wife to the Pattee Library where Charles W. Mann, Jr. , Director of Special Collections, awaited our arrival. Since Borges has had a long association with and love for libraries, he was most enthused by the tour which Mr. Mann gave him, spending much time handling the rare books in the collection. He was particularly pleased to hold in his hands many first editions of English and American classics.

The two librarians agreed to set up an exchange between their respective libraries. Afterwards, we visited the exhibit of Borges' books which I had arranged in the lobby; the author autographed several editions in the display and these were destined for the Rare Books Room.

Following a rest, Borges and his wife were the guests of Dr. Anthony M. Pasquariello, chairman of the Department of Spanish, Italian and Portuguese, at an informal luncheon at the Inn. Dr. Rodrigo Solera and I were also present. As is always the case where Borges is involved, the conversation was lively and far-ranging.

The inevitable siesta slackened the pace of the early afternoon, but after it I took the Borgeses for a car tour of State College and the surrounding areas. With the daylight he was able to distinguish better the forms and contrasts of landscape and cityscape, yet it was his imagination that brought a smile to his lips.

Later, while walking with Borges in downtown State College, we ran into Carlos Roll, a student in the Department of Spanish, Italian and Portuguese; when I introduced him to our distinguished visitor Carlos shook his hand saying, "Hola, Borges. ¿Cómo estás?" Borges, who was normally addressed in the formal Spanish manner, was much taken by the informality of the student and he had a good laugh.

That evening at the Inn Dr. Pasquariello hosted a dinner for Borges. Dr. Moser and I were there as well but Sra. Borges could not join us until dessert–the hectic pace of the days preceding their arrival had finally caught up with her and she was exhausted. However, Borges did not seem affected; he regaled us with anecdotes and witticisms, crowning his words with an inspired recital of the "Our Father" in Anglo-Saxon.

Warmed by a crème de menthe, which his wife did not fail to share, Borges began to talk about his approaching commitment to initiate the Graduate School Lecture Series. He did not like to lecture, he declared. Instead, he preferred to sit in open forums and to answer questions. Borges has always been attracted more by the unexpected than by the planned. But his larger audience waited in the Assembly Room of the Hetzel Union Building and our private time with Borges had to be curtailed.

A short ride to the Hetzel Union Building and we were faced with a throng. Only the front row of the auditorium was empty because it had been reserved for our party by our wives. Somewhat nervously,

Borges asked that water be placed on the speaker's table before he assumed his seat. The ploy gave him a few minutes of freedom. The aisles began to fill as the speaker made his way to the stage. Before Dr. Pasquariello's introduction was completed the crowd was overflowing into the hallway.

Borges sensed the excited mood of his public. He began to speak in a calm voice that carried his crisp, flawless English. He presented his philosophic subject, "Discussion on Solipsism," (the student newspaper had erroneously had it as Solecism) with great authority yet he avoided pedantry. He charmed his audience with his wit at the same time that he won them with his erudition. The ovation that punctuated his final words evidenced the success of the mixture.

The reception in the HUB Lounge drew a large segment of the audience. Faculty from many disciplines and their students, as well as Latin American members of the academic community and visitors from other institutions, took the opportunity to chat informally with Borges and to continue the question period that had followed the lecture. The same student we had met downtown asked him after his talk: "Borges, ¿tu crées en Dios?" From familiarity to impertinence, but Borges enjoyed it all.

It was after 11:00 p.m. when Sra. Borges asked me to "rescue" her husband because he so enjoyed these gatherings that he would lose all sense of time. My wife, Sally and I took the Borgeses to our car and, since he wanted a glass of milk, drove to our home. We spent a pleasant half hour together after which I drove them back to the Inn.

Rather than send Borges and his wife off alone the next morning, I picked them up and made the drive to his next destination, Pittsburgh, where he was scheduled to recite his poetry at the International Poetry Forum. Dr. Samuel Hazo, director of the Forum, hosted a dinner for Borges at which we were accompanied by Dr. Robert Clements of New York University and members of the Pittsburgh community of scholars and writers. Clements had been instrumental in publishing my translation of the first critical study on the author to appear in English, Ana María Barrenechea's *Borges the Labyrinth Maker* (NYU Press, 1965).

That same evening Borges appeared on the stage of the Carnegie Museum Lecture Hall before a full house. Dr. Hazo, who would read selected translations of Borges' poetry, introduced the program. I was asked to stand and be recognized as the translator of four of the selections. The warm introduction of the poet was followed by an inspired reading of the English versions; after each, Borges either recited the original, commented on the poem, or made an appropriate remark.

The evening closed with a reception at the Webster Hall Hotel where we were staying. Again Borges made himself available to all who approached him and again he had to be convinced to retire to his room after several hours.

The next morning, after we had breakfast together, I helped the Borgeses prepare for their return trip to Cambridge, Massachusetts. Dr. Hazo's secretary arrived to accompany them to the airport and I, having to return to State College, bid Borges and his wife farewell.

I did not know it at the time, but I was to be with them again shortly. Dr. Clements invited me to be one of three panelists in "A Conversation with Borges" to be held at New York University on April 6, 1968 under the joint sponsorship of the University and Grove Press, publisher of Borges' *Ficciones* in English. Sitting at Borges' right side, at the table with our host and the other panelists–Alexander Coleman (NYU), Ronald Christ (Manhattan)–I had an opportunity to converse once more with the genial poet, storyteller and essayist. The filming of the event by Grove Press provided an opportunity to preserve a rare moment. To my knowledge, the film has never been released.

After the panel discussion we adjourned to a cocktail party sponsored by the American publishing house at its Black Circle Lounge, next to the Evergreen Theatre. Later, Dr. Clements presided over a dinner at the Dardanelles; those of us present who had written about Borges took a few minutes each to convey to the others why we admired our guest. When my turn came, I recalled my first readings in Borges' writings at the post library in Ft. Dix, New Jersey and my first meeting with the man at Columbia. Everything had come full circle.

In the years thereafter I've been with Borges on many occasions. Next came the encounter in early December of 1969 when the University of Oklahoma sponsored a symposium on the Argentine author under the auspices of *Books Abroad* (now *World Literature Today*). Borges received the yearly honor accorded important writers by the journal. On December 6th I spoke on "Borges's Magic" and participated on a panel with many other critics. Unfortunately, the publication that ensued did not contain the text of the remarkable exchange of ideas that took place during this panel.

In Orono, site of the University of Maine, Dr. Carlos Cortínez organized and led a symposium on and with Borges in April 1976. I was on a panel on translating Borges with Willis Barnstone, Alan Dugan, William Ferguson, James Irby, and Donald Yates. The proceedings of the symposium appeared in *Simply a Man of Letters* (University of Maine, 1982).

Another occasion was at Carlisle, Pennsylvania when Dr. Cortínez, then teaching at Dickinson College, brought scholars together with Borges to celebrate "Borges the Poet" in April 1983. Borges was now accompanied by María Kodama, his doctoral student at the University of Buenos Aires and constant companion. I had lunch with Borges at his table and he thanked me for the insights into his work in the talk I had given before him that morning. The proceedings appeared in *Borges the Poet* (University of Arkansas Press, 1986).

Later on April 10, 1983 I brought Borges to Penn State again. He arrived with María Kodama at The Nittany Lion Inn at 4 p.m. and had dinner there with me, Paul West, Philip Young and Joan Searles. Generously, he consented to an 8:30 interview with Professor of English Leonard Rubinstein for the Penn State radio series "Odyssey Through Literature" sponsored by Comparative Literature.

The next day he visited the Nittany Lion Shrine on his way to the Comparative Literature Luncheon, where I introduced "Conversation with Borges." In the afternoon, after his rest, I took Borges to the Rare Books Room of Pattee Library, where Charles Mann had a display of books by the Argentine author, which I asked Borges to autograph for the collection. That night of April 11th at 8 p.m., after a dinner at the Inn, he spoke in the auditorium of the Kern

Graduate Center, as always to a sellout crowd; the Graduate School Lecture was on "Thoughts on Metaphor," in dialogue with Dr. Martin Stabb and me. Paul West was in the audience and had a brief discussion with Borges during the Q&A segment of the evening. Several newspapers in the area covered the event, carried his photograph and discussed his presentation.

On the morning of April 12th, Borges and María Kodama departed for their next stop, Franklin and Marshall College in Lancaster, Pennsylvania I saw them off at The Inn, thinking that, as in the past, there would soon be another encounter on the academic circuit.

But it was not to be. April 12, 1983 was the last time I spoke to Borges. I read of his marriage to María Kodama and of their residency in Switzerland. Within a few short months of moving there, Jorge Luis Borges died in Geneva on June 14, 1986. He was 86 years old.

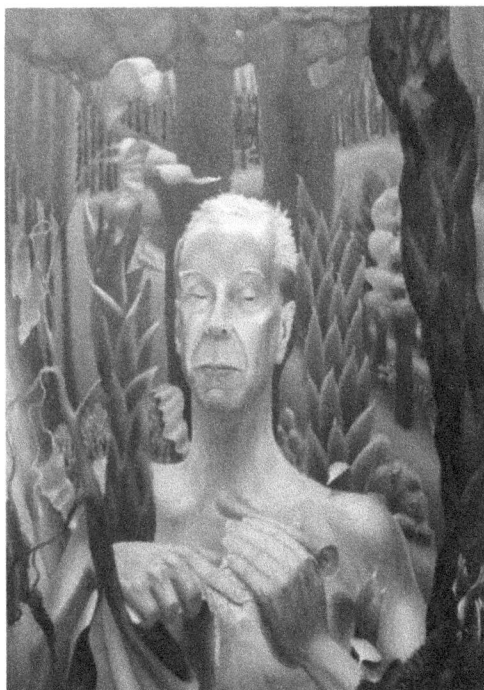

"Borges the Hierophant," Oil by Keith Lima

JOSEPH BRODSKY

The Miracle of Words

The Russian poet came to Penn State in late February 1973 from the University of Michigan, where he was Poet in Residence. His visit was under the auspices of Comparative Literature, which I chaired, the Department of English, the Department of Slavic Languages, and the Institute for the Arts and Humanistic Studies.

Josef Brodskii, Joseph Brodsky, as he became known in the English-speaking world, had been an outspoken critic of Communism and in 1964 was arrested; the charge was that he was "a social parasite." Although he was released in 1966 and permitted to return to Leningrad, he was still under the watchful eye of the regime. In 1972 he was exiled from the Soviet Union but found a welcome in the United States, where he lived and prospered as a man of letters. He would win the Nobel Prize for Literature in 1987 at the age of 47.

On February 22, 1973 he held an informal afternoon session with students, which I and several other faculty members attended. His

English left a lot to be desired and a translator passed his commentary to the audience. Despite the language barrier on both sides, the session was very successful. That same evening he presented a poetry reading in the Hetzel Union Building.

We are used in this country to listening to a poet read from a manuscript, journal or book. But Josef Brodky came from a different tradition, one in which the poet has committed his works to memory. And the words he delivered that evening were in Russian. Only a few in the audience could understand the poems but everyone *felt* them. How? Brodsky performed his poems. The cadence of the words, the musicality of the traditional stanzas, the choreography of his intense body language... all were elements manipulated by the consummate performance artist. There were moments of melodramatic gesturing, of deep sentiment, of epic stances. No matter the tone, the audience was *with* the poet. Had the phrase been in use at the time, Brodsky would have been dubbed a "performance artist."

As he recited, I hurriedly penned my impressions of what was evolving before me, a unique production of words, gestures, movements. The only other time I had experienced a similar performance was in New York City years before when Brother Antoninus mesmerized his audience at Columbia University with sonority and movement across the stage dressed in the white Dominican robes of his order; but on that occasion the poems he recited were in English. Not tied to the words now, but only to their sound, I was able to capture the effect upon me of the unusual recital.

MOVEMENT IN VOICES

Poems gifted without sense conveyed
reaching ears as epic song,
alien sound intrinsic in cadenzas
of a cantor's minstrelsy

Meaning sensed in body talk,
emboldened gestures, ritual mien,

orthodoxy's ancient liturgy
making theatre for the eyes

Utterance and movement meshed
to stir the deep resources,
just beyond the scheme of sense,
lying in the venue of the dream

Understandably, when the translator *read* the versions in English, they seemed flat. Real poetry–its vocalization, its rich cadences, its vitality–was personified that evening in the very memorable "reading" by Joseph Brodsky, who, despite his new American identity, retained the passion and verve of Mother Russia in heart and words. His were impassioned words, words that brought the audience into each poem he recited.

Saint Bernard had raised an army for the Jerusalem Crusade by preaching in the *langue d'oil*, which few of his listeners understood; the sonority of words and the passion of their delivery touched the consciousness of the listeners intuitively, even contemplatively. His preaching in a tongue foreign to his audiences achieved what could be termed a musical miracle for, as Ramón del Valle-Inclán has said in *The Lamp of Marvels*, "The words of poets, like those of saints, do not require grammatical decipherment in order to move souls. Their essence is the musical miracle." Such was the atmosphere at Josef Brodsky's memorable poetry performance.

He died in 1996 at the age of 56, a great loss of a poet so young!

GWENDOLYN BROOKS

A Voice in Black

In October of 1982, the important African American poet Gwendolyn Brooks spent a few days at Penn State University under the auspices of the Paul Robeson Cultural Center. During her visit she met with many faculty and students in informal sessions. I had occasion to attend various of these encounters but the most memorable for me was the poetry reading she gave on the last night of her stay. The locale where she read was "The Fishbowl" in the Hetzel Union Building and the glass-enclosed area was full (I had been instrumental in having the former open-air patio enclosed just for such events). As I looked around at the audience, I believe I saw represented all aspects of the cultural milieu in the student body and faculty; there were also people from town in attendance and they too manifested the racial diversity of the area.

There was a great expectation in the air and when the short, retiring, bespectacled figure got up to read after the introduction, a hush fell on the crowd. But there was nothing shy or retiring about the poet as she began to vocalize her works. Her voice had many ranges–from soft to startlingly powerful; her poems–soulful to jazzy–played many chords, and as the reading went on she became more and more vitalized as her audience reacted with warmth and, sometimes, raucous appreciation. She read many fine poems that night–"The Mother," "Sadie and Maud," "We Real Cool"–but the one that stood out for me concerned the plight of a small Black boy. Thinking about the theme and her full-body delivery of the powerful lines of the poem, I wrote a small tribute to the poet and her subject.

GWENDOLYN READING IN BLACK VOICE

"Ugly" is bad enough
but she stretched it out in black,
deep in her gut, and
brought it to the surface,
making it rise up throaty:

Ü Ü Ü G ' L I

The little boy in the poem
came alive through
her grave black voice
belching the ugliness he felt
when Black is supposed to be

B Ü ' T I F O O L

My poem was first published in 1987 in a collection of writings celebrating the seventieth birthday of the 1950 Pulitzer Prize poet. *Say that the River Turns. The Impact of Gwendolyn Brooks* was edited by Haki R. Madhubuti under the imprint of Third World Press in Chicago. It was in the South Side of "The Windy City" that Gwendolyn Brooks began her career as writer, activist and supporter of young writers by mentoring and financing their work. The poem again appeared in print in *Shooting Star Review* (Pittsburgh, PA, Fall 1989), together with an illustration (but not of Gwendolyn).

Gwendolyn Brooks (1917-2000) remains a cultural icon in American letters.

ANTONIO BUERO VALLEJO

A Committed Life

Antonio Buero Vallejo, the noted Spanish playwright, came to The Pennsylvania State University in 1966 at the invitation of Anthony M. Pasquariello, the department head who was one of those who arranged a lecture tour. My colleague Martha Halsey, who wrote on his plays, and I were asked to help host him during the several days that he spent here to attend a conference that had been arranged on contemporary Spanish theatre. He was to be the guest of honor. Among the sights I took him to see on and off campus, he was most interested in the theatres and in visiting the art department and its studio facilities. We happened to find a studio class with a nude female model and Buero was tempted to sit in with students to draw her figure. Besides his career as a playwright, Buero had also pursued his avocation as a painter and during his visit took time to sketch campus scenes.

Incarcerated in the early days of the Spanish Civil War, Buero eventually left his native country. But he was back in Spain in 1949 for the premiere of *Historia de una escalera*, the play which revolutionized modern Spanish drama. In time, Buero's international recognition as a playwright brought him to the Real Academia Española, one of whose numbered chairs is the greatest honor given to a writer in Spain.

When in Madrid to attend a conference, I was particularly taken by Buero's greeting as I was climbing the Art Nouveau staircase of the building housing the affair. Suddenly, from above came the exclamatory voice of the playwright: "Well, if it isn't Lima!" Everyone stopped to look at the figure on the staircase. It was a mere moment and could not come close to Andy Warhol's "Fifteen minutes of fame," but it did focus all eyes on my ascent to an *abrazo* from Buero. He was always generous in his friendship, as when on a later occasion in Madrid he invited Martha Halsey and me to lunch at one of the fine restaurants on the Plaza Mayor, where we sat outdoors to take in the mix of locals and tourists. He was interested in all comings and goings.

I was again in Madrid in October 1999, and saw the long-term accomplishments of the prize-winning playwright recognized by the premiere of what would be his last play produced during his life. The celebration of the fiftieth anniversary of Antonio Buero Vallejo's *Historia de una escalera* was marked at Madrid's Teatro Español with the production of his new play *Misión al pueblo desierto*, subtitled *Relato escénico en dos actos*. Buero's play looks back at the Guerra Civil through an unfinished personal narrative that is promoted as true by its reader and as fiction by another; upon its actualization, the scene returns to the present with a calculatedly ambiguous ending. The cast was headed by Manuel Galiana (in the role of Plácido), Juan Carlos Naya (Damián) and Paula Sebastián (Lola) under the direction of Gustavo Pérez Puig and Mara Recatero. Buero usually attended the early Saturday performance and when I saw it, he was brought on stage to take bows in front of a large photo-mural proclaiming the anniversary. He seemed uplifted by the audience's reception. Other kudos were offered in the four program notes by José María Álvarez del Manzano y López del Hierro (the Mayor of Madrid), Ricardo Doménech, Mariano de Paco, and Gustavo Pérez Puig. The program also featured four schematics of the sets, photographs from earlier plays, a chronology of Buero's *estrenos*, a list of his prizes, and a short personal statement on the motivation behind his plays.

After the performance, I waited for him on the sidewalk. He exited the Teatro Español by the front door on the arm of his wife, the actress Victoria Rodríguez. He looked older and more tired than during his brief moment of triumph on stage. I shook his hand warmly and said hello to his wife, who told me that Buero was too worn out to accept my invitation for a *café*. Their chauffeur held open the door of the automobile and they climbed in. It was the last I saw of him. He passed away not long after that on April 29, 2000 in Madrid.

Antonio Buero Vallejo, premier dramatist of his generation, left a legacy of commitment to social causes in his work. But his plays were never merely topical for, from first to last, they were always about the complexity of the human condition; in exploring ways to interpret it, Buero left a body of work that will endure as masterful dramas.

JOSEPH CAMPBELL

The Hero with a Liquid Face

From April 3 through 5 of 1975 scholars from the United States and elsewhere gathered at the University of Texas at Arlington to participate in a conference on literature and occult thematics, as ideated by Luanne Franck of the English department.

I was invited due to my pioneering work in the field since 1968. My course, **Literature of the Occult**, was the first university-level course on the subject ever taught for credit. Offered under the aegis of Comparative Literature, it included topics ranging from alchemy to voodoo as manifested in important literary works from many nations and periods. Over the years, there were assessments, among others, of S. An-Sky's play *The Dybbuk*, Mikhail Bulgakov's novel *The Master and Margarita*, Bram Stoker's novel *Dracula*, Henry James's novella *The Turn of the Screw*, Arthur Miller's play *The Crucible*, John Fowles's novel *The Magus*, Eugene O'Neill's play *The Emperor Jones*, Ira Levin's novel *Rosemary's Baby*, Nicholas

Condé's novel *The Religion*, Christopher Marlowe's play *The Tragedy of Doctor Faust*, and short stories by E.A. Poe, Wilkie Collins, Ambrose Bierce, Joseph Sheridan Le Fanu, Fitz-James O'Brien, M.R. James, Arthur Machen, Algernon Blackwood, and H.P. Lovecraft. Documentary films and slides on the variety of topics covered complemented the literature. The course was so in demand (I taught it for twenty years to as many as three hundred students each semester) that articles about it appeared in newspapers throughout the country from its inception. As a result, I received correspondence ranging from requests by colleagues for my syllabus to outrageous attacks by the fundamentalist fringe. To its credit, the university saw the merit of offering a course of such literary scope.

Having taught the work over so many years, I chose as my conference topic "Rite of Passage: Metempsychosis, Possession, and Exorcism in S. An'Sky's *The Dybbuk*." Other speakers ranged over Alchemy, Jung, Rosicrucianism, Satanism, Astrology, Art, and Music as applicable to literature from the Middle Ages to the Twentieth Century.

The list of participants included Wayne Shumaker and Joseph Campbell, who delivered the two keynote addresses. Shumaker addressed "The Uses of the Occult in Literature" and did a fine job of communicating his panoramic vision, while Campbell spoke on the mythic dimension of the topic in "The Occult in Myth and Literature."

The author of the seminal book *The Hero with a Thousand Faces* stood before the assembled crowd at the opening banquet. There was some good-natured banter after his introduction but it became clear immediately that Campbell was in no state to properly deliver the words he had put down on paper. His face was flushed and his body was unsteady at the podium, on which he leaned for support. A speaker with much experience behind him, it was not nervousness that manifested itself in the quirky behavior; the speaker was in his cups. Too much carousing during the opening festivities and too little time before his talk to sober up created the situation that confronted the audience. Everyone was embarrassed... except the man who was attempting to read lines that no doubt were a blur to his eyes and so emerged from his mouth in a flow of slurs.

Somehow he (and the audience) made it through the precarious presentation and he received polite applause. The less-than-enthusiastic reaction showed the disappointment over the "feet of clay" of the man many had granted near-mythic status. Campbell had now become anti-heroic, a clown with a flushed face and teetering body, a performer in a low comedy who couldn't get his lines straight.

In the conference proceedings published two years later, Joseph Campbell's essay headed the selected papers. I, for one, enjoyed reading the talk that he had botched and found the printed version to be up to the level of his other writings in insight and expression. Many important writers of any ilk, even mythographers, are often better read than met.

LEONORA CARRINGTON

Nude Descending a Staircase

In the summer of 1973 I made a trip to Mexico and after a stay in the capital, I went to visit the ruins at Mitla and Monte Alban, both pre-Hispanic sites located near Oaxaca. It was at the town's main plaza in Oaxaca one afternoon that I saw a woman looking for a place to sit and put down her purchases. I offered her a seat at my table, the only one with any room in the crowded sidewalk café. Gloria Feman Orenstein and I were both from Manhattan, had both done our doctoral studies at New York University, knew some of the same people, were both interested in Surrealism. It was a fated encounter and we became friends instantly.

In 1972 I had begun preparations for a major international event to celebrate the 50th anniversary of Surrealism, which André Breton had launched with his Manifesto of 1924. Gloria, who had written *The Theater of the Marvelous* and articles on the women of Surrealism, accepted my invitation to be a guest speaker at

Surrealism–A Celebration, to be held in November of 1974. So pleased was she by her involvement in the event that she suggested that the painter Leonora Carrington, whom she knew, might be interested in being invited.

It was Gloria who took me to meet Leonora Carrington at her Mexico City home a few days later. Leonora Carrington had left war-torn Europe in 1942 and through a marriage of convenience to a Mexican diplomat whom she had befriended in Paris, became a resident in Mexico City. She went on to marry the Hungarian emigré photographer Emeric ("Chiki") Weisz. They lived ever since in a townhouse in the Colonia Roma, a bohemian residential quarter of the city that has become upscale.

I had heard that Leonora was unpredictable and had been known to greet her guests by descending her staircase in the nude. I thought immediately of Marcel Duchamps celebrated painting "Nude Descending a Staircase," which had caused a furor when exhibited in New York in 1913, and on hearing of Leonora's penchant for nude descents I wondered if the painting had been her inspiration. Expectant or apprehensive, I waited for the door to her house to be opened. And it was Leonora herself who received us, her gracious welcome enhanced by her being fully and elegantly dressed. I was relieved at the same time that I was disappointed. We entered the house and our host showed us into the livingroom.

Leonora and the Surrealist painter Max Ernst had met in London and become lovers. During their many years together, he did many paintings and drawings for which she modeled. He called her "Bride of the Wind," the title of several of those early paintings. When her collection of stories La Dame ovale was published in Paris in 1939, the book carried the illustrations by Max Ernst. Then the lovers had had to suffer a separation when Ernst was incarcerated in a Nazi concentration camp. Leonora suffered a mental breakdown and had to be treated at a sanatorium in Santander, Spain. Later she returned briefly to her native England. Although she had painted and written earlier, it was during those reclusive years that she began to find the world of the marvelous that would define her painting thereafter. And the rest, as the saying has it, is history, for Leonora was to become an important Surrealist painter and writer in her own right.

And now Gloria and I set out to convince Leonora to attend the event as a special guest. Soon she was in the fold and promised that the Brewster Gallery in New York would make some of her works available for the exhibit that I was planning. She added that her son Gabriel was making a film on Surrealism and I asked her to invite him to give it its U.S. premiere at Surrealism–A Celebration. They would come together by train, she said, since Leonora refused to fly.

When I left Mexico I was a happy camper for I had garnered a gem for the celebratory event in 1974 and had an unexpected boon: the first showing of a new film on Surrealism. I envisioned, too, getting the Duchamp painting on loan from The Philadelphia Museum of Art and having Leonora Carrington pose next to it.

I did not expect to see Leonora again until late in 1974 but one day in 1973 I received a call from Gloria, who was still living in New York at the time, telling me that Leonora was in the city and that I had been invited to a party in her honor at her son's apartment in the area of Greenwich Village. Expecting to meet the filmmaker, I met instead the pathologist Pablo Weisz, another of Leonora's sons. As Gloria and I entered the walk-up apartment, we were greeted by a mass of humanity strewn about the small room in a variety of poses and positions.

From directly in front of us came a booming male voice that commanded "Take off your clothes!" I responded that it was not possible to do so since we had not yet been properly introduced to the throng. Pablo Weisz, somewhat nervous at the thought of the pending nudity that my retort implied, proceeded nonetheless to give names to the bodies around the room. Then, as if heroically offering to rescue us from the embarrassment of discarding our clothes, Leonora announced that she would take up the challenge. From the kitchen, where he had gone to fix us drinks, her son's voice cried out apprehensively: "Mother, nobody wants to see a 70 year-old woman's body!" Taken aback by her son's tone, or perhaps by his authority as a physician, Leonora desisted and settled back into her space in the crowded room.

But the situation took another interesting turn when the voice that had commanded us earlier boomed anew, this time offering to undress a comely maiden in black at whose feet he was seated. The damsel in distress was saved, literally, by a bell–the telephone rang and it turned out to be for the would-be despoiler. As he crawled to reach it, the man sprawled on his back and it was in that position that he spoke to the caller. "Hello, dear. Yes, dear, I'm having a good time. You too? Good. Don't worry, I won't drink too much. Bye, dear." Somehow regaining his knees, Boomer (who, I was to learn, was the guru of open marriage) scampered back to his prey and his clumsy hands began searching her skirt. No doubt having thought about what awaited her at his hands and having decided that the notoriety of being publicly undressed held some special reward, the woman in black let his fingers do the walking. She seemed amused by the procedure. It took some time for the buttons on the blouse to be unfastened and all the while everyone looked on with amusement as our inebriated companion struggled towards attainment of his quest. The blouse undone, revealing a well-filled black brassiere, the man was again called to the phone. Slithering like the snake that he was, he again spoke with his darling wife, assuring her that he was fine, was enjoying himself, and, no, he had not had too much to drink, and that he was in the process of denuding a worthy female. It was harder this time for him to return to his place but once there, he resumed his labor. The young lady's half-hearted protests notwithstanding, he managed to remove her skirt and we all saw her lustrous black slip trimmed in lace. Boomer, now panting after his several exertions and, no doubt, in great expectation of things to come, looked at the figure standing above him as if at a goddess (although not one on a pedestal). This goddess was all too readily within reach. A little more effort and his quest would be ended. Then, as he was about to remove her slip, the phone rang a third time. No one was surprised that the call was for him and that the caller was, yet again, his wife, no doubt concerned at her husband's public misdeeds. Crawling once more, Boomer arrived at the handset, mumbled something and fell soundly asleep on his back. The partly-clad lady-in-black, taking center stage, slinked to her would-be debaucher and placed a high-heeled patent leather shoe on his groin. But he remained oblivious and did not have to suffer the final indignity of seeing her put on the garments he had worked so diligently to remove.

The party continued, if not as animatedly, over his "corpse," an apt surreal image. When I asked what the phone calls were about, our host replied that Boomer was the author of an infamous, controversial and best-selling book that promoted sexual freedom in marriage and a sharing with one's partner of one's hijinks, that he and his wife practiced what the book preached, and that she–dutiful wife that she was–put aside her own pleasurable dalliance at another party just to make sure that her husband was having a good time. This happened with great regularity, according to Pablo and his guests. I need not have wondered at Boomer's unfazed telephone admission of his doings to his wife.

When I bid goodnight to Leonora, Pablo, Gloria and the other extant revelers, I wondered how Boomer's night out would end. Would wifey come to collect his sotted bones or would some good samaritan perform the onerous task? And once home, would wifey probe his sotted mind for a blow-by-blow description of his antics that night? Would he know? Did he ever after such drinking bouts? And when sober, would he care about his wife's own doings and listen attentively at the description of her own orgiastic revels? I wondered if they had ever had any. Some years later, in a sequel to the book, the authors admitted that while the theory was fine the practice left something to be desired. I know that I witnessed the beginning of the end of his marriage for the guru of "openness" with the telling telephone as the instrument of its demise. The evening had something of the surreal about it and it was fitting that Leonora Carrington had provided Gloria and me entry into the outlandish world of pop-culture.

But Leonora was to disappoint me deeply. Despite numerous letters, telegrams and phone calls to her Mexico City home as the opening of Surrealism–A Celebration approached, I never heard from Leonora, or her son. The opening ceremony was to highlight the premiere of Gabriel Weisz's surrealist film but neither he nor the print arrived. It was fortunate that I had arranged for some classic surrealist films to be on hand just in case. Leonora and Gabriel had stood me up but worse, offended the surrealists, art historians, literary critics, gallery owners, theatre directors, and audience-at-large that had come together for the unique event. There was never an explanation for the inconsiderate behavior of mother and son. Was hers a "fear of flying" or a fear of being among other surrealist luminaries? And what was her son's reason?

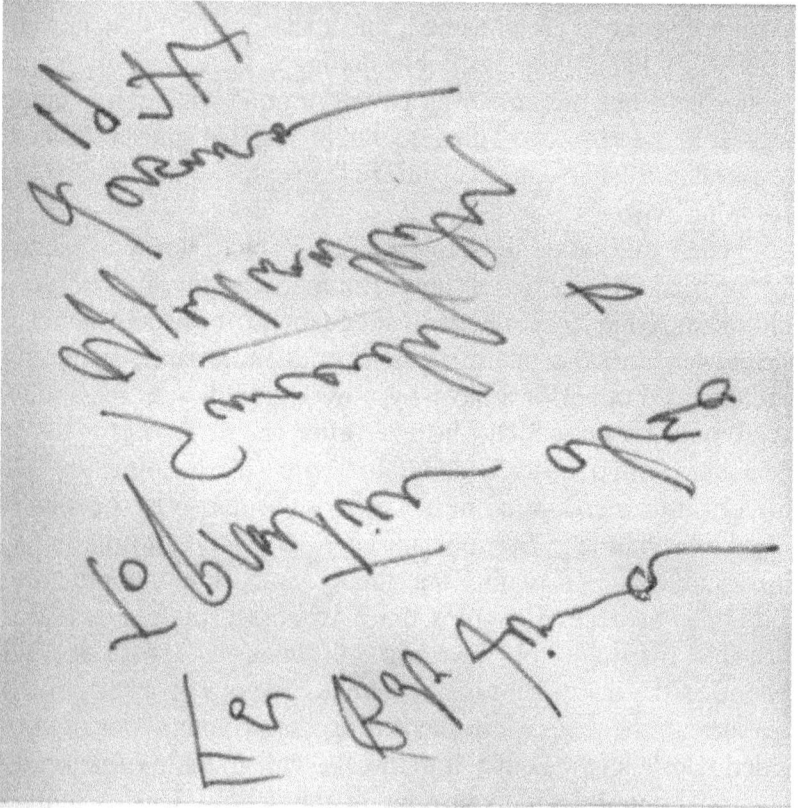

**BACKWARD-WRITTEN DEDICATION TO ROBERT LIMA
ON "MUJERES / CONCIENCIA" 1972 POSTER**

CAMILO JOSÉ CELA

A New York Moment

In the 1960s I wrote to the Spanish novelist Camilo José Cela at his Mallorca home, out of which he published *Papeles de Son Armadans*, a distinguished literary journal he had founded. I had started to research my doctoral dissertation on Ramón del Valle-Inclán and needed Cela to clarify certain biographical points regarding his fellow Galician. Both writers had been born in the northwestern region of Spain, Valle-Inclán in Vilanova de Arousa, Cela in Iria Flavia. Although separated by many years, the young Cela knew the old Valle-Inclán and had some interesting insights into his character, as well as details on his later life.

Although I didn't know him, Cela and I had a tentative connection. I had learned from my aunt Otilia, who owned property on Mallorca and spent part of each year there, that Cela was a frequent guest at her house and vice versa. Gallegos seem to find each other no matter how far they are from their home turf. That same aunt, while a very young girl, was traveling with her mother on a boat crossing the Ría de Arousa; the winsome lass won over a bearded, one-armed grandfatherly man sitting across from them and ended up sitting on Valle-Inclán's lap for the duration of the crossing. It seems that I was fated to contact Cela about his fellow Gallego.

Despite his fame as a novelist and a busy schedule as a celebrity in Spain and throughout the Hispanic world, Cela responded quickly to the queries of this graduate student. I had written to others of lesser renown to no avail and so it was to Cela's credit that he showed himself respectful of others and therefore a man worthy of admiration.

I had occasion to meet him a few years later while still studying at New York University. One of my professors, Francisco Ayala, had asked Cela to lecture and invited the graduate students in his class to help host the noted writer. I took the occasion to thank him in person for his earlier correspondence.

We went to his reading with excited expectations. The room was filled to the limit and some of us had to stand in the back. Curiously, it appeared to us, the first three rows were taken up exclusively by middle-aged matrons dressed to the nines, as the expression has it. Hats and furs were everywhere evident. We had no idea of who they were and thought that perhaps they had come to the wrong room. But the matter was resolved when they buzzed gleefully upon the entrance of the speaker; it became obvious that they were exactly where they wanted to be. During his preliminary remarks, Ayala thanked the Puerto Rican Ladies Club of New York for their joint sponsorship of Cela's lecture.

Ayala's introduction of Cela caused a momentary disruption and instigated the visitor's ire–real or feigned?–when his first and second names were inverted. From his seat, Cela reprimanded his host and pronounced his name in the proper sequence. We were all tense over the incident but Ayala's relaxed apology calmed the invitee. When Cela stood up to speak, he was not only the image of sartorial splendor in his impeccable grey suit and muted tie, but the picture of the distinguished man of letters. The three rows of the Puerto Rican Ladies Club tingled and teeheed in admiration of the stately, manly figure before them. Cela need not have said a word for the ladies to have felt they had gotten their monies' worth.

But things soon changed. Cela produced the manuscript from which he was to read. It was entitled *El toreo de salón*. Since it was not well-known, few had any idea of its content; Ayala knew and had primed his students as to what to expect. Suffice it to say that from the very onset, the reading stirred the room; it was a sight to behold as those of us in the back laughed so robustly that we shed tears while the refined ladies up front squirmed in their seats in indignation. What Cela was reading was a pornographic text, replete with "bad" words and vivid descriptions of sexual acts and bodily functions! The incongruity of the conservative figure at the podium and the salacious things he was mouthing made for one of the most entertaining and memorable sessions I've ever attended. But the Puerto Rican contingent, incensed at the licentiousness they were hearing and no doubt red-faced at having co-sponsored the event, followed the lead of the Señora Presidente and made a hasty retreat from the Hell-on-Earth of that room. Those of us who stayed were rewarded; Cela did not miss a beat as he continued to read through to the end of the work, shocking us into laughter and more tears.

It was a very different Cela that I met in Spain years later. On June 7, 1980, the playwright José Martín Recuerda invited me to accompany him and Ángel Cobo to Fuente Vaqueros, a town near Granada, for the inauguration of a monument to the village's illustrious son Federico García Lorca. At the same time was held a celebration of the Hermanamiento Lorca–Neruda, with the participation of numerous distinguished figures from the international world of letters and the arts. Among the luminaries was Camilo José Cela. Present too were Rafael Alberti, Isabel García Lorca (the poet's sister), Antonio Gala, Matilde Neruda (the poet's widow), Francisco Umbral, Gabriel Celaya, and Juan Carlos Onetti, among many others whose names I cannot recall. I sat on the stage erected on the town plaza and listened to the numerous tributes offered by Cela and others to Lorca and Neruda. It was the last time that I saw Cela.

Camilo José Cela, Nobel Prize in Literature, died on January 17, 2002.

ANTONIO CISNEROS

The Poet and the Chairman

When I arrived at the airport serving Lima, Perú and entered Passport Control, the officer on duty called over his subordinates and showed them my credentials; one of them accused me of using a false name. They had a big laugh over the consternation of this very weary traveler. I knew then that I was a marked man in Lima. My notoriety increased when *The Lima Times*, the city's English-language weekly, did a feature with the headline, "Lima Comes to Lima."

I was in Peru as a Senior Fulbright Scholar for the 1976-1977 academic year, both to do research and to teach. In the latter capacity, I had been assigned an American Literature course at the Pontificia Universidad Católica del Perú and a post as poet-in-residence at the Universidad de San Marcos, oldest in the Americas. The course I created was "La tradición metafísica en la literatura norteamericana" and I had about fifteen students at the first session. But things went downhill thereafter. Although I was required to present myself at the

Dean's office on teaching days and sign the register, giving my topic for the day, my students never came again. I spent the required time in the classroom in the hope that someone would come to hear my golden pronouncements but to no avail. Nonetheless, before leaving, I put the notes on the blackboard. On running into one of the young women from the first session, I learned that my students had been required to sign up for my course even though they had to take another offered at the same time that was required for the major. She told me that they took turns copying the notes and passing them around. Curious about their assigned readings, I ventured to the library to check on the books I had put on reserve; not a one had been signed out. Stoically, I followed my "normal" pattern of signing in and putting notes on the board. I was not assigned an office in which to work nor did any of my colleagues invite me for coffee in theirs, so after each stint on campus I headed to my residence, the Pensión Beech in the San Isidro district of Lima.

My residency as poet at the Universidad de San Marcos was even more frustrating. The Fulbright Office told me that because Maoist students had taken control of the university, as an American I would be in danger if I visited the premises. Although it was a great disappointment to learn that the second part of my Fulbright had been aborted, the upside was that I had much more free time to fulfill my avocation: archaeology. I took advantage of my newfound leisure by traveling often to nearby and distant pre-Hispanic sites.

As a Fulbrighter, I was invited to many private homes for dinners or *fiestas*. At one of these, I was introduced to the poet Antonio Cisneros, a lanky, cigarette-smoking, heavy drinking, good-looking Communist. Christopher Paddack, a pianist serving as the assistant Cultural Affairs Officer at the U.S. Embassy, thought it a good thing that I had met the poet; it seems that he had been offered a Fulbright to the U.S. but refused it for fear that accepting would ruin his chances of cultural support from the Communist bloc. I was "enlisted" in a new effort to win Cisneros over to "our side."

Despite our political differences, Antonio and I became friends and attended many cultural and social functions. Wicked Pisco Sours accompanied many of our sessions and one day, after several of the drinks at his house, Antonio invited me to join him on a personal tour of town and gown sites. I was concerned that his driving might be impaired but he proved himself an able chauffeur.

After pointing out some interesting sites, he told me that our real destination was San Marcos. Now I was really concerned and told him of the warning I had been given against setting foot on campus. But Antonio said that being with him guaranteed my safety; besides, I was a Cuban and was wearing a *Guayabera*, the typical shirt of my island of origin. Speaking native Spanish, no one would take me for a Yankee. And so we parked and I set a still apprehensive foot on the San Marcos campus.

Cisneros was a celebrity among the students, probably more because of his open Communism than for his stardom as a poet, although some of his work was politically oriented. He was greeted as *"Camarada"* as we walked along, sometimes stopping to talk briefly with a student, at which time he would introduce me as a Cuban poet. As we neared the buildings, we encountered a strange sight: blackboards, ripped from classroom walls, had been placed on the lawns and their surfaces covered with Maoist slogans. Antonio told me that inside the buildings doors from classrooms and offices had been removed so that professors could be watched while teaching, preparing lessons or advising students. There were hall monitors everywhere. It was a scene out of Orwell's imagination, if without the technology of *1984*.

We left campus and again set out to continue the sightseeing itinerary, or so I thought. Cisneros had yet another surprise for me. Back in a residential area of Lima, he parked across from a mansion. A red flag lay limply at half-mast. Antonio told me that we were across from the residence of the ambassador of The People's Republic of China and that the position of the flag acknowledged the death of Chairman Mao-Tse-Tsung.

Cisneros insisted that we cross the street for a better look and on doing so he took me by the arm and led me into the building.

He was known to the receptionist and we were ushered into a large room in which numerous people formed a receiving line. We were about to pay our respects to the ambassador and the other Chinese on the demise of their formidable leader. Antonio signed the visitor's book; I tried to pass it by but the keeper of the roll insisted that I sign as well. All too aware of the potential implications of formalizing my presence there, I scribbled my name. But Cisneros saw to it that the Chinese knew that I was an American and I was led back to the book and told that must sign my name legibly and enter my national affiliation as well. Having done so, the Chinese smiled happily and prompted me through the reception line. Everyone, from the ambassador on down, clasped my hand enthusiastically and said how pleased they were to see an American expressing sorrow at the death of the Chairman.

I was furious with Cisneros for having tricked me. But he was not through with me yet. As we proceeded along the front lawn of the mansion, he pointed to an automobile parked across the street. If I looked closely, he said, I would make out a man filming everyone who entered and left the premises. As if to drive the final nail in my coffin, Cisneros added that the film crew was in the service of the U.S. Embassy and that the film would find its way into the hands of the CIA operative there. Cisneros had a good laugh at my expense but I was sullen as he drove me back to my *pensión*.

The following morning, I went to the U.S. Embassy and asked to see the Cultural Affairs Officer. As I entered Frank Florey's domain, I put my arms in the air and confessed to him, his assistant and secretary to having been unsuccessful in trying to win Cisneros to our cause and had instead been lured by him into enemy territory the day before. They laughed! Soon I learned that they had seen the film and had noted my consternation as I berated Cisneros while leaving the wake. Instead of being led off in chains by the Marines as a traitor to country and the Fulbright Program, I was taken to the commissary for a cup of coffee and American camaraderie. Whew! Only after being exonerated by my fellow citizens was I able to ponder the death of Mao, put the strange interlude I had experienced in perspective, and set down on paper my impressions in:

FIRST RESPECTS

I hadn't thought of it at all.
The death had seemed to me
too far removed in many ways.

Yet, suddenly, I found myself
where large funereal wreaths
marked out a zone of sympathy
connected beyond space
to where the body lay
across the nautical
and the terrestrial miles.

Mao's visage here
surrounded by real faces
of inscrutable demeanor
[yet heavy with the weight of loss]
expressing in their stillness
last respects.

The cadences of formal rites
the bows, the handshakes
the occasion to imbibe
the moment's silence
in the presence of a death
that will not die.

Antonio Cisneros may have had a hearty laugh at my expense over the Chairman incident, as I termed it, but at least I got a good anecdote and a poem out of the experience. I never did succeed in winning him over to "our side," but may have had a positive influence on him since many years later he did visit the United States under government sponsorship.

Antonio Cisneros died in 2012.

SALVADOR DALÍ

Gold Cane, Mink Coat and Limo

"Avida Dollars" was the way André Breton baptized Salvador Dalí in a clever, perhaps apt, anagram of the great Spanish Surrealist painter's name. And Dalí didn't mind; indeed, he pursued notoriety and Breton's creation enhanced the image he pursued throughout his career. He even fashioned his moustache into a dollar sign for a famous portrait in the book *Dalí's Mustache*. [i]

I met Dalí only once. He was in New York City in conjunction with the opening of his latest exhibit at one of the city's major galleries. Learning that he was staying at the Hotel St. Regis, I asked at the desk if they would ring his room. The receptionist told me to call him myself; apparently he was not awed by the great man's mystique or, more in point, he was fed up with the painter's notorious antics and wanted nothing to do with him. Convinced that it was futile to insist, I asked the operator to ring his room.

Dalí answered the telephone on the second ring. I proceeded to identify myself as one who had written about Lorca, his intimate friend, and him in *The Theatre of García Lorca* and told him in brief about my desire to discuss a plan I had regarding Surrealism. Equally brief, he said he would meet me at the gallery in an hour.

I hastened to the Knoedler Gallery, located between Fifth and Madison Avenues at 19 East 70th Street. The curator of Dalí's exhibit became very nervous when I informed him that the painter would be arriving within the hour; he had no idea that Dalí would show up that day. Curator and assistants began to rush through the premises like worker beess preparing the hive for the queen; similarly, they had to make sure that their efforts would meet the artist's expectations.

He arrived in a black limousine of the traditional kind (those elongated behemoths had not yet materialized on the New York scene). His companion, a certain "Capitaine," opened the door and Dalí swept out of his regal carriage as if heading for a ball; he was sporting a gorgeous full-length black mink, his trademark gold-topped cane and, of course, the inimitable mustache. I was the first to greet Dalí and he was correct in shaking my hand. But before I could get to my proposal, the gallery staff swooped on him like harpies, addressing him in French since they were too uncouth to speak Dalí's native Spanish. Dalí led the way into the premises and the rest followed as an "entourage;" not wishing to be taken for a francophile, I re-entered the gallery at my own pace.

Dalí's attention went immediately to the display of his works–paintings, drawings, sculpture. He ignored even the curator and proceeded to reinstall some of the sculptures, changing their location. As always, he was concerned with the placement and interrelation of works presented to the public. That too was part of his image. Everyone bowed to his wishes. When I sensed that the time was right, I located myself at his right shoulder (like a Guardian Angel) and began to present my proposal. Unlike the Frenchified gallery tribe, I spoke to Señor Dalí in Spanish. I told him of my plan to celebrate the approaching fiftieth anniversary of Surrealism with a major international event. I had ideated a gathering of major figures in the field, artists, writers, museum curators, gallery owners, and art historians, along with a unique exhibit of Surrealist art on loan from museums, galleries and individuals. Dalí did not react to my narrative. He kept on fussing over the exhibit but he did not seem uninterested either. Hoping to bring matters to a head, I said: "Señor Dalí, we can speak later. I don't wish to disturb you now". If he had ignored me earlier, he certainly did not then. He swirled around, mink flying open, and thrust his cane in my face: "Disturb me! Disturb me!"

I suddenly realized that I was a participant in a "Happening!" Thus commanded to proceed with the improvisation, I did and conveyed to him–now again seemingly aloof–more details of my plan, much of which was already in place. Finally, I said that it was very important to the success of *Surrealism–A Celebration* to have him present as the Guest of Honor. But there was no response or reaction from Dalí.

Patience wearing ever thinner, I turned to Monsieur le Capitaine, who was behind me listening to my every word. Supposing that the Frenchman did not understand what I was proposing to Dalí, I reiterated my plan. He asked only when the event was to be held and, on telling him that it would begin on November 7, 1974, he said it would not be possible for Monsieur Dalí to attend because he traveled **only** by ship, and then exclusively on the *S.S. France*. Since the ship was not scheduled for an Atlantic crossing near the date of the celebration, there was no way for him to accept my invitation.

With great disappointment, I turned to leave the gallery but not before turning to say goodbye to Dalí. It was then that I spotted a pile of exhibit posters for sale. They were priced at a reasonable $25 and I picked out one that was in excellent condition. Naively, I approached Dalí and asked him to autograph it for me. He leapt back as if I had threatened his person with bodily harm (never mind that he had done the same to me moments before). His signature on the poster, he proclaimed, would greatly enhance its value (and I thought, recalling the "Avida Dollars," to heights that a mere academic could not afford to scale). It was a small but uncalled-for ego surge. And I had been the subject of its vehemence! I countered by replacing the he-would-not-sign-it-except-for-big-dollars poster disdainfully on the pile. I left the Knoedler Gallery without saying "Adios." I had shown the master of the outrageous gesture my own pique, if in no way comparable to his masterful disdain. The "Happening" was over.

Soon I was driving home with thoughts of what might have been. At least, I consoled myself, I had met a great artist and one of the oddest of characters. Through that proximity I had also "touched" Federico García Lorca, my favorite poet in Spanish.

But when *Surrealism–A Celebration* came to be and the magnificent grouping of artists, art historians, gallery owners, museum curators, writers, and literary critics from various nations came together and interacted so well, I came to realize that, as the Spanish saying has it: "No hay mal que por bien no venga." There were images of Dalí in the catalogs and several of his works in the exhibit but had Dalí been present, everything would have revolved around him and *Surrealism–A Celebration* would have been more about him than about the movement as a whole. Things had worked out for the better after all, as the Spanish adage had it.

Salvador Dalí, born in 1904, died in1989.

NOTE

Salvador Dalí and Philippe Halsman, *Dalí's Mustache*. Photographs by Philippe Halsman. New York: Simon and Schuster, 1954.

RONALD (RONNIE) DELANY

The Kneeling Icon of the Emerald Isle

Ronald Delany, the great miler from Ireland, became the kneeling icon of the Emerald Isle when, in the 1956 Olympics, he was photographed for the cover of *Sports Illustrated* as he knelt in thankful prayer. In winning the 1500 meter event, he had set an Olympic record.

I met Ron during our days as students at Villanova University and the fact that I was a senior and he a junior did not impede our friendship. Nor did his status as a celebrity even before his success in the Olympics; he had set numerous track records, including being the seventh man to better the four-minute mile, twice winning the IC4A's mile and two-mile races in one day, and setting the world indoor mile record. He had an indoor winning streak of twenty-nine races. Throughout his career as one of the top figures in world track, Ron was ever humble and personable, with a winning smile and a great sense of humor.

Even after my graduation in 1957, when I began attending law school at Villanova, Ron and I remained close. On those occasions when we double-dated, he with Susy Bruni and I with Sally Murphy, a grand time was had by all thanks in great part to his Irish wit.

After a year in law school, I decided to switch into the new graduate program in Theatre. And Ron Delany also opted for that career path, abandoning his major in Economics. We became fellow classmates in the fledgling program. We had different credentials–Ron having acted in Turf & Tinsel, the all-male musical spoof group, and I in the Belle Masque Dramatic Society–but we shared a passion for opera (we both joined the Opera Classica Society) and theatre. Under the direction of Richard Duprey, the program's founder, we performed in several plays on campus and at nearby colleges, as well as at competitions held by the National Educational Theatre Conference and other sponsors.

We may not have won any of these but we were noticed, largely due to Ron's fame. During a rehearsal for Christopher Fry's *A Sleep of Prisoners*, Ron arrived late. But his excuse was more than valid: he had been meeting with a television producer who wanted to cast him as the lead in a series; and we, his theatre companions, were to be featured as well! We were excited! We had hardly begun our studies for the M.A. in Theatre and Drama when this boon came our way; surely, we thought, our careers are made. The euphoria lasted for a few days while Ron pondered the decision to act or not to act in television. Our elation disappeared one day when he informed the producer that he would not pursue the offer; he never did explain why he had made the negative decision. And so we went back to rehearsals.

When I joined the U.S. Army in 1959 and had to go to Ft. Dix, New Jersey to serve my active duty, my contact with Ron was sporadic at best and by the time I returned to Villanova to receive my Master's degree in 1961, he was back in Ireland. Not long thereafter he married Joan, an Irish lass, and began working for Aer Lingus. As a national hero, Ron was very effective in his public relations position with his country's airline.

On June 27, 1964, seven years after our courtship began, Sally and I were wed. It seemed logical that having reduced the name of Murphy to her middle initial, it was necessary to compensate by having the first stop on our honeymoon be Ireland. I wrote to Ron and told him the date and time of our arrival; and, of course, we flew on *his* airline.

Upon arrival in Dublin, Ron was at the gate to meet us. It was a wonderful moment, a reunion after more than three years. He quickly passed us through the formalities and we proceeded to the baggage claim area. To our dismay, one of the beautiful white bags in the set of luggage I had given Sally was badly damaged; indignant, Ron went to the Aer Lingus office and immediately obtained a reimbursement check. After the mishap, he drove us to the Mt. Herbert Hotel, a pleasant small hostelry just off the city center. As we drove into the parking area, one of the maids came to get our luggage. Ron got out of the car to open the boot (trunk) for her and as he did so she froze in her tracks. Her hands were signaling wildly to her colleagues at the hotel and eventually her mouth uttered the excited words: "My God, 'tis Ron Delany! 'Tis Ron Delany himself." Her antics and the rich Irish intonation of her words are unforgettable. Ron, of course, was used to such receptions everywhere he went in Ireland and was soon signing autographs for the entire staff. Meanwhile, Sally and I waited in patient neglect by the automobile and our luggage sat on the gravel quite forgotten.

Once Ron bid farewell to his fans and told us he would pick us up the next day for dinner, the staff recovered their aplomb and saw us to our honeymoon suite. We were treated as if we were royalty because "Ron Delany himself" had brought us to the hotel. It is nice to have friends in high places!

Ron's house was a modest one in a modest neighborhood, somewhat reminiscent of Levittown in the United States. We were warmly greeted by his wife and given a tour. The most astonishing thing to us was the massive Waterford crystal trophy etched with Ron's most memorable moment, his Olympic triumph.

The photograph that had graced the cover of *Sports Illustrated* years before was magnificently captured in crystal. For lack of better accommodation in the small house, the valuable trophy sat on the floor at the turn of the stairs.

But we were in for another surprise, one of a very different ilk. While seated at the table for dinner, Ron kept on answering knocks at the door. He would take the single caller or small groups through the hallway into the kitchen. These people spent a few moments there, came out, tipped caps or bowed heads in our direction, and exited. It did not bother the visitors at all that the homeowners had guests and that we were all at the table. After several of these intrusions, we could not resist asking the meaning of the mysterious parade. Ron smiled and, apologetically, explained that he had the only refrigerator in the neighborhood; his neighbors just had to see that modern wonder for themselves and the Delany's kindly obliged. Between the Waterford trophy, the refrigerator "happening," and his excellent sense of humor, it was another fine evening with Ron Delany.

I returned to the Irish capital on two other occasions many years later and in each case Ron invited me to his club on St. Stephen's Green for lunch. By then he had left Aer Lingus. No matter when I visited with one of Ireland's favorite sons, Dublin was made all the more memorable by the friendship of Ronald Delany.

Staying the Distance, Ron's autobiography, came out in 2006 and the name on the cover is Ronnie Delany, by which he wishes to be known. The book, published in Dublin by The O'Brien Press, runs the gamut of Ronnie's life from childhood to fatherhood (of four children) and covers his stunning running career in hundreds of photographs. It is the story of one of Ireland's greatest and best-loved sports figures, for, as *The Irish Examiner* termed it, "Half a century on [his] achievements still resound." I treasure the copy he dedicated.

We almost reunited in June of 2008. Ron's class of 1958 was having its 50th anniversary at Villanova and I had been told that Ron would be attending. I quickly wrote to him and suggested that I could stop by the campus to meet with him as his schedule permitted. But it was not to be. Ron called me as the reunion date approached and said he was going to his summer home in the south of Spain instead of returning to Villanova. And, he said, he had arranged to take a course in Spanish, the better to communicate with his neighbors and the other locals.

Villanova University at last saw fit to honor Ron with an honorary degree in 2013 but although I had an input into his recognition, I was unable to be with him at the presentation.

Our personal reunion would have to wait for his next visit to the U.S. or my return to Ireland, maybe even to Spain during one of his summer stints there

JAMES DICKEY

A Good Ol' Boy

A conference in honor of the anniversary of the death of Pablo Neruda, Chilean Nobel Laureate in 1971, was held at the University of South Carolina from November 21 to 23 of 1974. Upon driving from the airport to the Hilton Town House Motel at which participants were to stay, I was greeted by an oversize banner over the parking area that proclaimed in bold letters: "WELCOME, PABLO NERUDA!" It was obvious that the Hilton's management was expecting the arrival of the poet.

It would be the most memorable and outstanding of all conference if the organizers had been able to reach into the otherworld and bring back Neruda to receive the honors "in person." No doubt someone aspired to attain the accomplishment of the feat through emulation of the "Magical Realism" of García Márquez. Or, perhaps knowing of my interest in things occult (I was teaching a literature course on the subject), those in charge expected me to head a seance to materialize the honoree. Whatever the ploy, Pablo Neruda never made the appearance heralded by the motel banner. I, for one was grateful that he knew his place.

But the conference proceeded with aplomb despite the letdown. Noted scholars in the field of Latin American literature included Jaime Alazraki, Enrique Anderson Imbert, Manuel Durán, Emir Rodríguez Monegal, Jean Franco, and Fernando Alegría (fondly called Freddy Happiness), among the one hundred eighty presenters from Europe and the Americas. Absent but nonetheless heard through their written tributes to Neruda were the American playwright Arthur Miller, the Spanish poet Vicente Aleixandre, and the Brazilian novelist Jorge Amado. Letters from Matilde and Laura, Neruda's wife and sister respectively, were read as well.

Despite the stellar field of participants, one figure stood out from the crowd: James Dickey, the distinguished poet in residence at the university. Not only was Dickey a very tall man, he was also one of the major poets of the United States with such recognitions as Poetry Consultant to the Library of Congress and the National Book Award.

The great United States poet came to honor the great Chilean poet and made his initial appearance at a cocktail party on the last day of the conference. If not before, Dickey was well into his cups early in the social event. Bourbon in hand, he stood his ground nonetheless and welcomed all comers. He was the university's pampered, can-do-no-wrong star. Mint Julep in hand, each southern belle in the room gravitated to him and he, ever the southern gentleman, bowed and kissed each hand proffered. It was a scene worthy of *Gone with the Wind*.

The social event over, we proceeded to the auditorium where the final session would be held. And Dickey was to "star" in that milieu as well. I was pleased to have been seated next to him. But I came to realize that mine was to be a "strategic" placement when the massive figure of the poet began to slide forward in his chair; it was clear to me that my role as the youngest (and fittest?) on the platform was to keep Dickey from toppling over into the audience. I performed my duty admirably (he didn't fall) as with discretion I had him by the collar, exerting great force to keep him in a seated position. What I couldn't do was keep his mouth shut. As he was scheduled to be the last speaker, he became annoyed at how long other talks were taking; out of his mouth came colorful expletives directed at the presenters. Even I was powerless to delete them. Somehow everyone carried through and duly finished their praises of Neruda. Then came Dickey's turn. I aided him to the podium (for which he thanked me profusely in a loud voice) and, with something to hold on to, began his speech with: "Well, folks, Pablo Neruda was a lousy poet, wasn't he? But he sure as hell got away with it." The audience was aghast. Some, I thought, would have thrown eggs, tomatoes or other missives had they been at hand. As if sensing that he would not get out alive, Dickey performed a miracle: he stood his ground before that alienated group and instantly turned to his favor by delivering himself of a fine appreciation of Neruda the poet, punctuated by lines from many of the Chilean's works. The rollercoaster ride had ended well.

Back in my room at the Hilton, where Neruda never did check in, I was moved by a muse of unknown identity to pen some lines so that the memory of the day's events would not dissipate.

The poem was published in *Sandlapper. The Magazine of South Carolina* (June 1975). Although this poem would not appear in the conference proceedings, many of the Neruda poems I had translated over the years were featured in the book *Simposio Pablo Neruda. Actas* (1975).

SOUTHERN DRAW

Columbia, S.C.
November 23, 1974

I: Reception

Good ol' boy J.D.
bowing with rocky grace
kissing the hands of belles
relentlessly tremulous
in their décolletage
admiring his colossus
of a man

He was bigger than life
in his mint-julep setting
bourbon in hand
e y e s
towering like beacons
sleeping
above the crowded room

II: Reading

He moved out loud
read with baited breath
as if he were tilting
at windmills
lurched emphatically
(recovered only slightly)
went on drawling Neruda
hip-shooter
with pin-ball moves

and mouthful words that stung
and a Jim Beam smile
the size of Carolina
that said hell was ok
if fair-haired was your game

III: Respite

In the end
it ended with relief
catharsis of applause
Good ol' boy J.D.
poet alive
carried it off
by the seat of his pants
with every possible hitch

SIR WILLIAM EMPSON

Yet Another Ambiguity

He came highly recommended. His *Seven Types of Ambiguity* was legendary as a way to comprehend English verse from Chaucer through Shakespeare to Eliot and Yeats. It had been an important touchstone in my English courses in college, as it had for countless others. He had also published the important *Some Versions of Pastoral*, which I had also used, and *The Structure of Complex Words*, which I had not read.

Then, in 1974, I met William Empson. As in many other instances where important figures from the creative and critical worlds came to Penn State, he had been invited by the Institute for the Arts and Humanistic Studies upon the urging of the Department of English.

Being the chairman of Comparative Literature at the time, I was involved in his visit, if only peripherally. I arranged for a seminar for him to teach and helped recruit graduate students. He was also to teach a course in the host department.

Born in England in 1906, Empson was already a frail man when we welcomed him to the university. Small in stature and very thin, he spoke in a quaint voice that was low and hard to understand, perhaps a remnant of his teaching days in what we thought to be the more soft-spoken ways of Japanese and Chinese institutions. Nonetheless, I and others thought he would be fine in an American classroom.

We could not have been more mistaken. A scant two weeks into the semester, students in both departments began to complain of not being able to understand him. One by one they began to drop the course I had tailored for him. Soon there were no students left in the graduate seminar in Comparative Literature. I believe that by a certain amount of cajoling the English course lasted a bit longer, but only.

The reason for William Empson's failure in these instances was not due to lack of expertise in his subject or in teaching–he certainly was an expert in both. We learned from interviewing students that he was distracted, unfocused and rambled. A man of sixty-eight, we feared that senility was taking hold (Altzheimer's disease had not yet become a common diagnosis). He was relieved of his teaching duties but, in deference to his renown, he was allowed to continue with his visiting appointment. He was out-of-sorts in academe, where once he had been a critic of great stature.

His condition also affected his daily life: he neglected his living quarters to the point that some of his hosts, myself among them, had to do kitchen policing of the piles of dirty dishes in the sink and other household chores to prevent the leased apartment from becoming rundown. The man could no longer take care of his surroundings. Or of himself. Sadly, he had become a pitiful figure.

All who were involved with his visit were highly sympathetic to his situation but were unable to do other than assist him in small ways. We were afraid to leave him alone in the apartment at night yet, the following morning, he would be ready when his "ride" came to take him to the campus. He himself seemed unaware of the shortcomings that concerned us. Yet, he remained a genial guest.

I had met William Empson and he had proven to be the eighth ambiguity.

Sir William Empson, beloved dean of modern British critics, died on April 15, 1984 in his 78th year.

PAUL ENGLE

Iambs in the Cornbelt

On October 26, 1978 I was invited to Iowa City to participate in the "Symposium on Latin American Literature Today" under the auspices of the famed International Writing Program of The University of Iowa. The invitation was extended by Jane McDivitt, director of the Latin American Studies Program. I was to learn that the Chilean poet Oscar Hahn, whose work I had translated for a symposium on Borges two years earlier, had been instrumental in the invitation. Arriving on November 26th, I was met at the airport and driven to the May Flower Apartments, where I met the Egyptian journalist Ali Shalash, the next-door neighbor with whom I shared a bathroom.

I had dinner with Oscar and his wife Nancy that Sunday and they invited several Latin American friends to meet me. The next day I was taken to lunch by Jane McDivitt and several of her colleagues, and given a tour of the town and the campus by Peter Nazareth. The event took place on the evening of November 27, 1978 and besides my own contribution to the discussion, I served as Moderator on a panel of writers from various Latin American countries. The writers were the poet Pedro Cateriano Delgado (Perú), the journalist Reina Roffé (Argentina), the short-story writer Edilberto Coutinho (Brazil), the poet Oscar Hahn (Chile), and the novelist Juan Carlos Martini Real (Argentina). The event was a success as the result of the panelists' informed presentations about literature in their nations and their interaction on previously prepared questions; the audience too volunteered comments. I had quite a time of it directing the discussion and keeping things on track and on time.

The famed program that provided writers from all over the world with residencies at the university had been founded in 1967 by Paul Engle, already the director since 1941 of the Iowa Writers' Program, and Hua-ling Nieh, the Chinese writer who was to become Engle's wife in 1971; it was the second marriage for each and each had two daughters. They had met in 1963 in Taiwan when Paul was doing research on Asian writers. The attraction was mutual but they could not marry until their previous unions could be dissolved.

Their compatibility in marriage was reflected in their creative co-direction of the IWP, which soon came to have worldwide impact. The couple was nominated in 1976 for the Nobel Peace Prize and the citation read, in part: "... it is a miracle in our time for such an effort to be made by two individuals with such matchless dedication. Hua-ling Nieh Engle and Paul Engle are architects of a unique program which realizes the dream of an international community of the spirit."

Although Paul had retired in July of 1977 and his wife had become sole director of the IWP, he remained as a consultant to the program. I met them at the Symposium and was taken by their friendly, open nature. Paul was a ruggedly handsome man of 70, a poet of great distinction who had been a Rhodes Scholar, winner of the Yale Series of Younger Poets Prize, a fellow of the Guggenheim, Ford and Rockefeller foundations, and a founder of the National Council on the Arts. The 53-year old Hua-ling had a beautiful oval face reminiscent of Utamaro's carvings, was an accomplished translator of James, Faulkner, Cather and Fitzgerald into Chinese, and had published nine books when she arrived at Iowa as a visiting writer.

Paul always gave her credit for ideating the International Writing Program.

Paul, Hua-ling and I hit it off so well that they invited me to lunch at their home the next day. On entering the country house I was taken by its eclectic nature: a spacious modern structure filled with exotica, including a magnificent collection of masks from the continents of Asia, Africa and South America (a collector myself, I appreciated their variety and artistry); Paul did not need encouragement to put on several, becoming highly animated by what each represented as if he were a street performer. But even more memorable was their camaraderie, including me in their banter as if I was a longtime friend. Then too there was the feast of Chinese foods that was laid before us by their resident Chinese chef!

I could not hope to duplicate the hospitality that the Engles had shown me but on returning to Penn State I began to mobilize various sectors toward inviting the dynamic couple for a residency. Since money is always a major consideration, particularly where two prominent visitors are involved, it behooved me to approach department heads in English, Comparative Literature, and Asian Studies but while all were in favor of inviting Paul and Hua-Ling, together they could not come up with the necessary funds. I then turned to the Institute for the Arts and Humanistic Studies, through whose auspices I had earlier brought Walter Starch and Jorge Luis Barges, as well as the participants in Surrealism–A Celebration. However, Stanley Weintraub, the then director of I.A.H.S. was not enthused and for reasons that he never explained allowed the matter to drop. As a matter of fact, he had never invited anyone affiliated with the International Writing Program to Penn State; I sensed, but could not prove, that some personal bias was behind the omission. As a result, I did not have the pleasure of hosting Paul and Hua-ling under my roof and sharing with them my own collection of masks and artifacts from many nations. It would have been a hoot to have seen Paul don some of these and improvise some antics as he had in Iowa.

Paul Engle, genial man of letters, born in 1908, died on March 22, 1991.

MIGUEL ENGUIDANOS

Eating High on the Hog

In early 2004, *The New York Times* carried the news that La Côte Basque, the epitome of French cuisine in New York City, was about to close its doors... forever. The distress of the writer was very evident for nostalgia oozed through every line of the report. It was as if the closing signaled the proverbial end of a way of life. And maybe it did for some.

As for me, once a twenty-year resident of New York, La Côte Basque represented the ultimate in social snobbery, sustained by the inexplicable appeal of dining a la française at outrageous prices, that made the restaurant accessible to the very wealthy or wanna-bes. Nonetheless, I had occasion to dine in its plush East Side premises on one memorable evening.

A group of academics had gathered in the lobby of The New York Hilton in late December to plan an outing to a restaurant after the final sessions of The Modern Language Association. We were an upbeat group looking forward to a last night on the town before returning to less glamorous cities and towns across the country.

Suggestions were abundant but no two people could agree. The matter was resolved when my friend Miguel Enguídanos, a debonair Spaniard from Valencia who had taught at many American universities, spoke on behalf of "a little French restaurant" at which he had eaten very well a few nights earlier. It was only a block or so away. When we accepted the suggestion, Miguel called for a reservation for the eight of us in the group.

Distracted by conversation as we walked on 55th Street, I was not aware of where Miguel was taking us; no one had thought to ask the name of the restaurant.

We arrived at 60 West 55th Street and stood before the famed La Côte Basque! I knew immediately that I and my companions were in for a very expensive evening.

La Côte Basque had been founded by Henri Soulé but he died in 1966 (in a bathroom on the premises) and, in time, the restaurant was revitalized by Jean-Jacques Rachou, the present owner and chef. When we arrived in the mid-1980s, the establishment was no longer a base for the likes of Truman Capote, who had written about the intrigues and peccadillos of its clientele in *Esquire* a scant ten years earlier. But ours was not to be an occasion for ogling and eavesdropping on the rich and famous; it was to be not only a culinary encounter of the French ilk but an eye-opener of the monetary kind.

The elegance of the premises impresses itself upon eye and mind the moment one enters: Sinuous red banquettes set off by brilliant white table linen on which sparkle high-end cutlery and crystal ware, large murals of French scenes, flowers, strategically-placed ornate mirrors, and a level of lighting that glamorizes the setting. It was intentional opulence, and it worked.

Then there was the typical haughty maitre d', who took a long look at the unsuitably-garbed academics, sighed (no doubt in longing for the good old days of gowns and tuxedos), and led us to our table. Menus were provided and suddenly, as if by magic, three waiters and a sommelier came to our service.

Miguel took charge of selecting the wines and we were soon nosing, legging, swilling, and imbibing some French vintage or other. I didn't even want to think of the price. But one of the women at our table inquired of the sommelier; she had been drinking a *blanc* and her sudden palor put its paleness to shame. There was no doubt that she was in shock over the revelation of the price. As if to diminish the impact, she put down her glass nervously.

Since we had asked for separate checks, even the women in our group received menus with prices listed. When our pale lady took one look at the amount next to each entrée, she blurted out that she was ill and bolted for the door, even before putting on her coat. She was so upset that the poor woman forgot to pay for her share of the wine.

With such as Foie Gras, Caviar, Lobster Bisque, Filet of Sole a la Moutard, Quenelles de Brochet and various Escoffier-inspired entrées, I tossed caution out the door with our deserter and ordered from the seafood selections, followed by a Crème Brûlé since specialty souffles had to be arranged for in advance. A variety of wines, courtesy of Miguel's expertise (if not his wallet), accompanied our sophisticated repast.

Having wined and dined elegantly and well, there was a price to pay. I'm certain that among many the thought stirred that perhaps they should have pleaded illness like our departed colleague and left before the catastrophic accounting. But each of us dutifully extracted a credit card and placed it in the guardianship of our headwaiter. And then, of course, there were taxes and tips to contend with in the final accounting. We paid the price for upscale dining.

Miguel Enguídanos, as if unaware of the early tension and of the one defection from the group, seemed rather pleased that the evening had gone so well. And, cost aside, it was a memorable dining experience for this participant. I'm certain that the others have not forgotten it either.

When he passed away in 1986, numerous colleagues, myself among them, joined in publishing *Los hallazgos de la lectura: Estudio dedicado a Miguel Enguídanos.*

WILLIAM EVERSON

The Friar in White

I met William Everson at the apartment of Doris Lindell, one of the regulars at the readings at Les Deux Megots, the East Village coffeehouse. Doris Lindell (Doe, as she preferred to be known) was a transplanted Pennsylvanian who, like so many in our group, had come to New York City to find what could not be sought or experienced back home. She was young, beautiful in a doe-like way, bountiful like an earth-goddess (or, was it, lush like the vegetation of a tropical forest?), quietly seductive, soft-spoken. I, for one, was taken with her and loved listening to the soft voice that always made her conversation an intimate experience. Doe thrived on her seductiveness and was fond of recounting such adventures as her being at the Italian Consulate where Giuseppe Ungaretti kissed her hand passionately and the Vice-Consul read some of her poems.

The special friendship that we shared had one manifestation in a poem she wrote for me and signed on September 10, 1962; it was titled "For Bob, On His Proposed Journey" when she gave it to me and was published in 1963 in her book *The Heart's Dark Street*, but with a new title: "May There Be Thirst for Wine. For Robert Lima." It was the first poem ever written to me, for me or about me. And I treasure it still, the framed parchment in calligraphy hanging in my study.

One of the many memorable times with Doe was the night of March 3, 1963 when she convened a small group of poets at her West 89th Street apartment. The occasion was the visit of her friend William Everson, then a Dominican known as Brother Antoninus. The West Coast poet had come to New York to do a reading at Columbia University. The poets David Ignatow and Allen Planz were there, as was Jack Gilbert, whose *View of Jeopardy* had recently been published in the prestigious Yale Series of Younger Poets.

Doe's apartment was candlelit for the occasion and the flickering light gave the craggy faces of Brother Antoninus and Jack Gilbert an eerie quality as they each read. Incense filled our nostrils with an exotic aroma. The rest of us also read that night, participating in what was a magical evening that lasted into early morning hours.

The next night, we arrived at Columbia to attend what we thought would be the reading. What it turned out to be was a performance of theatrical proportions: the poet striding back and forth across the empty stage, filling it with his larger-than-life voice and gestures as he recited from memory, all the while dressed in the black-and-white robes of the Dominican order. Afterwards, we visited backstage with Brother Antoninus. He gave me a copy of his book *The Crooked Lines of God* and wrote in it: "Inscribed for Robert Lima / in gratitude for the gesture of his own poems / and in remembrance of our meeting / Brother Antoninus / March 4, 1963 / New York City." A few days later, at Les Deux Megots, Jack Gilbert gave me a copy of his new book as well, taking the time to dedicate it to me with his sketched wishes and signature.

I was ever grateful to Doe Lindell for having been the catalyst of these special moments with Brother Antoninus, as well as with the other poets present on that singular occasion.

William Everson. born in 1912 passed away in 1994.

ROB FISHER

Rob the (Sculpture) Builder

When entering the United States through Philadelphia. one collects baggage and sundries and proceeds to the exit. On doing so, one enters an atrium, the International Arrivals Hall, which features an all-encompassing graphic representation of the Constitution of the United States. The extensive piece is "American Dream" and it was the winning entry from the 320 that were submitted in 2000. It is the creation of Rob Fisher.

An extraordinary artist who pioneered blending computer visualization and engineering principles to create large-scale pieces of sculpture, Rob's works are featured in banks, museums, hotels, restaurants, corporate offices, universities, and public spaces throughout the world.

I worked with Rob Fisher on two occasions and we remained friends until his untimely death in September 2006 from a heart attack. The memorial service was a difficult event for family and friends, but the tone of those who spoke, myself among them, was celebratory because his qualities as a person, husband, father, friend, and artist were so outstanding.

I met him in 1974. I was preparing Surrealism–A Celebration, an international event to commemorate the fiftieth anniversary of André Breton's First Surrealist Manifesto to be held at Penn State University in November. Someone on my organizing committee suggested that I meet an artist-in-residence at Penn State who was setting up an unusual work in the dining hall of Waring Building, one of the university's dormitories. I went there after teaching and was confronted by an immense black structure called The Membrane.

Rob explained that the multi-sided, latex and rubber wrapped "room" was a container for intimate viewing of slides rear-projected on a series of built-in screens. The dark environment in which the images surrounded the viewer, was to be experienced as if in a cocoon. We agreed that the Membrane would be a perfect element in my plans for Surrealism–A Celebration and I gave Rob full creative control in programming the slides.

On the last night of the international gathering, I led the participants from a rather jovial cocktail party at The Nittany Lion Inn on a cross-campus walk to the Hetzel Union Building, where the Surrealist Banquet awaited us. We were in a very good mood and despite some faltering steps and zig-zagging, we arrived at the ballroom which was to serve as our banquet room.

Rob had arranged The Membrane as the entryway to the festivities. One by one, each of us proceeded to the overlapping panels that led into "the thing," as several of our guests termed it. Some were reluctant to proceed into "the belly of the beast" and had to be coaxed by Rob and me, even though I had no idea of what to expect. Upon entering, we found that the floor undulated and footing was precarious but as each fell, we were cushioned by the aerated puffy material. On our backs, on hands and knees, or in a sitting position, we were exposed to an exotic visual and auditory bombardment: not the paintings of Surrealist masters or the compositions of Eric Satie or Kurt Schwitters, but the mouths of insects, grotesquely enlarged, chewing away at plants and each other! Some guests managed to scamper away from the Dantean hell but others remained in the prone position, unwilling to leave the odd spectacle or unable to figure out how to get up. In time, we all escaped from the dark dungeon of Rob's imagination. But he was not about to set us free. Once seated at the tables, and above the din of conversations, we came to realize that the insects had joined us at the banquet, their crude noises intruding ever more distinctly into our awareness. Rob enjoyed our discomfiture greatly.

Our second collaboration was neither dramatic nor gruesome. It was poetic. In 1985, I was serving on the executive committee of the Pennsylvania Humanities Council. Under our sponsorship, we launched "1985–The Year of the Pennsylvania Writer" as a statewide series of events. To the end of fostering local writers in Centre County, I put together two projects. The first was a series of articles by twelve local writers on living and writing in the area, to be published monthly in *Town & Gown Magazine* throughout the year. The second project was Poetry on the Buses, with the works of two local poets featured each month on placards carried by all Centre Area Transportation Authority and campus buses. Among the poets I selected was Rob Fisher. His poem is titled "Epilogue":

> As I returned
> The sun cut through,
> Sending extrusions of light
> From beyond the mountain.
> East defined,
> By surprise
> In a place unremembered.
> And suddenly
> My direction was clear.

Rob moved on to worldwide recognition as the creator of mobile and stable pieces of sculpture in numerous venues but I recall him as the collaborator who playfully shocked us in The Membrane and later who showed a tender side in his poetry.

REMEMBERING ROB

Our faces lit up when we saw each other near.
We had a history of friendship and respect,
and mutual admiration of each other's work.

And once, we'd shared in the Surrealism days
when in his fertile mind developed the Membrane
that led us to the culminating banquet at the HUB.

I saw his genius in and on the buildings of this town,
then in a New York Hilton restaurant, and on to
other sites, as at Osaka, round the world displayed.

His work encaptured light, refracted in metallic beams
or subtled in a scalloped form within a waterfall.
There was no end to his imagining, his mind itself aflow.

My face lights up on thinking of him all aglow,
dining in our home, telling of his trips abroad,
expressing with vivacity the plans for works to be.

My face lights up as I behold him living in my mind.

Rob Fisher, born in 1939, passed away on September 13, 2006.
His creative legacy continues through the efforts of his family.

ROBERT FROST

Coda

I saw Robert Frost at his last public reading. It was in New York City, at the Park Avenue auditorium of Hunter College, where I was teaching, that the renowned poet appeared before a standing-room-only audience. I had never been a fan of his poetry. Yet, I went to the reading. Why? Because I was there, in the same building, and his presence in the auditorium called to me; perhaps in fear that I might not have the opportunity to see him on another occasion, I ventured in and joined the standees.

He was already a frail man, not the blustery codger some had heard cursing or seen hoisting a few. The figure before me better suited the poet of "Mending Walls" and other icons of American literature. But I was more taken with having him before me than with the poems he read. The event was a disappointment but it would remain with me as a milestone of sorts.

Robert Frost, who died in 1963, was to be one of the poets I perceived to have "killed" by my proximity shortly before their deaths (Dylan Thomas in 1953, William Carlos Williams also in 1963, and Randall Jarrell in 1965 were the others). I had been close to them, like a Banshee about to screech out the fateful sound, and soon thereafter they passed on, hopefully to a reward greater than is the poet's lot in this life.

Many years later, I came across a black-and-white photograph by Margaret Duda of the mailbox at Robert Frost's country home. That image spoke to me of the man I had seen at the start of my teaching career and when I was a fledgling Greenwich Village poet. I sought to exculpate myself for the indifference I had felt then by writing a poem about what that mailbox signified and I did so in the simple style that he often favored.

R. FROST - FRANCONIA, N.H.

The flag is down beside your name,
painted folksily along the length
of your old battered box,
leaning slightly above knotty pole
(as once you must have rested there)
among wildflowers and the weeds.

No mail has been picked up,
delivered in these many years.
The flag is down beside your name:
a signal you're no longer here.

RANDALL JARRELL

On the Road

He had come to New York City from the Women's College of the University of North Carolina in Greensboro to talk to his publisher and to do several poetry readings. One of these was at the Bronx campus of Hunter College (now Herbert H. Lehman College) in 1964.

Since I split my teaching between that campus and the main center on Park Avenue, it was fortunate that I was in the proper place and thus able to attend Randall Jarrell's reading. Unlike the photograph in his books, he was beardless on the occasion of his reading at Hunter College. He had an easy manner, relaxing into the sofa from which he read, his voice verifying his roots in Nashville and his life in other southern locales. He prefaced the poems with brief introductions and then read with the ease of one "to the manner born." He was smooth and pleasant, like a mint julep.

After the reading, he autographed my copy of *Poetry and the Age*, which contains his famous essay "The Age of Criticism." I had read the important book in a college English class. His *The Woman at the Washington Zoo* had won the National Book Award in 1960 and he had served for two years as Poetry Consultant of the Library of Congress. His was a life replete with acclaim for his poetry and criticism.

All too soon Randall Jarrell would be dead. Born in 1914, he died in 1965 as the result of an automobile accident: suffering from depression, he had interned himself in a mental facility in Chapel Hill and while walking at dusk on a nearby road was struck, dying immediately. Some who knew his state of mind at the time said that his death was not an accident.

Randall Jarrell was one of four poets whom I would see shortly before they died; Dylan Thomas, William Carlos Williams and Robert Frost were the others.

I tried to capture elements of the man and poet on that occasion.

RANDELL JARRELL
WENT FROM TOWN
RIDING ON HIS PONY

At one moment
he was there
in life and big as
with his beard gone
(as he would be soon)
reading his poems
well and being a poem
sitting on the sofa
of a Hunter College
Bronx lounge

The next picture
has him with a coffeecup

and cookie crumbs
a co-ed at each side
relishing and touching
seeking signatures
on their libidos

He autographed their books

The man loved it all
as poetry

DENISE LEVERTOV

Now and Then

Denise Levertov had published *Here and Now* with City Lights Pocket Poets Series in 1956 and *With Eyes at the Back of Our Heads* in 1959, and was an established poet on the New York scene when I met her in 1959 at the Café Cino in Greenwich Village. That same year she published *The Jacob's Ladder*. Although she had earlier associated with the Black Mountain Poets and later was thought of as an avant-gardist, she disclaimed such associations. She also had the important post of Poetry Editor at *The Nation* at the time.

Twelve years my senior and quite a few steps ahead of me on the ladder of poetic recognition, we did not have a speaking relationship. But it was true that very few of those who attended the readings got to sit down with her for extended chats.

Denise was never at the Cino for long. She was in and out, often reading and leaving immediately thereafter with husband Mitchell Goodman in tow. She always conveyed a sense of urgency, of

116

important things to do elsewhere, that was in sharp contrast with the placidity of the other denizens. Perhaps it was Denise's English (or should I say part-Welsh on her mother's side?) reserve that made her seem rather unsociable, perhaps it was a dislike of the Café Cino scene or of the poetry read there that made her unwilling to share herself with lesser folk; whatever the reason, Denise Levertov did not come across as anything other than one more self-important writer. She did not allocate time for listening to other poets. It was soon clear that her attendance at the coffeehouse was self-serving.

Perhaps it was the poetry editor in her that prompted those hit-and-run visits. But if so, she never did seek out the emerging poets, invite them to give her poems to consider... And yet, when I approached her in 1961 to do an introduction for a poetry anthology that I was co-editing, she consented to read the poems I had gathered. She liked most of what she read and wrote "Voices are Speaking to Us," the introduction to *Seventh Street. Poems from Les Deux Megots*, published in New York in 1961 under the imprint of Hesperidian Press. It reads in part:

> When I was asked to write an introduction for this book, I said I could only do so if I liked all the poems in it. As I took a first look through the mss. I realized how foolish I had been to say this. Does one expect to "like" a whole roomful of diverse people?... Of course there are poems here I don't care for, as there must be for anyone in any anthology; yet, I am honored to have been asked to write this foreword; and I am writing it not for the sake of those poems I like best, but because of a spirit which runs through the whole collection, and to which I respond. How to define it? Perhaps this way: these writers have in common a love of the poem.... They mean what they say. They are worth listening to.

Denise had certainly opened herself to those of us who had left the Café Cino to form our own open readings, first at Tenth Street Coffee House and then, definitively, at Les Deux Megots, both on the

East Village. In our eyes, at least, she had left her pinnacle and recognized the worth of those "other voices."

Many year later, I was instrumental in bringing her to Penn State through the auspices of the English Department's Jack McManis, himself a poet. During the visit, I conversed one-on-one with her over lunch. On this occasion, I found her to be a very different person as we shared memories of our Greenwich Village years.

Denise Levertov, born in 1923, passed away on December 20, 1997.

FRANCISCO GARCIA LORCA

The *Público* **Manuscript**

While working in the early 1960s on the manuscript for what would be *The Theatre of García Lorca*, a critical study of the playwright's entire dramatic opus, I was stymied by the inability to locate the text of *El público*. I knew that the surrealist text, of which only two disconnected scenes had been published, was among the last of Lorca's plays and that several copies had been given to friends in Spain prior to his departure for Granada in 1936.

Federico's decision to forgo a South American tour to be with his family when civil war was imminent proved to be his undoing. By being in Granada when war erupted, he put himself in jeopardy. And indeed, despite efforts by family and friends to move him around the city, he was abducted and never seen again. All attempts to piece together what occurred during his arrest and execution have proven futile; the facts have never been fully clarified nor his body located.

As a result of his disappearance, the manuscripts he had handed over for safekeeping, including that of *El público*, also seemed to have vanished. In the years that followed the civil war, it was not prudent to possess material deemed detrimental to public morals, as FGL's plays were sometimes adjudged. His works were censored and his name could not be publicly mentioned.

I posed the dilemma of locating the manuscript to my publisher, Gaetano Massa, and he contacted another FGL, Francisco García Lorca, the playwright's brother, who was teaching at Columbia University. Through this mediation, a meeting was arranged.

Some days later, I took the IRT Subway Line to 116th and Broadway, in the very heart of the university. A short walk took me to the apartment building on Riverside Drive and 116th Street where the meeting was to take place (Federico himself had lived nearby in John Jay Hall while enrolled briefly at Columbia in 1929). I was greeted cordially and invited into his abode by Don Francisco García Lorca. I was thrilled to be in the presence of Federico's brother, the only such contact with the playwright, if an indirect one, I had ever had. In his youth, he somewhat resembled Federico but before me was a man who had lived the many years Federico never had.

FEDERICO & FRANCISCO GARCÍA LORCA

After preliminary conversation, typical of Spanish social gatherings, I began to ask questions regarding Lorca's life–details I needed to flesh out the biographical chapter that opened my book. My first queries concerned Salvador Dalí, his sister Ana María and their relationship with Federico. Don Francisco provided the details that he could but since he had spent a lot of time away from his brother over the years he could not verify everything I wanted to clear up. I did not dare bring up the sensitive matter of his brother's last days. And then came my big question: What had become of *El público*?

Don Paco (nickname for Francisco) looked at me intently for a time. Then, without a word, he left the room; I was alone in the living-room wondering what would ensue. Some minutes later, he returned. In his hands he held a box tied with a ribbon of a nondescript color, obviously affected by time. Again hesitating, he came to me and placed it on my lap. "Ábrala," he coaxed. Intuiting that I was about to see something important, perhaps of great value, I proceeded to undo the ribbon as he had commanded.

What lay in the box sitting on my lap was the typescript of *El público*!

There have been few occasions in which words have failed me; this was one of them. Not knowing what to say, I said nothing. But I did take up page after page with great care, perusing rather than reading the full-length play. I was holding in my hands the very pages that Federico had written! What had been lost was now found: *El público* was Lorca's prodigal son. And from the all-too-brief perusal, it was evident that Lorca had returned to the Surrealist mode.

Eventually I got up the nerve to make an outrageous request of my host: Could he possibly have the manuscript copied at my expense for me to read? Don Paco neither laughed at my naiveté nor scoffed at my audacity. He merely said that it would not be possible because he was planning to publish the work and did not want it studied until after it appeared in print. Calmly, he took back the box, re-tied the ribbon and returned it to its secure place among the books in his study.

Upon his return, I thanked him for allowing me to interview him and for the privilege of holding the treasured manuscript of *El público*. Perhaps the last play that Lorca had finished before his death, it would be many years before another manuscript of the play was disclosed and published by Lorca's friend Ramón Martínez Nadal. Francisco García Lorca never published the version of the play that he had shown me. There have been several editions of the play but these came well after my book was published in 1963 by Las Américas. Thus, my critical study of Federico García Lorca's plays was published without a chapter on the "lost" *El público*.

The photograph that heads this piece dates from circa 1966, when Francisco García Lorca was at Martha's Vineyard. The image was provided me by his daughter, Laura García-Lorca, who heads the Fundación Federico García Lorca in Madrid. In the photograph, Don Paco was very much as I remembered him during our New York session.

A successful university professor and writer in his own right, Francisco García Lorca, born in 1902, died in 1976 and is buried in Madrid's Cementerio Civil.

ERNESTO GUERRA DA CAL

A Gallego-Portuguese Voice

The dapper man I met in 1960s New York named Ernesto Guerra da Cal, was Professor and department head of Spanish and Portuguese at New York University, where I would eventually enroll as a doctoral student. I met him at Las Américas, the publishing house and bookstore on 23rd Street founded by Gaetano Massa that was a center of Hispanic culture in the city. Nearby was the famed restaurant La Bilbaína.

Da Cal had been born In El Ferrol, a seaport and naval base in the north of Galicia, Spain and although his career would focus largely on Portuguese literature and culture, he never relinquished his love for Celtic Galicia. Born Ernesto Román Laureano Pérez Guerra on December 19, 1911, he spent his early years on the family villa in the town of Quiroga. Thereafter, he was raised in Madrid, where his mother taught.

He became active in the Ateneo de Madrid and attended the *tertulias* at the Café Regina, a center for Galician intellectuals, among them Ramón del Valle-Inclán, and met luminaries Pablo Neruda and Federico García Lorca, helping establish La Barraca, the touring theatrical group led by Lorca and funded by the Second Republic. Having opposed the government of Primo de Rivera, he espoused the republican ideology and took up arms with the Milicias Galegas against the Franco Nationalists. Upon the defeat of the Republic in 1939, Da Cal remained in New York City, to which he had been sent on a mission, there becoming involved with Galician and other expatriates, among them the jurist Emilio González López and the writer-cartoonist-politician Castelao.

On becoming an American citizen in 1954, Ernesto Guerra added his mother's maiden name, da Cal. It was in New York City, then, that Da Cal found his calling, publishing the highly influential book *Lingua e estilo de Eca de Queirós* in 1954; it was the title that made his academic career. Two years later he collaborated on *Dicionário de Literatura Portuguesa, Brasileira e Galega* by writing the entries on Galician literature. Subsequently, he also published four poetry collections: *Lua de álem-mar* (1959), *Poemas* (1961), *Rio de sonho e tempo* (1962) and *Motivos de eu* (1966).

My relationship with Da Cal was multi-faceted. Having left employment at a film company, I joined the New York City office of the Voice of America as the assistant to the producer of Spanish and Portuguese programming. It was there that I re-connected with Ernesto da Cal when he entered the studio to broadcast to Portugal and Brazil. Many years his junior and only starting my career in radio, I became the producer of his shows! But he was a professional and handled the disparity with aplomb.

Knowing that my position at VOA was tentative pending my security clearance (being Cuban-born, it was necessary to show that I was not sympathetic to the Castro regime), he was kind and generous in offering to recommend me for a teaching position at a high school in Queens. But our mutual friend Massa intervened by promoting my cause at Hunter College, a lectureship in Romance Languages that I accepted in 1962.

Although I no longer worked with him as his producer, I was soon a doctoral student at NYU and had occasion to take an independent study course with Da Cal in the setting of his museum-like office. We became friends and he extended an invitation (and ticket) to attend his performance at the theatre of Barnard College where, on All Soul's Day, November 2nd, he played the role of Don Juan Tenorio in Zorrilla's play of that title. I recall that he was the embodiment of the romantic figure and that females in the audience suspended their disbelief and sighed openly over his seductive charm, any one of them willing to take on the role of his paramour. Da Cal performed the Don Juan role yearly over a long period.

In 1964, he interviewed Camilo José Cela for the Voice of America, the noted Spanish novelist having been invited by Francisco Ayala and New York University. One evening, Cela addressed an audience composed of graduate students and a large number of Hispanic ladies from a social group which co-sponsored the evening event. After Ayala's introduction, Cela read "El toreo de salón," a piece replete with porno, foul words and indecencies of many kinds. Those of us who knew his works, expected no less yet we rocked in our chairs with laughter and couldn't hold back tears. The ladies, however, had a very different reaction: following the leader of their congregation, they noisily stood up and stomped out of the room. Cela, of course, continued his outrageous performance without batting the proverbial eye. And we roared on!

It may have been after this night of mirth that Da Cal interviewed Cela, probably for the VOA; the recording is at The Hispanic Society of America in upper Manhattan.

I left New York City in 1965 and did not see Da Cal again. I leaned that when he retired from NYU, he returned to Portugal and that from 1977 he lived in Estoril, there continuing to publish his poetry, among others the books *Futuro imemorial* (1985), *Deus, tempo, morte, amor e outras bagatelas* (1987) and *Espelho cego* (1990). He passed away in Lisbon on July 28, 1994 and is buried there.

WALTER LOWENFELS

A Real *Mensch*

Walter and Lillian Lowenfels came occasionally to the Les Deux Megots, the East Village coffeehouse, for the poetry readings. It was there that I met them and we soon became friends. On one of those evenings–it was during the Christmas season of 1964–Lillian came to the readings with her newly-issued book of Hispanic poetry published by Corinth, *Modern Poetry from Spain and Latin America*, which she and Nan Braymer had translated. Besides an extensive collection of the works of César Vallejo, who looks wistfully from the cover in a June 9, 1938 drawing by his friend Picasso, the contents featured another eleven poets, among them the Cuban Nicolás Guillén, the Spaniard Rafael Alberti (who belonged to the same generation of poets as García Lorca), his countryman Blas de Otero, and a group of four Catalan poets; the introduction was by Walter. Lillian stood, read a few of the selections and then passed the book around. She autographed my copy "For Bob, from Lillian Lowenfels. Xmas 1964."

My most memorable evening with Walt and Lillian took place in the spring of 1965 at the apartment of Allen and Doris Planz. I was accompanied by my wife, Sally Ann Murphy, whom I had wed on June 27, 1964 after a long (seven years) and long-distance (NYC-Philadelphia) courtship. Sally was expecting our first child (June 9th) and we would soon thereafter be leaving New York City for far-western Pennsylvania, but those thoughts were dispersed by the special atmosphere that evening. Walter–Surrealist, avant-garde, political radical–was full of "the gift of gab" (you don't have to be Irish to have it) and regaled us with stories of his outlandish deeds as an ex-pat in Paris in the 1920s, and as a Communist in the 1930s and 1940s, for which activism he was jailed under the Smith Act.. When he emerged from prison, he settled in New York City and became a touchstone for many avant-gardist writers and political dissidents.

Besides being talented as story-teller and raconteur, Walt was a shrewd purveyor of his poetry. Prior to the reading that evening, he passed his books to us, each one given a copy of *American Voices* and *Some Deaths*, ostensibly so we could follow along. Later, he told us to keep them... for a price. I bought the two books and he joyfully autographed each, referring to the first as "this forgotten book," and signing the second for "my fellow translator." Perhaps because the poet's books are often forgotten, Walter Lowenfels had to swallow his pride and resort to self-promotion. In Walter's case, his literary stature and his personable manner justified his *chutzpah*. Rather than feeling put upon, I felt good about helping a fellow poet by buying two books of great creative worth. When we said goodnight to Allen and Doris (not knowing we'd never see her again due to her death), Sally and I were pleased to give Walt and Lillian, who was an invalid, a ride home. Three years later, in remembrance of that special night of poetry and friendship, Walt sent me *To an Imaginary Daughter* with the inscription:

> "Dear Robert–This is for that
> baby you were having
> when we met,
> and for your poems!

Thanks
Walt Lowenfels
Peekskill
1968."

Now that he and Lillian are gone, I have left the vivid mental image of that night, a few of Walter's letters from the years thereafter, and the cover photo of *Some Deaths*, the visage of the teeth-gritting 1930s revolutionary who was sent to jail until freed on appeal two years later for lack of evidence. There is a record of his poetry readings and political discussions on PennSound.

He was a *mensch*, a man who could push his wife's wheel-chair with a tenderness that belied the ferocity of his photographic image.

Walter Lowenfels, born in 1897, died in 1976.

JACKSON MAC LOW

A Clockwork Poetry

One of the more unusual of the many such in Greenwich Village was Jackson Mac Low. He was the strangest of the strange types that read at Les Deux Megots, the East Village café that was home to a group of poets during the decade of the 1960s. He was a Chicagoan who assaulted New York City with his "chance operations" a la his mentor John Cage. MacLow had begun using this technique in his poetry, music and plays in 1954.

Aloof by nature (or was he shy?), he read obscurantist, discordant pieces that alienated the majority of his listeners by their impenetrability. By the time he started reading at Les Deux Megots, he had perfected his esoteric technique: he read his strange poems ("asymmetries," as he called them) with a stopwatch in hand, clicking it on and off; the interstices were markers for the audience, invitations to interject their ideas into the reading–but only in silence.

He took poetry into such a personalized level of meaning that the process of communication became a private rather than a public occurrence. It was the apparent quirkiness of his experimentation that perplexed many of his listeners, some breaking into nervous laughter during the silences between spoken words, some (including poets) walking out purposefully during his reading. Although he seemed unaffected by the alienation of the audience, I saw his plight during one such indignity and tried to capture his isolation in the poem:

FIGURE OF JACKSON MACLOW

You, sitting there
across four pieces of wood,
shaped,
wait the meantime
of the air-conditioner,
the espresso machine,
pulling your hair beard
away elastic face
to your breath.

You, whispered
in laughter in another across
abused and nervous
until yourself were an across
harsh in constrained bitterness
of defense–
excommunicated.

But if he and his poetry weren't always understood or appreciated, Jackson had other acceptances. His play, *The Marrying Maiden*, for example, was produced at The Living Theatre by Judith Malina and Julian Beck, who sometimes came to Les Deux Megots to hear him perform his "chance operations." We all enjoyed knowing the producers of the most avant-garde theatre in the United States, perhaps because they were famous (or notorious). Jackson was one touchstone to that theatre world I also aspired to enter.

One day, Jackson, whose image included long dishevelled hair and beard, entered Les Deux Megots a changed man. Perhaps in an attempt to appear "normal" to his listeners, Jackson entered the premises one evening with an wholly different appearance: he had been to a barber and his once-long scrufty black locks had been shorn to a near-GI cut. The unexpected effect stunned those sitting with him and whispers began to make the rounds of the coffeehouse. But the full impact of the metamorphosis was felt only when Howard Ant introduced his reading–some hadn't recognize him until then. The loss of his mane prompted me to write in "Poems of Les Deux Megots."

II
The hair falling from him
                              fell
from the scissored comb
                              slowly

dejectedly
already feeling.

The quiet lion had been shorn
and now he roared.

But the pieces he read that evening had not been shorn of their obscurity and remained unassimilated by his audience. To this day, Jackson MacLow has remained faithful to his special calling; to use a hackneyed phrase, he marched to a different drummer until his death in 2004.

JOSÉ MARTÍN RECUERDA

Stages of Collaboration

I met D. José Martín Recuerda, the noted Spanish playwright, in March of 1980. The occasion was the world premiere of my English-language version of his work *Las arrecogías del beaterio de Santa María Egipciaca*. The event took place at The Pennsylvania State University, situated in a then-idyllic locale known to many as Happy Valley. The distinguished playwright was the guest of honor at the symposium Contemporary Spanish Theatre. Martín Recuerda's play, in my adaptation–translation and under the direction of Manuel Duque, was the centerpiece of the conference.

The process of adapting, translating and rehearsing had gone on for nearly two years. When, at last, the opening of the symposium was at hand, José Martín Recuerda arrived from Spain accompanied by his protegé Ángel Cobo; it was the first visit to the United States for both of them and they found it strange not to be in a large city but in the very geographic center of Pennsylvania, keystone of the federal union of states

136

that formed the nation. We had reserved a room for him and Angel at the then Sheraton Hotel (now Day's Inn). But despite the well-appointed room and the hotels amenities, including a swimming pool, our guest was not a happy camper. He told his companion Angel that he felt ill and throughout the night complained of chest pains. He called Manuel Duque at an outlandish hour, when the entire town was asleep, and dramatized his woes: "¡Manué, Mánué, me estoy muriéndo!" Fearing for the man's life, Manuel Duque put on his robe, got in his car and drove to the hotel. On entering the playwright's room he found Pepe stretched on the bed holding a stethoscope to his chest and moaning, "¡Me muero, Manué!" Manuel recognized the symptoms of hypochondria and saw no other solution to the dilemma but to take Pepe home with him. Once ensconced in a hospitable Hispanic home, an atmosphere where he could enjoy the tender loving care of Manuel and his wife Gale, there occurred a miraculous transformation, a true apotheosis through which José Martín Recuerda's symptoms dematerialized and he was able to repose without further cries of near annihilation. The following morning he ate a hearty breakfast and was very jolly, in contrast to his hosts who had been left sleepless in State College.

In the days that followed, Manuel and I met daily with the playwright in the Pavillion Theatre, the theatre-in-the-round where his play would be performed. We spent quite a long time viewing, walking through and commenting on the scenic design created by Anne Gibson.

But I had also contributed to the set, an element important in my version of the play: the *torno*, a circular cylindrical apparatus with a door that upon being turned permits the introduction of objects from one side of a wall to another, all without the person on either side being seen. It would function as a way of introducing into the convent proper foods, messages and... the rebel flag that plays an important role in the proceedings. This innovation, necessitated because there was no other way to introduce the flag into the convent in the setting as designed. The idea for the *torno* came from a deeply imbedded personal experience from my childhood. As a child in Havana, whenever I misbehaved (which, of course was rarely), my parents would take me to a convent of cloistered nuns, there to place me in the street-side *torno*; on ringing the bell, the voice of a nun would ask why she had been called and my father would tell her that I'd been so disobedient that they were giving me away to the convent (no doubt they had seen or read *Canción de cuna*, the play by Martínez Sierra). Satisfied that the reason was legitimate, the holy woman would make the *torno* revolve. And in a matter of a second, I was swung around to the opening on the convent courtyard. On seeing me curled up in fear and crying loudly, the sweet nun declared that I was too beautiful a child to be bad, convincing my parents that they shouldn't abandon me; I, for my part, swore never again to disobey Mamá and Papá. The nun would then give another turn to the diabolical machine and I would emerge anew to the light and the loving embrace of my parents. It was all a very serious matter then but as an adult I came to realize that it had been pure theatre, each participant playing his or her role to perfection while I improvised in that theatre of cruelty. My introduction of the *torno* into the scenic design of the convent in the play was my homage to my own incarceration in that real contraption of a convent in Old Havana.

The *torno* proved effective during rehearsals and all other aspects of the production were finely tuned and we all gathered for the opening of *The Inmates of the Convent of Saint Mary Egyptian* on the night of March 27, 1980. Despite the fact that Martín Recuerda knew of my interpolations and changes to his play, I was nervous throughout the performance. As any theatre practitioner knows, there's no monologue, dialogue or soliloquy that can't be altered by actors on stage, be it during rehearsals or in performance (Are even the soliloquies of a Hamlet or Segismundo exempt?) Because of the language barrier, Martín Recuerda could not hear the variants of my text that the actors mouthed from time to time. I sat irately whenever my sacred words were violated but Martín Recuerda was blessedly ignorant of the periodic travesties and of my discomfiture.

At the end of the performance, something unexpected and unforgettable occurred: Martín Recuerda received the great applause with notable satisfaction, standing at his seat. But, as the clamor grew, he descended boldly to stage center. There, he removed his jacket and with a dramatic flair let it fly into the seats as if he were a torero tossing his cap to the crowd in an Andalusian arena; he then knelt and began throwing kisses to the adoring public on the three sides of the theatre, from whence could be heard a battery of "Bravo" and "Olé". It was no less than a "Happening". But Martín Recuerda did not ignore his collaborators in his momentous triumph and soon called Manuel Duque and me to share his euphoria at center stage. Before the antics of Pepe, we could do no more than bow to each side.

Martín Recuerda returned to Salamanca full of joy over his newfound success, his first in the Americas. That he was pleased with my version of his grand work went beyond the words he uttered before his departure for shortly after his return to Salamanca he invited me to lecture at the university under the auspices of the Cátedra Juan del Encina, the theatre department that he headed. Installed in the august lecture hall where Fray Luis de León had taught his classes, and seated on the very throne-like chair, his *cátedra*, I was tempted to begin my lecture as had the great maestro upon returning from his imprisonment, beginning by speaking the lapidary phrase, "Como decíamos ayer." But I resisted the temptation.

A few days later while in Madrid, I was astonished at the recognition I received as translator of Martín Recuerda's play. Awaiting me at the hotel was a luncheon invitation from the Cultural Affairs Officer of the U.S. Embassy and I was regaled with newspaper clippings and magazine articles on the U.S. premiere of *Las arregogías* and my role as its adaptor and translator. I was also very well received by the theatre world of Madrid, including by the playwrights Lauro Olmo and Antonio Buero Vallejo, the critic José Monleón, and the Fundación Juan March, in whose library of Spanish theatre I was given a private office.

My days basking in the glory of my fame in Madrid were short for upon the completion of the academic year at Salamanca, Martín

Recuerda, accompanied by Ángel Cobo, met me in the capital and took a heading south to Granada. Upon arriving, we met Juan, Pepe's brother and, instigated by his exuberance at seeing us, let him take us from plaza to back street, visiting bars and cafés where the flamboyant brothers were as famous as movie stars. Even though I knew Granada from two previous visits, I found myself introduced to aspects of the city and its life which were wholly new to me. It was as if I were on a secular pilgrimage through streets and back alleys of another city. And I was in excellent and distinguished company.

I stayed with Pepe, Juan and Angel at their home, "La Torrecica," in Salobreña, on the Costa del Sol and was wined and dined at various al fresco restaurants, on which occasions I met many of Pepe's admirers, some of whom were writers. On June 7, 1980, the playwright invited me to accompany him and Ángel Cobo to Fuente Vaqueros, a town near Granada, for the inauguration of a monument to the village's illustrious son, Federico García Lorca. At the same time was held a celebration of the Hermanamiento Lorca–Neruda, with the participation of numerous distinguished figures from the international world of letters and the arts. Among the luminaries present were Rafael Alberti, Isabel García Lorca (the poet's sister), Camilo José Cela (the future Nobel Prize winner), Antonio Gala, Matilde Neruda (the poet's widow), Francisco Umbral, Gabriel Celaya, and Juan Carlos Onetti, among many others whose names I cannot recall. Thanks to the intervention of Martín Recuerda, I was invited to join the dignitaries on the stage erected on the town plaza and listened to the numerous tributes offered by Cela and others to Lorca and Neruda.

Many years later, I was to be with the playwright again on Spanish soil. José Martín Recuerda was to be recognized in October 1999 for his achievements. His native city of Granada spearheaded a series of events throughout the month of October and into the first week of November in celebration of his sixty years as a dramatist. On October 15-17 his *Las arrecogías del Beaterio de Santa María Egipciaca* was performed in the Aula Municipal de Teatro de Pinos Puente under the direction of Javier Ossorio. Then on October 23rd a marathon reading of four of his plays (*Las salvajes en Puente San Gil, La Trotski, Como las secas cañas del camino*, and *Las ilusiones de las hermanas viajeras*) was held in Granada, followed by the awarding of the José Martín Recuerda Theatre Prize, which in turn was followed by an *homenaje* presented at the Teatro Alhambra by the Teatro Español Universitario of the city, featuring scenes from *La llanura*, *Las arrecogías* and *El engañao*. A cycle of three lectures on the dramatist took place from the 26th through the 28th of October.

Invited by Don Mariano Sánchez Pantoja, Director of the Teatro Alhambra in Granada, to present one of three lectures on the dramatist (the others were given by Ángel Cobo and César Oliva), the night of October 27th I offered some words in appreciation of Martín Recuerda for his generosity, kindness and gentility as well as in recognition of my professional admiration of his plays. Mine was not a critical study of his dramatic production but an anecdotal assessment of a friendship that began as a long ago long-distance collaboration.

The festivities were climaxed by the professional presentation from the 28th of October through the 7th of November at the Teatro Alhambra of *La llanura*, which the award-winning Helena Pimenta had directed earlier in Seville as part of the *homenaje*. These events, sponsored by the Junta General de Andalucía, were admirably coordinated by Mariano Sánchez Pantoja.

**ÁNGEL COBO, ROBERT LIMA,
JOSÉ MARTÍN RECUERDA AT THE HOMENAJE**

On his death on June 8, 2007, I wrote his necrology in the professional journal *Hispania*. Today, in the town of Salobreña where he lived, the municipality has created the Fundación José Martín Recuerda.

GAETANO MASSA

The Affable Bookman

Gaetano Massa was very important in my life. I met him in 1962 when, having finished a manuscript on the Spanish playwright Federico García Lorca, I went to the bookstore of Las Américas Publishing Company on East 23rd Street in New York City to speak to the publisher.

Upon arriving at the second floor of the building, I entered a world of books. They were everywhere–on metal bookcases that reached for the tin ceiling high above, on nondescript tables here and there, stacked on the floor throughout the premises. At the end of the room that faced the street, a large desk was partially obscured by more books, periodicals and catalogs.

Behind the obstructions, a compact dark-haired man of indeterminate age sat reading. Behind him was the large window with lettering that let the outside world know that these were the headquarters of Las Américas. Despite the disarray, the light behind him gave the figure an aura of serenity. The man first looked at me over his reading glasses and then stood to greet me. Gaetano Massa was smaller than me by about three inches and was dressed simply in a white shirt, black pants and a blue cardigan yet he exuded a cosmopolitan air and self-assurance that made his size and appearance seem unimportant. After the introductions, he presented his wife Gilda, who was secreted in a corner at another desk similarly defended by a parapet of books.

Massa found a chair for me and we sat at his desk. I heard about the operation of the bookstore, about its focus on Spanish and Latin American books, about its service to New York area universities by providing literary and linguistic texts for their courses. He showed me through the store and it became instantly obvious that the man had a passion for books that went beyond his role as bookseller. It was the income from the store, he told me, that made possible the publishing side of Las Américas.

He showed me novels he had published by the Spanish novelists Ramón Sender and Francisco Ayala, and the criticism of the jurist Emilio González López, all of whom had left Spain during the Civil War of 1936-1939. These and many others he had published, including notables from Latin America, appeared on the shelves. Any Hispanic writer who passed through New York City came to visit Las Américas and its affable bookman, Gaetano Massa.

The catalog he showed me included creative writing, critical studies, and cultural materials; there were dictionaries and histories of literature, some of which he co-published with houses in Spain. Re-issues of the classics of Spanish and Latin American literature were published to make them accessible to the area students.

Our conversation was interrupted several times by buyers in search of particular titles and Massa would guide them through the labyrinthine stacks to the exact place where the items could be found; if a customer said he had looked there and not located the book, Massa would roll back his sleeve and search in the back of the shelf; inevitably, he came up with the item and, upon dusting it off, proceeded to price it (nothing in the store had a label, although some had the price inside written in pencil). If the buyer needed change,

Massa reached into his pants pocket, pulled out a roll of dollar bills and completed the transaction; nowhere in the store was a cash register in evidence. Gilda would keep inventory of items sold in a ledger. Massa and his bookstore were definitely not hi-tech. But both were charming.

Returning to his seat, Massa asked about the manuscript I had mentioned when I called for an appointment. I produced the typescript. He paged through it, first assessing its length with the savvy of a publisher; then he perused the Table of Contents and the Introduction as I sat by his side. He said he would consider the work and that he would pass the manuscript on to a reader. When I left Massa and Las Américas I was feeling that all was right with the world and even if many weeks would pass before I would receive word on the fate of my manuscript, I intuited that it would be accepted. Although not a follower of Norman Vincent Peale, I've always believed in the power of positive thinking and I was certainly sending out mental messages of the sort as I descended to 23rd Street.

Whether my emanations worked or my karma dictated it, or my writing would have found favor on its own remains moot. But my manuscript was accepted and was scheduled for publication in 1963 as *The Theatre of García Lorca*.

I returned to Las Américas to sign the contract and there met Robert O'Brien, the tall sandy-haired editor who had approved my manuscript for publication. We found we had many interests in common and soon thereafter began a collaboration that would last until his premature death. Bob had a commission from the American Educational Theatre Association and I soon joined him in preparing *Spanish Plays in English Translation* (1963), an annotated bibliography ranging from medieval to contemporary drama; in it are listed various of my own translations. Subsequently, I worked with Bob on another commission, the revision of Max J. Herzberg's *The Reader's Encyclopedia of American Literature*, a tome of 1280 two-column pages, published by T.Y. Crowell; I would also work on their revision of *Roget's Thesaurus*.

I also began to publish articles, translations of poems and plays, and a bibliography on the plays of Federico García Lorca in the pages of *La Voz*, a journal issued by Las Américas. But Massa's effect on my career was not to end with publishing.

I was then working in the New York City office of The Voice of America, the propaganda arm of the United States Information Agency. With the worsening situation in Cuba, where I had been born, the security clearance I had once held while in the Naval Reserve Officers Training Corps in college came under scrutiny. Although I was performing many fulltime duties as the number two person in Spanish and Portuguese programing, I would not receive a regular appointment until the security matter was settled. I expressed to Massa my frustration over the long wait I was undergoing and the insecurity I felt about my future. A few days later, it was in early September of 1962, he called and informed me that he had made an appointment for me with the chairman of the Romance Languages Department at Hunter College. When I asked why, Massa said that he felt I would make an excellent teacher. I was flabbergasted! I had never taught a day in my life nor even taken education courses. Furthermore, I had never taken a course in Spanish or Latin American literatures. I had written about Lorca as my thesis project for the M.A. degree in Theatre and Drama. Before that I had been an English major. But Massa was not deterred by my disclaimers. He told me that I had to keep the appointment or else he would lose face! He knew that he had me there because he had surmised that I would not allow another to suffer that indignity. He had read me perfectly. But I also thought that the fate of my book might be in the balance were I to refuse; this supposition was unfounded, for I learned the better I knew him that Massa was a man of honor who was never petty or vindictive.

Bearing the onus of Massa's face-saving, I kept the appointment with Professor René Taupin. He had one of the professors show me around the multi-storied Park Avenue facilities of Hunter College. I was then back in the main office. Taupin explained the position of Lecturer in Romance Languages for which I was being considered, which entailed teaching the Spanish language and literature; the appointment would be renewable on a year-to-year basis. I *knew* that the job was not for me but I listened respectfully. I figured that I would be contacted later on with either an offer or condolences at having lost out to another candidate.

And then it happened. Dr. Taupin sat forward on his chair, looked me in the eye, and pronounced these French-accented words: "Well, Monsieur Lima, are you interested in the position?" There was an impish tone in his voice and I thought that the game was afoot. I heard myself reply that I was interested. Imagine the shock I experienced when Taupin's voice, full now of satisfaction, responded: "Excellent! You begin this afternoon."

And so it was that I entered academe, wholly unprepared for the "slings and arrows" that awaited me five days a week in five different courses that ranged from Spanish language instruction through the entire gamut of Spanish literature and culture. Hunter was at the time one of the top women's colleges in the country, which meant that the intellectual level of my students would be very high and that I had to prepare my lessons with great care. I became aware immediately upon entering my first classroom that fateful day that as a young male, and single at that, I faced other challenges.

Once I began to come to grips with my strenuous situation, my vanity kicked in. I must have been quite the candidate to have been offered the teaching position so enthusiastically! Despite my dearth of experience in the classroom, my other shining qualities must have stood out and overcome my deficiency. When next I visited Las Américas, I expressed these thoughts to my mentor. He soon set me straight. He now felt that I could be told the truth: a professor had suddenly vacated his position and with the first day of classes at hand, Taupin was panicked. He had approached another faculty member, Emilio González López, to aid in finding a replacement. The noted Hispanist, himself a Spanish exile, in turn sought Massa's counsel. And I was the unwitting and naive sacrificial offering. I came to learn through this experience that Gaetano Massa was the great mover of Hispanic culture in New York City.

It was in this way that he became the impresario of the play that was my life, changing it dramatically first by publishing my first articles, translations of poetry and a play, and book and then by channeling me into a career path I had never expected to take. That I stayed with the academic life for forty years until my retirement in 2002 is powerful evidence of the wisdom of his intuition.

Among the other aspects of my involvement with Massa at Las Américas was meeting writers and artists. Zilia Sánchez (Cuba, b. 1928) appeared in the store one afternoon and we were introduced. She had come to show Massa some of her drawings and, on seeing them, I felt that she could do justice to the cover of a book about Lorca — mine! Massa agreed with me and assigned Zilia the task; the book appeared with a red band with a cratered moon on a grey field, signifying the blood, sand and moon tropes in the playwright's works.

Another individual whose writings Massa had published was the Spanish exile Ramón Sender (Spain, 1901-1982). His novels prior to the Spanish Civil War often dealt with anarchic and Communist themes. Sender had known Lorca and was enthused by the plan to publish my book on his plays; he asked Massa to send him the galleys so that he could do a review in his newspaper column. That review of my book, the first to appear, was very complimentary of my work and greatly helped in boosting my academic career.

When in 1964 I told Massa of my impending marriage and plan for a European honeymoon, he reached into that deep pocket and presented me then and there with a roll of bills, and they were not singles! His generosity made it possible for Sally and me to honeymoon more comfortably during our three-month-long journey to Ireland, England, Spain and Portugal. I wish that I had thought of visiting Italy in honor of our benefactor, Gaetano Massa.

After passing the reins of Las Américas to his principal employee, Massa went into retirement in his native Italy, settling in Rome. But neither he nor Gilda took it easy. They thrived abroad and were very active in the cultural life of the city. Gaetano (Gae, as Gilda called him) wrote regularly for *L'Observatore Romano*, the Vatican's newspaper, and Gilda worked in various Vatican offices. Gaetano also lectured throughout Latin America and Europe and was the director of Dowling College's Mediterranean Conference, held annually in different countries. He was also awarded a Doctor of Humane Letters by Dowling and the Italian government named him Commendatore.

There was a great deal more to the bookman than a pocket full of bills. And it is to my chagrin that I last saw him in 1982 and lost contact with him thereafter. Gaetano Massa passed away in February of 2009 in Rome; he had lived a very long life since his birth in Taurasi in 1911.

He and his wife Gilda are buried in the family tomb in Gesualdo, together with his sister.

RAYMOND MCNALLY

A Vampirical Obsession

On October 5, 2002, *The Boston Globe* reported the death of Dr. Raymond McNally, Professor of History at Boston College, which occurred three days earlier; his obituary would not appear in *The New York Times* until October 20th. He was 71. In light of McNally's interest in Dracula and other Undead, the *NYT* may have been waiting for the certitude of the scholar's demise before issuing his obituary or the editor may have wondered if it would be within the newspaper's theme of "All the News That's Fit to Print."

When someone you know dies, you remember to think about him, even if you hadn't in years. This was the case with Raymond McNally. Many years ago, I was instrumental in bringing him to Penn State University as a speaker in a campus-wide lecture series. His topic, of course, was to be Dracula, about whom he and his colleague Radu Florescu had published numerous books and articles, most notably *In Search of Dracula* (1972) and *Dracula: A Biography of Vlad the Impaler, 1431-1476* (1973).

I had been teaching Bram Stoker's *Dracula* since 1968 in a yearly Comparative Literature course I created called "Literature of the Occult." The hundreds of students who signed up for the course each time it was offered had also been assigned many other pieces, including a dramatic version of the novel and the plays *The Dybbuk* by An-Sky, *The Crucible* by Arthur Miller, and *The Tragedy of Doctor Faustus* by Christopher Marlowe; the novels *The Devil and Margarita* by Bulgakov, *Rosemary's Baby* by Ira Levin, *The Magus* by John Fowles, and *The Turn of the Screw* by Henry James; along with these came a hearty selection of great tales of terror and the supernatural by the likes of Edgar Allan Poe, Ambrose Bierce, Wilkie Collins, Joseph Sheridan LeFanu, M.R. James, Arthur Machen, and H.P. Lovecraft, among others.

But it was Bram Stoker's novel that most horrified, thrilled and pleased my students. It was natural (is that the proper term?) therefore to invite Raymond McNally, as an expert on the subject, to discuss the nefarious deeds of Count Dracula. McNally and Florescu had traced the historical Vlad Tepes, the great war lord of Wallachia in the Transylvania region of Romania, whose bloody deeds against the Ottoman Turks in defense of his nation brought him notoriety as an impaler and made him feared among his enemies. Out of this historical figure, Stoker devised a novel that cast the heroic (to his people) Vlad Tepes, whose symbol was Dracu, the Dragon, as an evildoer of unprecedented proportions. To the real man he added the image out of folk beliefs of the Revenant, but not as a ghost, rather as one of the Undead. As such, Dracula was made to prey only on females–an interesting Freudian bow to Victorian tastes–in order to quench his thirst for blood, "For the blood is the life," and remain eternally functional in the world of the living.

In the twenty years that I taught the course, 1968-1988, the Penn State campus had gone from being a hippie-like commune to a backlash conservative community. But when McNally was invited in the mid-70s, the far-out culture was still thriving... but so was the Christian right set on restoring old ways. A very noticeable part of the latter was a fanatical sect led by a character who called himself Bro Cope, a once ne'er-do-well who found his calling preaching outside

Willard Building and harassing female students by calling them whores. The enlightened university administration, no doubt fearing the wrath of the unkown backers of the preacher, failed to protect the students from the verbal abuse hurled at them daily. And so it came to pass that when McNally's upcoming lecture was advertised, Bro Cope decided that it was time for a confrontation with the forces of evil. He let it be known that he and his followers would disrupt the lecture.

Some of my students, chagrined over the threatened disruption, brought me the news. I, in turn, alerted the campus and local police forces. Bro Cope was warned that he and his followers would be arrested if they carried out their plan. When the day arrived for McNally to present his historian's findings on Dracula, uniformed and plainclothes officers provided security in Schwab Auditorium, which was filled to overflowing. Bro Cope and his cronies did make their predicted visit but the police presence and the threat of immediate arrest dissuaded them from pursuing their disruptive plan.

The speaker was never aware of the tension caused by the potential incident. When we met later for dinner and I told him what had transpired, I detected a smile of pleasure on McNally's face. I believe that he enjoyed the notoriety that his vampirical obsession brought him.

Our paths crossed several times more when we both made presentations at the annual Conference of the Fantastic in the Arts, held at Ft. Lauderdale, Florida in the spring. But so many things went on and so many other people interjected themselves that we did not have another opportunity for relaxed conversation about our favorite obsession.

With his internationally-recognized voice silenced by his demise, we are now faced with the onslaught of such desecrations of Bram Stoker's novel as the film *Van Helsing*, in which the professorial Dutch expert on vampirism has been transformed into an Indiana Jones type who confronts Mr. Hyde in Paris, the Wolf Man in Budapest, rescues Frankenstein's Monster, and finally does in Count Dracula in his eerie Transylvania digs. But come to think of it, Van Helsing emerges as a handsome and dashing hero in this portrayal, unlike that in the off-off-Broadway play in which he was trans-sexed into a dominatrix. I wonder what Raymond McNally would have thought of such transgressions.

MARIANNE MOORE

A Millinery Statement

Some thought of her as "The Mad Hatter" of poetry, if a female version. And she earned that sobriquet by wearing some outlandish head cover or other throughout her public and private outings. Even the photographs on her book jackets depicted her with a head cover of indefinite form and uncertain provenance. Apparently, eccentricity meant more than comeliness in her eyes. The look was quixotic.

She was thus crowned when I went to one of her readings on October 26, 1962 in New York City. It was difficult to keep one's eyes off the hat and pay undivided attention to the poems she was reading in a soft, measured voice. I don't remember the words but I haven't forgotten the image of the aged poet with her "signature" hat.

After the session, she consented to autograph the books proffered by admirers. I was among those who approached and sought her signature. When it was my turn, she took the *Collected Poems* I held and, like the schoolteacher that she had been in early career, proceeded to flip the pages of the book. Stopping at several, she made changes in the printed text, wielding the pen like a weapon against the inept Macmillan typesetters who had betrayed her poems. She raged as her pen corrected typographical errors (I think she also muttered some utterances the proper St. Louis-born lady must have learned during her enlightening years at Bryn Mawr). I understood her rage in light of my copy being the ninth printing (1959) of the *Collected Poems.*

When she finally got to actually autographing the book, the entry read "Robert Lima's Collect (sic) Poems not corrected." Did she write "Collect" rather than "Collected" to mimic the typesetter's omissions? Whether intentional or not, I then held a personally corrected copy. The only thing missing in the book (and did she also resent the omission?) was a photograph of the poet-with-outlandish-hat. Even without that picture, the quirky image of the poet remains vividly imprinted on my mind.

Marianne Moore, born in 1887, died in 1972.

HOWARD MOSS

Hard Hearing

The poetry editor of *The New Yorker*, Howard Moss was invited by the English Department of The Pennsylvania State University to read at its English Colloquium on September 26, 1978. Having authored several books of criticism, published nine collections of poems, and received the National Book Award for Poetry, the invitee had all the right credentials.

The evening for his appearance arrived and the room in the Kern Graduate Building was replete with faculty and students, many of them hoping to find an "in" to the poetry pages of the famed magazine. There was the expectation that Howard Moss would give a good reading.

As some poetry readings go, this one began weakly, with some mediocre poems read badly. He stood like a stick figure and spoke flatly, without intonation, as if afraid that giving nuances to the words would offend. Neither was there a setting that would put the poems in context. Perhaps the poet was feeling his way around the audience, I thought. But the hope that matters would improve never materialized. He went from bad to worse and some in the audience exited well before the merciful conclusion of the event. It was apparent that his host had never heard Moss read in public or, if he had, he didn't know anything about public performance values.

I stuck it out to the final spoken word, perhaps expecting something to be said (or read) that would rescue the evening and redeem Moss. But I was already thinking of a few words of my own that would express what occurred and didn't that evening.

C L O S E D   H E A R I N G

The words hang on the ears
like Spanish moss,
dangling, nearly lifeless
without feeling or innocence
intruding on one's expectations
with dank, loose greyness,
never quite touching,
hanging about fecklessly,
Moss having grown in years
within the schema of tall buildings
without a single bound
rather than on tree limbs
of some vital swamp
wherefrom it could hang
and mean

So bad was the experience of the reading that I passed up the opportunity to socialize with Howard Moss at a private reception later that evening. I could have attended and ignored him but in a small house I would, sooner or later, have had to speak to him. And what I would have said was better left unsaid. Better not to have attended than to have heaped verbal criticism or to have lied. In conscience, I could not do the latter and thought that the former would be wasted on him. In this instance, at least, omission was better than commission.

Howard Moss may have been revered by the establishment and gifted with its laurels, but I suspected after his dismal performance that much of the recognition had come to him because of his powerful position at *The New Yorker* during forty years. It never hurts to have connections but in this case it was the listeners who suffered the consequences of such Moss-barreling liaisons.

Howard Moss went to his reward on September 16, 1987.

MOTHER TERESA

A Mystical Encounter

Born in Macedonia in 1910, the woman who would become known worldwide as Mother Teresa early on felt the call to be a missionary and after training in Dublin was sent to India to teach. In time, she received permission to work among the poor in the slums of Calcutta, her commitment extending from 1948 until her death in 1997. Her selfless work made it possible for her to found her own order, The Missionaries of Charity, which would become an international congregation of dedicated women and men. In 1979, she was awarded the Nobel Peace Prize. And I was to meet this saintly nun.

In 1991, I went to L'Aquila, Italy to participate in an international congress to celebrate the centennials of the birth of St. Ignatius Loyola, the founder of the Society of Jesus (the Jesuits), and of the deaths of St. John of the Cross and Fray Luis de León, three major figures in Spain's religious history. The event, aptly held at Il Forte Spagnolo from June 24th through the 30th, was the Congresso

Internazionale di Semiotica del Testo Mistico. I had been invited by the organizers, Gilbert Paolini in the United States and Giuseppe De Gennaro, S.J. in Italy. Hundreds of participants came from the United States, Europe, Latin America, and India. On the bus that took a group of us from Rome to L'Aquila, I was the only non-Russian; surprisingly, the U.S.S.R. delegation was one of the largest at the congress.

The gathering was multi-faceted, with presentations in many languages that were translated simultaneously, with roundtable discussions, visual displays, festive luncheons in the dungeons of the fortress, encounters with colleagues new and old, dinners at the best local restaurants... A group of musicians and dancers from the Sangeet Abhinay Academy of Bombay regaled us throughout the event with performances of sacred dance, music and song.

But the most inspiring presence at the Congresso was Mother Teresa of Calcutta. The diminutive nun made only one appearance but that was sufficient to give the participants the feeling that they were in the presence of a living saint. Garbed in her traditional white robes trimmed in blue stripes, she addressed us briefly and offered a prayer for the success of our endeavor. Very feeble, she was led from the podium while the room erupted in applause.

Mother Teresa was not to return to the congress hall. Too ill to venture through L'Aquila, she was taken to a convent on the outskirts of the city where she could rest and receive medical attention. But despite her infirmity, she stayed in contact with us through modern technology: daily, she faxed her hand-written message to be projected on the screen at the auditorium for all to read. One of these, dated 28/6/91, reads:

> My dear People of L'Aquila,
> This brings you my prayer and blessing. Keep the joy of loving each other as Jesus loves each one of you. Remember, love begins at home–by praying together you will help each other to remain together. Let us pray.
>
> God bless you.
> M. Teresa

A small group of us received permission to visit her at the convent. It being a cloistered house, Mother Teresa was borne on a wheelchair to a barred window, spoke to us briefly and gave us her blessing. Were it not that the woman on the other side was a saintly nun, the moment would have been reminiscent of the Spanish tradition of wooing the *doncella* at her window, the lover said to be "eating the iron bars" in his desire to be near the beloved. We too were anxious to be near the holy woman but it was Mother Teresa who had wooed us to her side by her humility and saintly ways.

There is no doubt that her life of selfless commitment to the poor until her death in 1997 will result in her elevation to sainthood. The Catholic Church has raised her to the tier of Blessed. To those of us who experienced her in person, she was a living saint.

NICANOR PARRA

Portrait of the Anti-Poet

It was the afternoon of December 29, 1972. Having experienced intellectual indigestion from seemingly endless papers absorbed during the two professional meetings I was in New York to attend (at the Modern Language Association and the Association of Teachers of Spanish and Portuguese, at the NY Hilton and the then Americana hotels respectively), I set out with some equally discomfited colleagues to seek a luncheon respite at one of the numerous restaurants that then inhabited the basements and ground floors of West 56th Street. Between the Avenue of the Americas and Fifth Avenue we entered a place called Steak Pommes Frites, which a member of the group recommended. Francesca Colecchia, Martha Halsey and John Gabriele were three I remember being in the group. The food was adequate and plentiful, the white and red wines obscure but palatable, the conversation sparkling and wide ranging.

Afterwards, my companions returned to the academic fray but I set out by taxi to meet the "notorious" Chilean poet Nicanor Parra, promoter of a style dubbed *Antipoetry*, which, in his words, "seeks to return poetry to its roots" by eschewing rhetoric and decoration, by revitalizing poetic language through the use of unencumbered metaphor. In this his ideas were not unlike those of William Carlos Williams but Parra's antipoems open the mind of the reader to the absurdity of life in the contemporary idiom. He reveals the irony of life, often with subtle satire, often with shattering force; his is not poetry for the poetaster but for readers with robust constitutions. Parra is a guerrilla of words.

Parra had first reached an English-speaking audience by way of *Poems and Antipoems*, published by Lawrence Ferlinghetti's City Lights Books; his second book in English, *Emergency Poems*, translated by Miller Williams and published by New Directions, had appeared earlier in 1972.

I was anxious to meet Parra and show him the translations I had done for a feature in *Latin American Literary Review* that would appear in the Spring 1973 issue, along with my introduction on the man. After listening to the political and social opinions of the man-on-the-street cabdriver on the long ride to Greenwich Village, I was happy to alight at the 30 East 9th Street address off Fifth Avenue and proceed to apartment 3K, on the third-floor, that the doorman indicated.

Did *Antipoetry*, I mused, also allow for a poet to live in a building served by a doorman? Was the poet one of those upper-crust types typical of literary dabblers in Latin America? Was his use of the *tú* form of familiar address on the telephone when we discussed getting together just a disarming ploy that would be abandoned for the formal *usted* upon our meeting?

Less sure now of how the afternoon would go, I reached his door just as his wife and small child exited; they were on their way to nearby Washington Square Park. A brief greeting and they were off. I was grateful that I would have the opportunity to converse alone with the poet, whatever he might be like.

There was nothing smacking of upper-class formality in our meeting. Parra greeted me in his robe, bare legs, slippers and unkempt hair. He looked the way a poet might look in midafternoon. He used the *tú* form of familiar address and his warm reception set me immediately at ease. The reputedly fierce anti-poet was also an amiable antiformalist. It was good to be in the company of Nicanor Parra.

We sat in the well-appointed livingroom of the apartment he was subletting. Appropriately, the walls were lined with bookcases and the tone of the place provided the right atmosphere for our conversation. Except for several telephone interruptions and the delivery of a telegram (a belated Christmas greeting, he told me), we talked animatedly of his poetry and mine, of the translations of his poems I had brought for him to read, of politics in Chile and Cuba, of his seminars at Columbia and New York universities, of the late Luis Heiremans (a Chilean playwright I had met during his final illness), of his readings at several campuses and of many other things.

Parra showed me his newly published work, which had arrived from Santiago de Chile in that morning's mail. *Artefactos* is not a book but a box containing illustrated antipoems printed on postcards (these, he noted, could be sold individually, thus reaching a wide audience). The collection is in some instances witty, in others raucous, in still others irreverent... In all cases *Artefactos* makes a poignant assessment of contemporary society.

The author was overjoyed at having the collection in his hands not only because he found it artistically satisfying but especially because its publisher, a Catholic university press, had taken a courageous step in issuing what some were certain to criticize as a confluence of pornography, diatribe and vituperation. They would no doubt be seen as non-poetic as well. Parra was elated that the university press had understood what lay beyond the first impression conveyed by his antipoems and the art that accompanied them; those responsible for the publication of *Artefactos* had recognized the intent of the author: to show the corruption, hypocrisy and loss of grace which typify the modern scene. In these and all his antipoems Parra points out with a literary jab where truth has gone awry.

The deep satisfaction and sense of fulfillment which his face and voice expressed as he handled Artefactos effectively underlined for me the nature of the man behind the anti-poet. I knew then for a fact what I had surmised from his writings: Parra was a man of convictions, a person who would not hesitate to attack frontally when he finds that a cause he has supported or an individual he believed in has abandoned or betrayed the ideal which bound them together. *Artefactos* makes this explicit, as in the case of Fidel Castro, beneath whose effigy Parra writes "Marxism" with a swastika instead of the x.

With the postcards still spread out on the table, we listened to Dylan Thomas reading "Do Not Go Gentle Into That Good Night" and I was touched as many times before by the wondrous power of voice and word that was the Welsh poet's. Parra then played a recording by Violeta, his sister, a folksinger who had committed suicide at the height of her professional career. I dared not ask why. The Thomas poem, with its exhortation to "rage against the dying of the light" acquired a strange cast in the context of her death. Parra and I exchanged a look but not a word was said. We listened and we drank the coffee he'd prepared, not the espresso I would have thought a sophisticated Chilean might prefer but instant, perhaps a brew more suitable to an anti-poet.

Having shared both public and private echoes of his life during the long session, it was all too soon time to leave. I left my translations. We agreed to keep in touch and he promised that his agent would forward permission for the publication of my translations. I thanked him and, after a latino *abrazo*, was soon out on the streets of Greenwich Village.

The day had started out fragmented, like the antipoems on the postcards of *Artefactos* but it had come together meaningfully, as they did during the three hours I'd spent with Nicanor Parra.

A few days into the new year, I received a letter from Patricio Lerzundi, Parra's agent, which said in part: "I just talked with Nicanor and he told me of his meeting with you. He was very impressed by you and your fine translations and asked me to authorize you to use them in the *Latin American Literary Review*." Nicanor Parra had been true to his word, as he was in his antipoems.

My article and translations, "The Anti-Poems of Nicanor Parra," appeared in *Latin American Literary Review*, published at Pittsburgh's Carnegie—Mellon University, in the Spring–Summer issue of 1973.

Born in 1914, Nicanor Parra continues to be the ferocious anti-poet.

GREGORY RABASSA

Formidable Translator of the Masters

In 1973, through the auspices of Penn State's Institute for the Arts and Humanistic Studies, I invited friend and fellow translator Gregory Rabassa to Penn State. During his five-day residency in 1974, he did numerous visits to classes besides his formal presentations. I introduced his first talk, "Negritude in Brazilian Literature," at the Comparative Literature Luncheon on April 9th; that evening he was the starring member of a panel on translation theory and practice jointly sponsored by the English Colloquium and Comparative Literature, where I was introduced by Robert Secor (English) as chair and interlocutor between him, Judith Moffet (English), Lois Hyslop (French), and David Stewart (English). On the 10th he delivered his major lecture, "Beyond 'Magical Realism': Thoughts on *One Hundred Years of Solitude*," for the Department of Spanish, Italian and Portuguese. All of his presentations were well-attended for his reputation went beyond the boundaries of Hispanic and Lusophone literatures; among those present, many came from other Humanities departments, especially English. As always, Rabassa's knowledge and wit won over his audiences. He continued to charm those in attendance at the reception I hosted at my home after his lecture.

Gregory Rabassa is the most prolific promoter of modern Latin American and Peninsular literatures to the English-speaking public. He translated 40 books by authors from Argentina, Colombia, Guatemala, México, Perú, Brazil, Portugal, and Spain, and he co-shared the inaugural National Book Award for Translation in 1967 for Julio Cortazar's *Hopscotch*. Numerous other titles followed, including novels by Nobel Laureate Gabriel García Márquez. Most notable was his brilliant rendering into English of the "magical realism" of *One Hundred Years of Solitude* (1970), and *Autumn of the Patriarch* (1976), for which he won the PEN Translation Prize. Other PEN awards followed for foreign novels he made accessible to new readers.

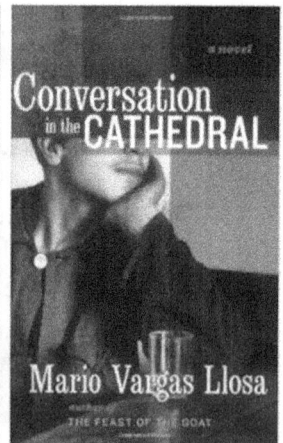

THREE OF THE MAJOR NOVELS
TRANSLATED BY GREGORY RABASSA

As with so many other notables, I met Gregory Rabassa through Gaetano Massa, the publisher at Las Américas in New York City. It was in the early 60s as I was embarking on my writing career and he had yet to become the translator of major literary works. We were both in academia, I studying for my Ph.D. at New York

University and he a full-time Instructor at Columbia University having completed his Ph.D. He would eventually become a professor at Queen's College while I would teach at Hunter College, both institutions part of the City University of New York. And so we coincided at some cultural events.

In later years, I remember his penchant for wearing a military-styled belted great coat topped by a beret jauntily worn and the effect accessorized with a swagger stick, cutting a dashing figure as he strolled the campus alongside me during his residency at Penn State. He told me what he was free to narrate of his service in WWII as a cryptographer with the OSS, having been recruited out of Dartmouth. He was based first in Algeria and later in Italy, and I surmised that he may have had an impact on some important missions in Africa and Europe. But that he could not divulge. My peacetime Army service at Ft. Dix, NJ as a cook at Mess Hall #4 paled in comparison.

We also shared memories of Cuba, of my childhood there until coming to the U.S. in 1945, and of his Cuban father's business as a sugar broker until the market burst in the 1920s and the family moved to the U.S. where his father owned land in New Hampshire; we also left our island home in 1944 because of an economic downturn. Another touchstone was that he had been born in Yonkers, and I came to live in nearby Manhattan, so we also shared being New Yorkers and working at universities in the city.

We reminisced further over a single malt and dinner at my house near the Penn State campus, after which he graciously signed several of the masterpieces he had translated, including García Márquez's *Leaf Storm and Other Stories* and *One Hundred Years of Solitude*. These have a special place next to autographs by Borges, Vargas Llosa, Amado and other literary giants.

A group of us, including Brazilianists Earl Fitz and Gerald Moser, set up a return visit for April 1981 for him and wife Clementine, again as guests of the Institute and the department of Spanish, Italian and Portuguese. But after the arrangements for his stay on campus at The Nittany Lion Inn and for his honorarium, we received a letter informing us that earlier tentative arrangements had come to fruition and he could not join us.

His memoir, *If This Be Treason. Translation and its Discontents*, appeared in 2005 and won him the PEN Art of the Memoir Award. His career was capped by invitation to the White House to receive the National Medal of Arts, presented by President George W. Bush in 2006.

**GREGORY RABASSA
WITH PRESIDENT AND MRS. G.W. BUSH
AT THE WHITE HOUSE PRESENTATION
OF THE NATIONAL MEDAL OF ARTS**

At 92 as of this writing, Gregory Rabassa remains the major star in the constellation of translators of Hispanic and Lusophone literature into English.

MARIA REICHE

Keeper of the Lines

The preservation of the Nasca Lines in the Pampa del Ingenio and Pampa de San José in Perú was the self-imposed labor of two people. The first was Dr. Paul Kosok, an American anthropologist who in 1941 first viewed the earth drawings. The second was Maria Reiche, a German mathematician who has devoted her life to the study of the lines since 1946, publishing *Secret of the Pampa* in 1949. It was that book that first brought the lines international attention. She was responsible for raising awareness of the site, promoting its preservation by the government of Perú, for erecting a viewing platform from which some of the mysterious lines could be seen, and for constructing a site museum.

While in Perú in 1976-77 as a Senior Fulbright Fellow, I had occasion to visit many archaeological sites. One of my excursions from the capital took me far south along the Pan American Highway, first to Arequipa, the beautiful colonial "white city," via a series of "colectivos," shared taxis, and a few days later, returning north by the same network of taxis, to Nasca, which the Spanish had named Villa de Santiago de la Nasca.

I booked a room at the Turistas Hotel. Bypassing the lure of the swimming pool and bar, I immediately arranged for a flight over the Nasca Lines. My pilot was a Peruvian of Japanese descent, one of many whose ancestors had been imported as laborers. He and I took off from the small airstrip and were soon over the drawings inscribed on the desert floor four hundred thirty meters above sea level on a rocky terrain containing ferrous oxide; nearby hills protected the pampa from erosive winds as well as from being covered by sand. The pictographs and rectilinear forms had been made thousands of years before the time of Christ and even though modern vehicles had crisscrossed the images, they still held their integrity.

Below me was a spectacle of incredible proportions and variety. There were the long-distance lines that went straight to ancient destinations of unknown significance, lines whose terminus had once been marked by standing posts. These linear drawings were of many types, most notable being the extended triangles and rectangles but there are many variants in their patterns; that they sometimes intersected on the plains may indicate that new lines superseded the old when the need arose, much like cave artists often superimposed new work on the old. But as fascinating as these were, I was more interested in the zoological images. There was no duplication among them. There was the great monkey with its huge tail in the form of a perfect spiral; various birds: a pterodactyl-like creature, another with the beak of a hummingbird, a parrot-like avian, a fourth more elongated than the others with massive wings, beak, tail and talons; the spider with its bulbous sac; a shark; and other beings of abstract shape with hands outstretched. On a distant hillside that would have been visible from the sea, there is a humanoid figure and elsewhere another image dubbed the candelabra. It was difficult to take it all in considering the many questions that the mind raises on perceiving such magnificent works of early times. Elated but mentally exhausted by the viewing, I alit from the plane, thanked my pilot and made my way back to the hotel and its amenities.

The next morning I had a poolside breakfast at the hotel. The manager, a man in his thirties who had befriended me, joined me at the table. As we conversed about the lines, he pointed out a white-haired woman at a nearby table; it was Maria Reiche, he told me, known as The Keeper of the Nasca Lines. Dressed in what I learned was her "uniform," khakis and a white cotton shirt, she was totally immersed in the books and papers before her. She had recently moved to the hotel after many years in the ramshackle Hacienda San Pablo, at Ingenio, where she had her minute home and field office. The hotel management considered her a national treasure and gave her complimentary room and board there.

Maria was very thin, frail even, and it was apparent that the years of desert living had not only deeply tanned her face and arms but also taken their physical toll yet she was very vibrant when I was introduced to her. Although I was reluctant to interrupt her work, she generously invited us to join her. The three of us sat for a long time and discussed her work, both her earlier assessment of the straight lines in relation to heavenly events of import to farming communities and her more recent attention to the zoomorphic figures. Maria had been working for years on the method(s) used by the ancient land sculptors to plot out the massive figures with such precision and she had constructed a measuring technique based on the length of the human arm; she believed that the designers had first made small-scale models of the drawings and then transferred the measurements to ropes or cords, increasing them to the desired size upon reaching the site for the construction of the figure. But although it was easy to theorize that the purpose behind the endeavor was ritualistic–either religious or astronomical–even she could not say with certainty. She posited that the site was a vast astronomical calendar drawn with great mathematical accuracy, as her measurements unveiled and as she wrote in *Mystery on the Desert. A New Revelation of Ancient Peru*, a copy of which she inscribed to me at our meeting. But to date the mystery of the Nasca Lines remains unsolved.

MARIA REICHE AMONG THE NAZCA LINES

Not long after I returned to the United States in mid-1977, the Peruvian government awarded Maria Reiche the Order of Merit for her more than three decades of study, dedication and preservation efforts at the Nasca Lines. She continued her efforts into 1998, when she died at the age of ninety-five. As an international news headline put it "Maria Reiche to Rest with the Enigmas She Unraveled." And, indeed, after being given a wake at the Museo de la Nación, and paid homage at several schools that bore her name, her body was taken to Nasca to be interred in the place to which she had given much of her life.

Today, the drawings she protected and explicated form an important part of the Peruvian patrimony and have been designated a World Cultural Heritage Site by UNESCO (United Nations Educational, Scientific and Cultural Organization). Maria Reiche is commemorated in Perú with a site museum in Nazca, also named after her.

HAROLD GILL REUSCHLEIN

The Singers Dean

When I entered Villanova College as a freshman in the Fall of 1953, I met Dean of the Law School Harold Gill Reuschlein. That meeting was to prove of great import in my life.

The Dean, as everyone called him, had only recently become the founding Dean of the Villanova School of Law, which opened its doors to the first class that Fall Semester of 1953. At forty-nine years of age, he was a dynamo.

When Villanova decided to proceed with plans to create a law school, the search began for an individual to head the new institution. A nationwide search was conducted and the position was offered to Professor Harold Gill Reuschlein, then a faculty member at the University of Pittsburgh School of Law. He was appointed Dean in March of 1953. The Villanova School of Law opened its doors in September of that year. Dean Reuschlein built the school from the ground up and in 1956, the first class of 28 graduated. In that same year, the American Bar Association granted full accreditation, while in 1957, the law school was tendered membership in the Association of American Law Schools. A subsequent recognition of its status was the granting in 1961 of a chapter of the Order of the Coif, the national law honorary; Villanova School of Law was the first church-related law school to be so honored.

Not only had the Dean undertaken the complex job of constituting a law school in 1953, he had also been approached by a group of undergraduates and talked into taking on another project of a vastly different nature. His reputation as the music director and organist at St. Paul Cathedral in the Diocese of Pittsburgh, along with other music activities over the years, had become known in the process of his candidacy for the deanship and so the students asked him to found a male choral group.

He accepted that challenge as well. The Villanova Singers began in 1953 and I was one of the original members of the group, singing in the Second Tenor section. The Dean had great patience with those of us who were less than perfect in the execution of the liturgical, religious and secular music he had chosen for the repertory. Many of us had sung in high school choirs but the expectations of the Dean were of a higher caliber than those of our earlier directors. He was after perfection. He honed us into a finely-tuned chorus of male voices.

Performing at area colleges and other venues with the Dean as conductor over my four years as an undergraduate at Villanova was a major aspect of my university education. And making "a joyful sound" as we performed popular tunes or conveying the deeper tonalities of a Mass or of a classical piece were exalting experiences. One felt the Dean's own emotions as he led us in the variety of song and even though he was not an alumnus of Villanova, the singing of the "Alma Mater" stirred him greatly for the sound he elicited from us was indeed ethereal.

The Dean passed away in 1998 at the age of 93. He was born on December 2, 1904 in Burlington, Wisconsin. He graduated from the University of Iowa in 1927 with a degree in history and on April 24,

1930 married Marcella Christien, his wife of nearly 69 years. Before attending Yale Law School, Reuschlein was an instructor in History at New York University, a position he continued during his law studies, as well as acting as choirmaster and organist at a New Haven church. He was multi-tasking before the phrase became commonplace.

After graduating from Yale Law School in 1933, Reuschlein continued his legal studies at Cornell on a fellowship, where he earned a JSD, an advanced doctorate in law. Thereafter, he worked briefly at a Philadelphia firm as assistant general counsel but left when offered a position at Georgetown University in 1934. It was the beginning of a career in legal education that would span five decades, interrupted only by service in the Judge Advocate General's department in the U.S. Army during World War II, earning the rank of Colonel. After Georgetown, he taught law at Notre Dame, Syracuse and Pitt.

Having retired from Villanova in 1972 as Dean Emeritus, he became the Katherine Ryan Distinguished Professor of Law at St. Mary's University of San Antonio. But he returned to Villanova in 1984, remaining an important force in the law school he had founded until his death.

Through the sheer force of his personality and indefatigability, he shaped the law school from its founding and watched over it through many decades. "The Villanova Law School is largely the story of one man and his contribution to American legal education," said the late John G. Stephenson III, a noted legal academic, in 1972. "No individual has given more to the cause of American legal education than Harold Reuschlein," read the certificate presented by the American Bar Association, during an awards ceremony in 1992 in which the Dean was honored with the Robert J. Kutak Award.

The then President of Villanova, the late Rev. Edmund J. Dobbin. O.S.A., said, "Dean Reuschlein's inspired vision and leadership established Villanova as a premier law school in an incredibly brief period of time."

Thanks to the commitment and vision of the Dean, just as the Villanova Law School has thrived and has had an impact on the legal profession, the parallel organization he founded in 1953, The Villanova Singers, continues to make a vibrant contribution to the cultural life of Villanova University, the Philadelphia area, and far-flung places throughout the U.S and the world.

The alumni of the Singers have created the Villanova Singers Legacy, an organization that has met at the university in 2007 and every two years thereafter.

The Villanova Singers Legacy is a tribute to Dean Harold Gill Reuschlein as founder and inspiration to the directors who followed him in the creation of a brotherhood of song.

ANDRÉS SEGOVIA

The Personal Touch

My one up-close-and-personal encounter with Andrés Segovia, the masterful Spanish classical guitarist, was highly memorable, even moving. A graduate student at Villanova University, outside of Philadelphia, I read the notice that the internationally-renowned musician was to perform at The Academy of Music, then the city's premier music venue.

I hastened to the box office and purchased the best seat I could afford–an aisle seat in the very last row of the orchestra section, on stage left. It was a disappointment not to be able to obtain something closer to the proscenium. I was not so much concerned with hearing his performance (the Academy is famed for its acoustics) as with being close enough to see his deft fingers on the instrument. Nonetheless, I had obtained one of the last tickets available and I felt a great sense of expectation at being at one of the Maestro's performances.

When the day came, I arrived early enough to wait at the stage entrance of the Academy of Music for Segovia's arrival. The doorman assured me that Segovia had not yet appeared. After some time–it seemed interminable to me–a limousine approached. Although I could not see inside because of its dark glass, I sensed that the time had come. I beat the driver to the passenger door and opened it. Segovia was indeed inside. I spoke to him in Spanish, offering my hand to help him exit; having done so, suddenly, he handed me his guitar case. This total stranger had been entrusted with one of the great string instruments extant, the guitar played all over the world by Andrés Segovia!

The Maestro noted the great care I took with the famed instrument and thanked me when I returned it to his hands at the stage entrance. He went inside and I, full of an indescribable elation, went into the Academy to claim my seat for the much-awaited performance.

Segovia appeared on stage to thunderous applause. It was not the applause usually tendered a conductor upon taking the podium but the kind that a renowned and beloved artist earns over years of dedication to his music and his public. He walked to the center of the stage, sat on a simple wooden chair, and propped his leg atop the low bench in front of him. The vastness of the stage loomed all around him. The silence too was overwhelming to all but him. It was a moment akin to meditation. His and the audience's. Then he began to play.

The program contained many of the Spanish pieces by Sor, Rodrigo, Castelnuovo-Tedesco, Albéniz, Ponce, Granados, and Moreno Torroba that he had recorded over the years and while I was familiar with each, there was no substitute for hearing them performed in person by the master of the classical guitar. He also played several works by Bach, each arranged by Segovia for the guitar, one of his numerous contributions to expanding the literature available to other instrumentalists. The final chord of each piece was greeted by resounding applause, which Segovia acknowledged with a humble bow of the head.

At the conclusion of the announced program, Segovia consented, as was his wont, to an encore. But instead of proceeding immediately to play a piece, as do many virtuosi, he prefaced the selection by saying in his Spanish-accented English: "I dedicate this piece to my young friend who carried my guitar to the stage door." He had not mentioned my name but I felt as if all eyes in the audience were fixed on me; I was awash in emotion and had to exercise great control not to stand and announce to all the identity of the dedicatee. I remained the secret "groupie," to use the later term, of the Maestro.

Andrés Segovia's generous gesture in recognition of my simple act will always stay with me and be a reminder that greatness does not preclude the human touch. I saw him perform on several other occasions but none had the immediacy of that first in-person encounter with the Maestro.

Today, I live with a pen-and-ink drawing of the Maestro playing his classical guitar, a gift of my wife's aunt, the late Philadelphia artist Mildred Dillon. The piece hangs in our living-room and whenever I look at it, I am reminded of my singular experience with Andrés Segovia at The Academy of Music.

SIR WALTER STARKIE

Blood Brothers and Nobel Friends

Not long after arriving at the University Park campus of Penn State University in 1967, I was asked by Anthony M. Pasquariello to take charge of the Lecture Series of the Department of Spanish, Italian and Portuguese. In those days we had access to National Defense Education Act funds for humanities programs and so it was possible to bring speakers of the first rank to campus. I set out to create an impressive list of potential visitors and as each academic year's roster was finalized, I designed and edited a brochure.

Walter Starkie (1894-1976), the renowned British writer and folklorist, was my first choice for the 1969-1970 Lecture Series, the earliest opportunity which he could find in his busy schedule.

He had published several books on Gypsy lore–*Spanish Raggle-Taggle Tales* (1934), *Don Gypsy* (1936) and *Sara's Tents* (1953)–, which he knew intimately from his travels with the Romany tribes, ultimately becoming their blood brother; done vibrant translations of Cervantes's

Don Quijote de la Mancha (1954) and *Exemplary Novels* (1961), and had written *The Road to Santiago* (about Spain's most important pilgrimage site). He had also published books on the playwrights Jacinto Benavente (1924) and Luigi Pirandello (1926). Most of his titles were reprinted.

Starkie gained his vast cultural, historical and folkloric knowledge from numerous endeavors: as a theatre and music critic, diplomat, academician, and world traveler. He first taught at Dublin University, publishing drama and music reviews, eventually becoming the director of the famed Abbey Theatre, the National Irish Theatre. For over fifteen years, he served the United Kingdom as its representative in Spain, with postings on the British Council, the British Institute (which he came to head), and as Cultural Attaché at the British Embassy. He taught at the Universidad Complutense de Madrid and lectured at others throughout the country, as well as in Portugal and Spanish America; subsequently, he was a sought-after visiting professor at the universities of Chicago, Texas, New York, Kansas, and Colorado. In 1961 he was appointed Professor-in-Residence at UCLA until his retirement in 1970.

Over the years, his diverse labors and accomplishments where recognized by many nations. Among an impressive list of decorations are the Order of Alfonso XII (Spain), Legion of Honor (France), Order of the Crown (Italy) and Order of the British Empire; he was inducted into the Royal Spanish Academy of Letters, the Irish Academy of Letters, and the Royal Spanish Academy of History. In 1965 he became the head of the Gypsy Lore Society; no one could have been more suited for the post.

I had met him during his visit to New York University when I was a doctoral student in the early 1960s; I had been impressed by the talks he gave there and by the humility of the man who, despite his fame, was generous with his time and professional counsel to all who approached him.

When I approached Pasquariello, the department head was very supportive of my idea of inviting the world-renowned Hispanist to our campus. Starkie arrived at University Park in late April 1969 for a week-long residency. He used some of the time to do research in the Rare Books Room of Pattee Library with the assistance of its curator Charles W. Mann and to interact with music, theatre and literature faculty members. I had occasion to host him at a small dinner in my home and to accompany him on his university rounds during the week. He was always jovial, made interesting conversation and charmed all who met him.

On April 24, 1969, Walter Starkie gave the first of three presentations, a talk on *Don Quijote*, for the Department of Spanish, Italian and Portuguese. A second lecture, for the Comparative Literature Luncheon, which I chaired, was entitled "My Nobel Friends," and included anecdotes on Jacinto Benavente (in 1922), Luigi Pirandello (in 1934), Eugene O'Neill (in 1936), Ernest Hemingway (in 1954), and Juan Ramón Jiménez (in 1956), among others. His longtime contact with these literary luminaries added much to our knowledge of each as writer and person. His name-dropping lecture was a unique feat in that he had known so many men of letters so well for so long.

Then on May 1st, he spoke on "Gypsies of Many Lands," afterwards regaling the large audience with a solo rendition of traditional Irish and Scottish tunes on his fiddle, some of them learned "on the road" with tinkers. All three appearances were a resounding success but the latter "brought down the house" after the lively performance by the spry folklorist, who resembled a leprechaun as he performed on his fiddle. We had found the legendary pot-o'-gold in Sir Walter Starkie.

**ANTHONY PASQUARIELLO, ROBERT LIMA
AND SIR WALTER STARKIE AFTER HIS
LECTURE AT PENN STATE**

Sir Walter Fitzwilliam Starkie, CMG, CBE, Litt.D, born on August 9, 1894, died on November 2, 1976.

DYLAN THOMAS

The Bard of Laugharne

I saw him only once, at The White Horse Tavern in New York City. I'd been told that he always went there when in Manhattan; he liked being at a remove from the tourists of Greenwich Village and The White Horse, on the corner of Hudson and 11th Streets, fit his needs perfectly. And that of others as well. The West Village bar was a favorite of the likes of Anaïs Nin, the singular diarist and woman of mystery, Norman Mailer and Jack Kerouac, when not on the West Coast. A disapproving hand signaled displeasure at the Beat's founder by writing on the bathroom wall: "Go home, Kerouac!" There were no such graffiti against Dylan Thomas. In time, the walls of the White Horse bore images of his time there.

Despite his reclusiveness, I was determined to see Dylan and one night, early in my first year of college in 1953, I wandered over to the tavern on the chance that he might be there. I was in luck. I was too young to drink but not to sneak into the place and take a peek at the

190

rotund, disheveled figure sitting alone at the bar. His curly-haired head was hung low and he was as desolate a human being as I had ever seen. Had I been older I might have approached him and told him how much I admired his poetry, loved the sound of his recorded voice. But all I could do was stand by the doorway and take in his figure, trying to fix it in my mind.

I was soon hustled out of the premises by the bartender. And yet, I had caught my glimpse of the great poet. Despite his drunken state, I felt privileged to have seen him in person. Not long thereafter, he was dead. He passed away at New York City's St. Vincent's Hospital on November 9, 1953. I had celebrated my 18th birthday two days earlier. I was never to experience hearing him read in person.

Dylan Thomas had been and continues to be one of my literary touchstones. Since seeing him not long before his death, the spirit of the great Welsh poet had called me to visit his homeland. So it was natural that while on a 1979 journey around the circumference of the United Kingdom to visit archaeological sites, I should take time off from that endeavor to give vent to the long-held desire to visit his haunts. I traipsed the streets of Swansea, where Dylan had been born a Scorpio, to several pubs that he had frequented or otherwise been associated with; thereafter, I headed to Laugharne, where he had lived.

My first stop was the cemetery. There I found not a great monument to the town's and Wales's greatest poet but a simple plot topped by tufted grass. At the head of the burial was a wooden white cross simply inscribed: "In memory of Dylan Thomas Died Nov. 9th 1953 – R.I.P."

It was a disappointment not to find a better homage to the creative genius who had penned "Fern Hill," "A Child's Christmas in Wales," the play *Under Milk Wood*, and that highly resonant poem "Do Not Go Gentle Into That Good Night." But since such matters of remembrance are left to the living and many of them did not appreciate the drunkard that they saw all too frequently, or the man whose raucous arguments with wife Caitlin were legendary, it is perhaps understandable that no marble monument celebrated his life.

The hard living, however, could not undermine the monument of a body of work that will ever stir those who read it and hear the recordings of Dylan's sonorous voice.

But if the cemetery was a disappointment, the poet's house was not. Perched atop the promontory overlooking the sea, it too was a simple affair, a modest wooden structure now turned into a museum, if one of minute proportions, run by the Ffynone House School Trust. I took my time during my visit in the house, silently thanking the poet for letting me have the place to myself once past the door attendant.

Behind the house stood the tiny shed-like study where he wrote or polished so many of his fine works, as the placard above the entrance proclaims: "In this building / Dylan Thomas wrote / many of his famous / works seeking / inspiration from the / panoramic view of / the estuary." I entered the one-room outlier where he went daily to write as if approaching the holy of holies. For me it was a sacred site, the home of Dylan's spirit. And it seemed that Dylan looked at me from his desk, surprised to see me intrude into his poetic reverie.

But I was alone in the room. I sat at the small table he had used as a desk and marveled at the beauty below that had fed his creative soul. Caught up in the mystique of the place, I was moved to write a paean at his desk.

DYLAN'S WALK

Above the estuary of Laugharne,
seeing gentle as the water rolled
ashore and out again to sea,
he strode on his high walks
with power of figure, mighty ken,
and rolling voice that carried,
like the tide, its own eternal gait.

Above the estuary of Laugharne,
poised within his flimsy wooden perch
[aerie for the eagle in the man],
he overlorded sea and land
and made them his through Bardic voice.

Mine was not a poem in praise of an Apollo but of a very human poet who had put to paper some of the most memorable lines ever penned. And it is our fortune to be able to hear still that "Bardic voice" with which he was gifted by the gods of Wales as it recites those unique verses from his poems and plays.

Putting aside his human frailties, Dylan Thomas remains my poet of poets. He may have passed away in 1953 at the age of thirty-nine but his voice, be it in writing or in the spoken word of his recorded poetry, remains as a testament to his poetic genius.

MARIO VARGAS LLOSA

The Internationalist

When I first met Mario Vargas Llosa in Lima, Peru in 1976, he was already a novelist established on the Hispanic scene. But his reputation was becoming international. He was so highly thought of by the Cultural Affairs Office at the American Embassy in Lima, that I was recruited to entice him to participate in a television program devoted to Saul Bellow upon his being awarded the Nobel Prize for Literature. I was able to win him over to the idea; we were soon joined by Luis Alberto Sánchez, dean of Latin American literary critics, and the U.S.I.A.'s Christopher Paddack, who moderated *Discourse of the Americas*. The program was videotaped at CETUC, the television facility at Pontificia Universidad Católica del Perú with which I was affiliated, and aired throughout Latin America. The program explored many aspects of the literature of the United States in the context of Bellow's place therein and also focused on inter-American literary relations.

Thereafter, when the University of Texas was preparing a volume of *Texas Studies in Literature and Language* in honor of Vargas Llosa, I was invited to participate. Having recently returned from Peru, I submitted several poems I had written while in Lima that seemed appropriate to the themes that Vargas Llosa covered in his novels and stories. The poems "Debacle" and "This City" (now "Lima") opened the volume:

DEBACLE

The Sun

d
e
s
c
e
n
d
s

like gold

wasting

its

substance

to render

v i e w s

through

our

pollution

*

LIMA

————

t h i s
c i t y
w i t h o u t
s k y
l o o k s

t o
e a r t h
a n d
s e e s
s a n d

Another poem, "Extended," was featured on a later page:

E X T E N D E D

——————————

The houses share
external walls,
the brick and stucco
butting into each
unlike the lives
behind the buttressing
façades

The special issue of the journal, containing articles by literary critics Jean Franco and José Miguel Oviedo, among many others, appeared as the Winter 1977 volume.

I was with Mario on other occasions, most notably during his visit in 1991 to the University of Pennsylvania, where after his lecture the stage was stormed by a large boisterous man in a camel-hair overcoat intent on hugging the speaker. As he rushed the stage, security guards ran after him. It was to no avail. He reached his target unimpeded and was soon upon him. Mario received the bear hug offered by Yevgeny Yevtushenko with aplomb, pleased to see his rambunctious Russian friend. Later, as we three walked on Penn's campus to the banquet held in Vargas Llosa's honor, my daughter Debra photographed us for the campus newspaper.

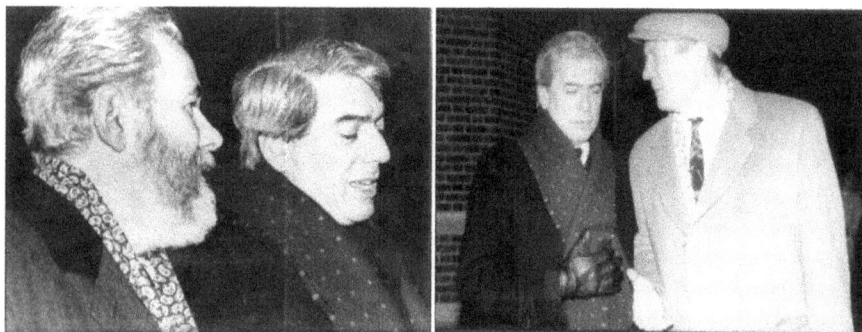

At the banquet, to which the Russian poet invited himself, Vargas Llosa and all of us in attendance, listened as Yevtushenko monopolized the affair.*

More recently, I was asked by *The Baltimore Sun* to review a new book. *The Language of Passion* features items from the biweekly newspaper columns Vargas Llosa wrote between 1992 and 2000 for Madrid's *El Pais*. The indefatigable journalist chose from those numerous columns forty-six pieces ranging through literature and other arts, politics, cultural affairs, lost friends, lost causes, religions, travel, social issues, then current events... He is passionate about what he discusses but does not allow emotion to cloud reason; in matters of world events, he is scrupulous in presenting the facts.

I am reminded that he began his public writing career as a journalist at the age of fourteen and that his commitment to "telling it like it is" stems from long years in that field. He went on to have parallel lives, with a worldwide readership for his prose fiction and a Hispanic following for his columns, which are internationally focused and were written in various countries. Most pieces are between five and seven pages long. Their appeal is to general readers as varied as the book's contents.

There are touching portraits of individuals, as that of a romance novelist in "The Lady from Somerset," of Bob Marley in "Trench Town Rock," of writers from his Barcelona days, of an old Jewish Pole with bunions, of a sacrificed Inca maiden of rare beauty... I confess that I found such bio sketches more satisfying and pertinent than the topical discussions on ethics, national identity, contraception, immigration, and politics although some may still have currency. Vargas Llosa's real strength lies within the realm of character development and I find such sketches attuned to the early Pío Baroja (he who was to influence Hemingway) and "Azorín" (pen-name of José Martínez Ruiz), masters at capturing the essence of human nature and life's minutiae with brevity. Vargas Llosa's sense of loss at the demise of the Reading Room of the library at the British Museum is reminiscent of Baroja's when recalling a bygone carousel. Having said that, I am enthusiastically aligned with his condemnation of Foucault, Derrida and other Postmodernists as "charlatans" and supportive of his unabashed promotion of the criticism typified by Lionel Trilling and Edmund Wilson.

A prize-winning novelist who has created indelible characters and a columnist who has observed reality and tersely reported on its vagaries with valuable insight, he is also a teacher to readers of his journalism. As the title of his column, "Piedras de toque," posits, these pieces are touchstones to the heart and mind of Mario Vargas Llosa; his "language of passion," expertly captured in Natasha Wimmer's excellent translation, makes for informative reading.

On April 10, 2008, I had yet another opportunity to be with Mario. He was named the recipient of an award established at Penn State University through the Institute for the Arts and Humanities.

Mario was first the guest of Patty Satalia, who was to interview him on WPSU-TV, the university's PBS affiliate. Prior to the interview, I spent twenty minutes with him in the television studio's Green Room, where we renewed our friendship by talking of previous encounters in Perú and at Penn (the Yevtushenko affair), of mutual friends Raquel and Eugenio Chang-Rodríguez, José Miguel Oviedo, Luis Alberto Sánchez... We were cut short by the two-minute warning of the upcoming interview.

I sat in the audience before the impromptu platform on which guest and interviewer sat on two orange-colored chairs. Patty Satalia was very well informed about Mario's life and writings; she asked astute questions on a variety of literary and political topics, the latter focused on his failed candidacy for the presidency of Perú in 1990, all of which he answered at length with aplomb and fluency. In his trademark open-neck shirt, Mario was in his element.

Later that evening, dressed more formally for the occasion, he received the 2008 IAH Medal for Distinguished Contributions to the Arts and Humanities before a capacity audience in Schwab Auditorium. The previous recipients of the honor had been Salman Rushdie and architect Daniel Libeskind, the former being a good friend and cohort (together with Umberto Eco, who had dubbed them "The Three Musketeers" for their many joint appearances on the world's stages).

Mario delivered a lecture titled "The Road to Fiction," in which he harkened to prehistoric times, imagining the fundamental role of the ubiquitous storyteller, keeper of the people's traditions, in the evolution of modern fiction from oral narrative practices. The lecture returned to a theme that was at the core of his 1987 novel *El hablador*, which focused on primitive traditions of Perú, as perceived by the narrator and as remembered by an anonymous Machiguenga Indian. The audience was enthralled by his panoramic presentation and great applause ensued upon its conclusion.

An exhilarated but very tired Mario Vargas Llosa returned to his overnight abode at The Nittany Lion Inn, where he could sit for an hour with his wife and me, enjoying the company of a few old and new friends at an intimate reception at the Alumni Lounge.

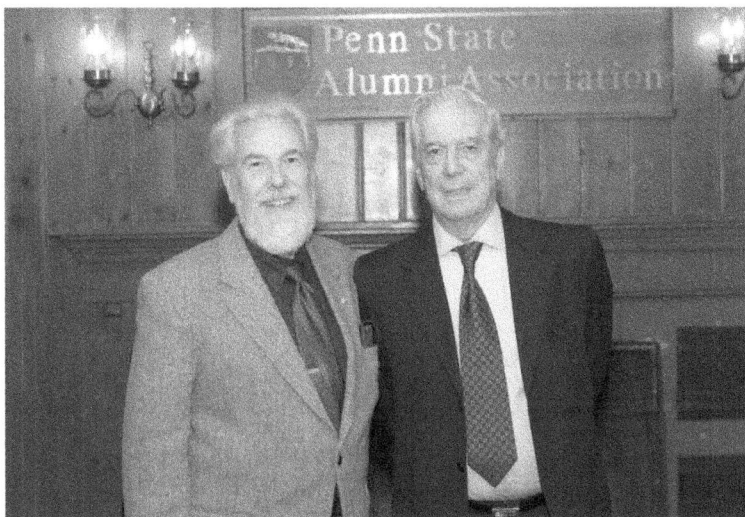

ROBERT LIMA AND MARIO VARGAS LLOSA

Refreshed, the next morning he met with graduate students for a seminar and then set out for New York City, where he would participate on May 2nd in the International PEN–American Center event "World Voices" with many other writers of renown, including the other two members of his Dumas-inspired "trio." During that stay in New York City, Mario also attended the gala dinner of the Museo del Barrio, at which he was an honored guest and delivered a speech. The museum. dedicated to the city's Hispanic culture, earlier presented the film "La fiesta del chivo," based on Vargas Llosa's novel of the same title.

*See the essay on Yevtushenko.

PAUL WEST

Quadruple Alliance(s)

My friendship with Paul West began more than forty years ago and I have focused on four events that distinguish that relationship and give a sense of the man. My literary appreciation of the writer of novels, poetry and memoirs appears elsewhere.

In the mid-1960s, I received a request from a Spanish priest stationed in the Philippines for an essay by Paul West, noted novelist, memoirist, poet and critic. Knowing that the author and I taught at the same university, he had taken it for granted that I would have access to the piece. I didn't. Since I was at a campus other than University Park, where Paul West taught, I didn't know the author either (to my chagrin, not even his name). Checking the meager holdings of my small campus library for a book of his that might contain the piece, I drew the proverbial blank. But since collegiality is the hallmark in the best of all possible worlds, the academic, I wrote the author a note explaining my friend's pressing need for the essay (he was working on his doctoral dissertation) and his offer to pay for it (I don't recall if in Spanish *pesetas* or Philippine *pesos*).

Some time thereafter, I received a letter from the author explaining that the essay would reach me as soon as the English Department secretary got around to Xeroxing it. I guess she never did for I received instead a package via inter-campus mail which contained not one but two copies of Paul West's *The Wine of Absurdity*, in which the desired essay on Graham Greene appeared. And the books were gifts from the author, one for the needy priest and one for me! It was my first opening to Paul West.

The largesse of my newly-discovered colleague toward two strangers not only impressed me as a humanitarian (or should I say, humanistic?) sort of thing, but also verified my Panglossian belief in the utopic nature of collegiality. Over the years, where others have caused deep erosion of my naiveté, Paul West has continued to uphold his status by periodically bestowing upon me many and sundry titles–novels, essays, stories, memoirs, poetry. These works have made manifest to me what a reviewer writing in *The New York Times Book Review* has termed "his ability to make language behave the way he wants it to."

When I moved to the University Park Campus of Penn State in 1967, I met Paul West and have had many occasions to interact with him, including dinners at my home and at sessions I hosted with Jorge Luis Borges, Walter Starkie and other distinguished writers I had brought to campus. But the strangest have been two disparate events, one in the United States and another in his native England. A third is the result of Paul's most recent illness.

The next anecdote I entitle *"Doppelgänger, Or My Other Self."* I have lectured at many universities in the United States and abroad but never at Cornell. In itself, there's nothing unusual in this–there are numerous other institutions I have not visited as a speaker–but a rather strange circumstance related to Cornell makes it imperative that I narrate what follows.

Paul West has a house in Ithaca, New York with his wife, the writer Diane Ackerman. They had invited me to visit but I had never found the occasion to do so. I had been to Ithaca and the Cornell campus only once, and that was as a brief stop on a summer trip returning to Pennsylvania from Canada; I didn't think it appropriate to foist my wife and four children on Paul and Diane. I have never visited Cornell again, although I would have gone there had my candidacy for a deanship some time ago moved beyond the exchange of letters.

On encountering Paul on the Penn State campus on one occasion thereafter, I was surprised by his aloofness. More than that, he seemed annoyed. Not one to let pass a friend's snub without questioning its motive, I confronted him. It turned out that he felt I had snubbed him and Diane. Somewhat dumbfounded, I pursued the inquiry. What I learned was a revelation of supernatural magnitude.

Paul explained that I had failed to contact him and Diane when I lectured at Cornell recently. I told him that I had not lectured or even been there since the family outing years before. He persisted, however, telling me that I had been the guest of the Romance Languages Department and Comparative Literature. He claimed that I had offered a seminar under their auspices and that a woman friend had sat in on my presentation. I reiterated my case, offering that perhaps my name had been misunderstood, or that someone had impersonated me, and Paul offered to have the matter mediated by the friend who had vouched for my presence at Cornell.

In the meantime, I ran into a former student who informed me that someone was going around town and campus claiming to be Robert Lima. This was too much of a coincidence coming as it did so close to my Cornell situation. I asked the informant if he could identify the impersonator and heard him described as a short, fat, red-headed youngish man. Not even close. If imitation is the highest form of flattery, as has been said, this proved the adage to be skewed. This was obviously an inane hoax but it was my second encounter with identity theft. I never did locate the rascal and the matter never escalated.

When Paul contacted me some days later, we met in his English Department office in South Burrowes Building. I recounted the other act of impersonation, wondering if the Cornell case could be assigned to the same perpetrator. But I was nonplused when he told me that the friend at Cornell had checked that it was indeed my name on the announcement of the seminar and that those present verified my participation. Yet, what flabbergasted me most was that she described me perfectly! She added, perhaps as an incentive for me to own up to my alleged visit, that I had been "brilliant." Paul rested his case.

I *knew* that I had not been there, brilliant or not! I also knew that the matter had gone beyond the possibility that Paul was pulling my leg. Having created and taught a course entitled "Literature of the Occult" for many years, I had recourse to the only explanation left to me: a non-rational, supernatural answer for my supposed visit to Cornell. While I knew that I had not been to Cornell on that occasion, I concluded that it must have been my *Doppelgänger*, my apparitional double! This being must have acted my part convincingly since my description was so precise but I wondered why it had not been mentioned that *its* feet never touched the ground, a dead give-away of an unnatural double. Perhaps the seminar attendees had only seen my *other* seated.

I think I managed to convince Paul–or was he merely tired of my protestations–that I had not committed a breach of etiquette because I had not been there to do so and that, as hard to believe as it was, I was oblivious to the presence of a supernatural impersonator, even if it was my alter ego in that seminar room. To this day, I have not found out the answer to the enigma.

Nor have I ever received payment for my "brilliant" presentation at Cornell University. Consequently, the question remains: If the honorarium was paid to the *Doppelgänger*, what did he/it do with the money? Did he/it take it and disappear into the realm of the supernatural? If so, it may prove that capitalism rules there as in this world.

My hope however is that when I cross over, I will have awaiting me the start of something like a savings account, the result of an honorarium for services rendered by my *Doppelgänger*. No doubt, the funds will have been earning interest at an elevated rate.

And when I meet Paul on the other side (trusting that both of us will have earned entry to the elevated locale), I will treat him to a great single malt and a heavenly dinner, to be paid for in the currency of that realm from the earnings of my other self.

My following anecdote is headed "*The Other Paul West.*" I was in London briefly and had time on my hands. I remembered that Paul West had told me that he would be staying in his London flat that summer. He had invited me to visit on the next occasion and this was it. But I had left the address and telephone number at home and had to resort to the telephone directory. I found his number easily enough and placed the call.

The voice that answered did not sound like him and I asked if I could speak to Paul West the writer. He identified himself as such and I proceeded to identify myself and to inform him that I would like to visit during my brief time in London. I hoped, I said, that he was free and we could get together as he'd suggested back in the States. He sounded rather tentative about the whole thing but came round to accepting my suggestion. I too felt awkward, as if I was intruding into other plans that he would have to set aside to accommodate my visit. Nonetheless, he gave me instructions to his place and we agreed to meet at six that evening.

I located his house–not a flat–and arrived promptly at the appointed time. A very dapper fellow in tweeds and an Ascot opened the door and greeted me. As I had seen him moments earlier on the street carrying a bag of groceries, I imagined that he was Paul's man servant. It may not be usual for a writer and academic to have a butler, but I figured that since Paul had done very well in his writing career he could afford that luxury. I gave the man my name (hat and coat would have followed had it been the season) and asked for Paul. He said that he was Paul West and invited me in.

He may have been Paul West but he was not *my* Paul West! On the phone I had asked specifically for Paul West the writer and this man had identified himself as such; clearly, he was usurping my friend's identity and living in his house. Seeing my consternation, he admitted that my name had not been familiar but that during a recent tour of universities in the States he had invited several academics to visit him when in London; although my name did not awaken memories of an earlier encounter, he had seen fit to have me over. He was indeed Paul West and he was indeed a writer–of television programs. I explained about my friend the noted novelist and memoirist and the Paul West present before me acknowledged that he had read some of his works; and he was gracious enough to laugh at the case of mistaken identity, even if taken *ad absurdum*.

I absented myself despite his protestations, not even accepting the gracious offer of a whiskey. I don't know that I have ever been as embarrassed in my life, both by my original faux pas and then by my flustered exit. But the authentic Paul West, the one I had sought in that house in a London suburb, had a hearty laugh when, back in the U.S., I recounted my failed attempt to meet up with him. I wonder if this anecdote will materialize in some future edition of Paul West's *Portable People*.

Recently, I received a package from Ronald Christ, on whose doctoral committee I had sat at N.Y.U. and who now is the publisher of Lumen Books in California. The package contained a copy of Paul West's latest poetry collection, *Tea with Osiris*, which Ron had published. Amazing the triple-play interconnection of Lima–Christ–West that brought Paul's book into my hands!

On reading the note accompanying the book, I learned that Paul West had suffered a stroke. What mixed emotions: excitement over the new book of poetry–his first in many, many years–and great sadness over its author's illness! Truly, there is no justice in the world when a wonder of letters is felled while beings of little or no worth go on living without tragedy or trauma. However, I think of Paul as indestructible as his wonderful words and I'm pleased that *Tea with Osiris* proves that he continues to be irrepressibly "ornery" and indefatigably brilliant. He may be next to Osiris in this book but Erato has not left his side and Amaryllis awaits him for further sporting. He no doubt will go for it with great tenacity in spite of his setback!

That he has was made evident when I received an inscribed copy of his article "Mem, mem, mem," which appeared in *The American Scholar* in the summer of 2007. Paul not only had suffered a stroke but its aftermath was aphasia, which for a man of words was catastrophic. In this article, he details the process of combatting the language-crippling effects of the disease and his successful garnering of moments in which to write and speak, if only for a few hours daily, toward the recovery and continuity of his talented voice.

"Mem, mem, mem" is a unique document of a dark time, a time that he has brought into the light with inimitable language and narrative skill. And humor, for Paul West did not lose that quality of his writing while fighting through the shadows. He laughs as if at someone else's antics when describing his naked run through hospital hallways in the wee hours of the morning, the sisters (British for nurses) chase after him and ultimately return him to his cubicle. Or when he muses over the strange mutterings emanating from a mouth not able to formulate proper words. Or the contrast between an ineffectual arm and thin but functional legs. Or over the communication of "three voices" in his head.

When he speaks of such voices, I think immediately of Julian Jaynes' *The Origin of Consciousness in the Breakdown of the Bicameral Mind*. The late Princeton psychologist posits that prior to 2000 BCE humans–from Mesopotamia to Perú–lacked consciousness and were cued to action by the voices of gods, as in *The Iliad*, which he analyzes as typical of such in ancient Greece. What Jaynes assesses is akin to what Ramón del Valle-Inclán (1866-1936) had to say in *The Lamp of Marvels* (my translation):

The Golden Age was dawning and the Greeks, divine herdsmen, were still contemplating pale stars. They did so wrapped in the silence of flocks, on hills dappled with olive trees, among guardian dogs. Their souls came forth at dawn; those goatherds possessed the sovereign eyes of eagles and an intuition wrenched from the celestial core of the Sun. Their souls were filled with sacred paths leading to groves, crystalline brooks, grottoes out of which flew long-winged birds at twilight, the shadows of laurels, and distant, golden shores of a blue sea. With eyes open in amazement to the light, they received all images as if they were the eucharistic species, images so frequent and diverse that they summed up the norms of all knowledge.... They did not receive their understanding of the world like a cold inheritance from the urn of words... To those herdsmen, ideas meant numbers and forms under the rhythm of the Sun.... What they learned impulsively was enjoyed in quietude. (*LM*, 55-56)

In his ironic "quietude" perhaps Paul West is being endowed with celestial awareness and will no doubt attain Gnosis.

Paul's condition also calls to mind Goya's famous etching "The Sleep of Reason Produces Monsters" (*Caprichos*), wherein "monsters" are metaphors of the human mind gone awry, of a mind that has lost contact with its primal holistic nature. Long distanced from its original state of being, the mind has been constrained by the rules of civilization and its processes distorted thereby. As the artist sees it in the etchings collected in *Caprichos* (Crazes), *Disparates* (The Follies) and *Desastres de la guerra* (The Disasters of War) and his so-called *Pinturas Negras* (The Black Paintings), anything that cannot be explicated by the norms of logic can become monstrous in modern life. Monsters created by modern man's mind gone astray demonstrate how disparate is its state from that of the ancients, who held discourse with the gods through a mind open to divinity in a way that ours is not.

In those moments when incommunicado, Paul West too is experiencing the "monsters" of irrationality, a "static-racked" voice of the old gods trying to break through after so many centuries of having been displaced by the operations of consciousness that Jaynes describes. But through the process of fighting his aphasia, Paul is recapturing his ability to recompose language, if in a context highly affected by the introspection imposed by his illness.

There are bound to be many more revelations in *The Shadow Factory*, the longer manuscript regarding his state of being, of which "Mem, mem, mem" is but a sliver of his unique, if harrowing journey through the brainscape of memory.

WILLIAM CARLOS WILLIAMS

The Parkinson Syndrome

Working at night with the Staten Island Music Theatre as set designer, stage manager, sometime actor and chorus member, I met Diane Logie who, with Nick Rinaldi, co-produced our presentations on the professional theatre at Sailors Snug Harbor or at the venue of The Elizabethtown Players in New Jersey. We put on fully-staged productions of *Carousel*, *New Girl in Town*, and *Damn Yankees*, among others, using the talents of professional actors, dancers and musicians who were at liberty, as well as community theatre people.

Knowing that I was a poet, Diane offered to introduce me to William Carlos Williams, the legendary doctor-poet, perhaps the most American of poets, champion of free verse, author of forty books and winner of most major literary awards, who lived in East Rutherford, New Jersey. Diane's father, the writer Fred R. Miller, one-time publisher of the proletarian magazine *Blast*, had been a longtime friend of Dr. Williams (who had prompted Oscar Baron to publish Miller's *Gotbucket & Gossamer* in his Outcast Chapbooks in 1950) and often took the young Diane along when he visited; over the years, she remained very close to WCW and Florence Herman, his wife.

Our visit took place on April 15, 1961. We arrived at the modest house and were warmly greeted by Flossie, as Williams called her (although she was Floss in his poems, plays and a novel). Her husband was seated in the living-room by the front window; around him on the floor and on a table were groupings of books and literary journals. He could not rise to greet us but not because of his seventy-eight years. A victim of stroke, he was greatly incapacitated. There were moments when his lucid speech was interrupted by a silence imposed by his condition; in those hiatuses, his eyes would be highly expressive of the thoughts his mouth could not utter. He went in and out of that state throughout our visit. Diane, who had seen him in better days, was very moved by his condition, as was I. It was a situation in which the adage "Doctor, heal thyself!" was applicable but modern medicine had yet to learn how to cure such devastating illnesses.

I had brought two books for WCW to sign but when I realized that he could not use his right arm fully, I withdrew my request. But he would have none of it. His wife handed him my books and he painstakingly proceeded to write his name in each. I witnessed him struggling to inscribe a signature in each, his hand trembling from lack of total control. I was feeling great guilt over having put him through the ordeal but William Carlos Williams smiled at me when he had finished writing. As a consequence of his selfless action, I now possess two treasures: *Kora in Hell. Improvisations*, in The Pocket Poets Series of City Lights Books, and *The Collected Later Poems*, published by New Directions; each bears only his signature in the shaky letters dictated by his condition.

I took away from the visit many images of the man and the poet, the latter urging me to write "naturally" and to forgo traditional forms towards a more open, freer poetic expression. He cajoled me: "Say it! Not in ideas but in things." Those words have stuck with me through the years.

His death in 1963 brought not only the sorrow of seeing pass a major voice in American poetry, but an emotional response that centered on the man and his spirit. Despite his debilitating illness, he had taken the time to meet with me and to consider the poetry I had brought for him to critique. I wrote a few lines in celebration of that humanity.

TO WILLIAM CARLOS WILLIAMS
"In Memoriam"

It is
your joy in having
still the thought–
"Our sons"–
in timelessness

Not as
new images of
your Paul,
your Bill,
but as
"Our younger,"
"Our elder"

And your
children's children
still,
as it should be,
"Our own"
is set
in your reality

Forever
should be
ours

YEVGENY YEVTUSHENKO

Che's Corpse at Dinner

February 14, 1991, St. Valentine's Day, provided me with a singular opportunity: to meet again with Mario Vargas Llosa, both of us invited to the University of Pennsylvania by José Miguel Oviedo, the noted critic of Latin American literature. The event was sponsored by International PEN. Vargas Llosa gave a lecture followed by a conversation with Oviedo and then took questions from the audience. It was all very academic and proper... until a member of the audience stood up and shouting something in Russian, rushed the stage. There were no security people who could catch and restrain him and so the intruder leaped up the steps and ran to Vargas Llosa. The audience gasped and Oviedo was startled, to say the least. But Vargas Llosa recognized the interloper, stood up and received a Russian bear hug from the poet Yevgeny Yevtushenko. No doubt relieved that nothing untoward had happened, the audience applauded the "happening."

The impromptu appearance of the Russian required that Oviedo invite him to the intimate dinner planned for Vargas Llosa. And thus we proceeded on foot from the auditorium to the designated dining-room; as we walked, a photographer from Penn's newspaper took photographs of our group; she happened to be my daughter Debra, who was studying at the Philadelphia university. Her photos show us in various conversations: Mario and Yevgeny, Mario and me... Besides the remembrance of the event recorded in the photographs, which are in the Vargas Llosa chapter, I commemorated the strange doings by Yevtushenko before and during dinner in:

AFTERWORDS

PEN AT PENN February 14, 1991

After words that Vargas Llosa & Oviedo said,
the Russian loomed up suddenly on stage–
quite tall & gaunt, with ruddy face & hair,
a raunchy tie of orange-red set off against
the jacket's camel hue–to take possession
of the honored guest and of our ears.

At dinner, Yevtushenko rambled on and on.
Directing his accented twang to Mario's face,
the table-hopping voice curtailed all speech
but his, its so-so Spanish nurtured years ago
in Castro's Cuba and Bolivia's heights,
where he had haunted Che Guevara's path.

Tyrant of the banquet table all night long,
he soon insisted that we clear away our talk
like dirty dishes and listen only to his voice
declaim a poem (in Spanish) he had written down

in honor of the Comandante's savage death
that fateful day when hunters felled their prey.

"A la izquierda, siempre a la izquierda," said
as he ranted from my right (his left, of course),
made his impassioned utterance first rise then fall
like the Bolivian hills where Che Guevara died.
The leftist words he'd spoken to the captors then
had nearly cost the Russian poet his own life.

Emphatic in recounting that old death, Yevgeny
placed Guevara's corpse where plates had been
(a somber Valentine) in front of dinner guests.
A tired Vargas Llosa had retired to bed by then
and was not forced to witness how surrealistically
a fatuous symbiosis was attempted on that night.

When I again met Mario Vargas Llosa on his visit to Penn
State, I gave him a copy of the poem and he read with amusement of
that encounter in 1991 and, with a hint of nostalgia, told me that he
had lost contact with the exuberant Russian poet, he of the unexpected
Russian bear hug in the City of Brotherly Love.

II

CORRESPONDENCE

CORRESPONDENTS

ALTMAN

Robert F Lima Jr.
Faculty Chrm
Cultural Affairs Committee
P.S.U.
Beaver Campus

Box 269
Pine Grove Mills
Pa.   16868

Feb. 27- 1967

Dear Mr. Lima

Thank you for your letter of Feb 15th inviting me to exhibit my work at the 2nd Annual Spring Art Exhibit and sale to be held on April 8-9.

I should like to do so and I would appreciate information on how the work is to be sent to the exhibit and how it may be returned.

I would be sending matted graphic work (etchings and lithographs.

Please send me whatever information you can concerning the exhibit.

Sincerely Yours

Harold Altman

222

Prof. Robert F Lima Jr.   Bot 269
Penn State University   Pine Grove Mills
Beave Campus. Monaca Pa. Pa. 16868

Dear Prof. Lima   May 9 - 1967

    I have just unpacked the carton of my prints which were returned to me on Friday, April 28th

    22 prints were in the carton — Since I had been paid for the sale of "Three Trees" the only missing print which is unaccounted for is "Conversation V" priced at $60.00

    Could you advise me as to the whereabouts of this print?

        Sincerely

        Harold Altman

AMMONS

711 Triphammer Rd
Ithaca, N. Y.

July 9, 1966

Prof. Robert Lima
The Pennsylvania State University
The Beaver Campus
Broadhead Road
Monaca, Pennsylvania 15061

Dear Prof. Lima:

Actually, I'm not supposed to be reading translations for the CHELSEA issue (the regular editors are doing that) but I don't think they would mind my accepting Borges's Cyclical Night on their part. I don't think it probable that another translation of that particular poem has already arrived to them.

Your own poems are good but, I think, make little "technological" connection. That they don't is, of course, nothing against them.

Many thanks for letting us hear from you.

Best,

A. R. Ammons

Dear Prof Lima:
      Yes, your poem is in the issue. The issue itself was expected, as of last report, for "late spring." That's now—so a copy should be reaching you before long.

Good wishes,

A. R. Ammons

Dear Prof. Lima:

Yes, I'd like very much to see some of your Borges translations. Send soon — or the <u>Chelsea</u> issue I'm editing is about to close.

Good wishes,

Archie Ammons

BALABAN

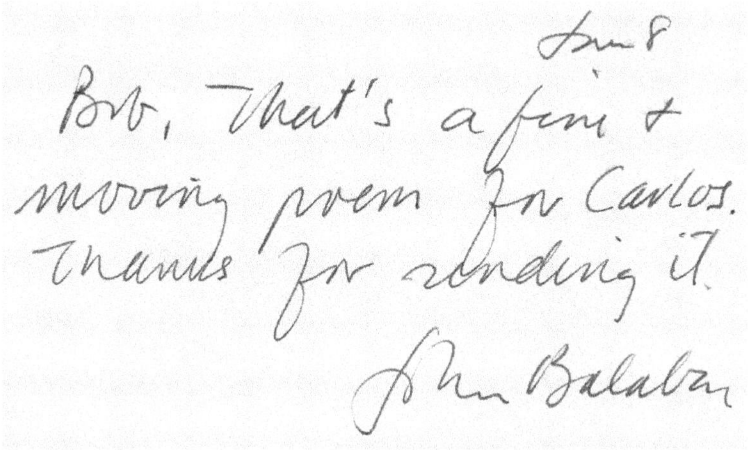

Jan 8
Bob, That's a fine &
moving poem for Carlos.
Thanks for sending it.

John Balaban

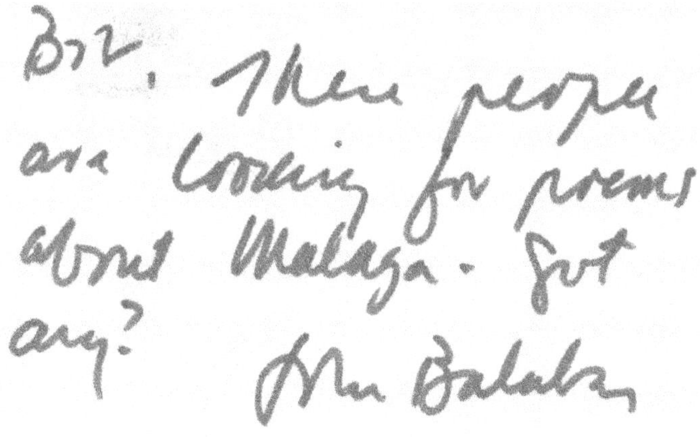

Bob, These people
are looking for poems
about Malaga. Got
any?

John Balaban

Feb 29, 1982

Dear Bob,

I'm on sabbatical in New Mexico
and am not in touch with the Writing
Committee (headed by Bob Downs, the
Director of the Option). Since I
don't know Keys' work (although
his name is awfully familiar?)
perhaps it would be better for you
to contact the English Dept about
him.

How's your play translation
doing? Any further productions?
Pretty exciting.

All best.

John Balaban

Date: February 4, 1991

From: John Balaban

To: Bob Lima

Thanks for being willing to consider my nomination for an
Institute Fellowship. Enclosed is my <u>vita</u> and the catalog copy
for the two new books which are now in galleys. Poseidon is
division of Simon & Schuster; Copper Canyon is the small press
participating in the National Poetry Series (in which <u>Words For
My Daughter</u> was a winner).

Besides this prize my earlier poetry won the Lamont Selection
of the Academy of American Poets and a nomination for the
National Book Award. I have also received two each of the
following national fellowships: Natl. Endowment for the Arts,
Natl. Endowment for the Humanities, and Fulbright.

I'd be grateful for your support, but please do not feel
obliged in any way.

BALAKIAN

Dear Robert,

Again, Congratulations on your book. It looks terrific and I hope will be prominently displayed at the MLA.

I won't be attending this year. It is too cold to go to Chicago.

I am continuing with my writing & lecturing, particularly this year with the Breton Centennial coming up in 1996. Have you thought of getting a colloquium together in 1996 on Breton & the Hispanic World? I still remember your celebration of the 25th Anni.

Wishing you
a Christmas
bright with beauty,
warm with joy.

I have collected my essays on Breton & on Latin American Surrealists but haven't been able to place the collection with a publisher. I must add that I haven't tried too hard. Have you any suggestions?

Best wishes for the New Year,
Anna B.

New York University
A private university in the public service

Graduate School of Arts and Science
Department of Comparative Literature

19 University Place, 4th Floor
New York, N.Y. 10003
Telephone: (212) 998-8790

March 2, 1988

Professor Robert Lima
Department of Comparative Literature
Penn State University
University Park,16802

Dear Robert,

I have been following all your literary activities in the
last decade or so, your poems particularly which you have been
so kind as to have sent to me. And now I see that you have
a major work coming out on Valle-Inclan. I wish you the best
of success on what should become a major literary milestone.

I remember with so much pleasure the Surrealism Festival
under your direction at Penn so many years ago.

On another topic, you may know (I already had it in mind
at the Surrealism conference) that I have been translating
Rosamel Del Valle's Eva y la Fuga. His widow, Therese, entrusted
it to me because she thought I would be closest to understanding
his surrealist way of expression. It is a beautiful little
narrative-poem, in the genre of Nadja and I have completed the
translation and notes for a while now but have been waiting
for an appropriate time and place to have it published.
Evelyn Picon Garfield wants me to let her see it for her new
Latin-American series. I am hesitating; I would very much
like your opinion, and also your suggestions as to what kind
of publication would be best for a virtually unknown author
who writes with poetic imagination,* freely mingles dream and
reality as few of the French surrealists ever achieved-
I'd say he is closest to Bunuel's cinematic style- and who, in
my opinion is indeed a remarkable poet.

Do you think a trade publisher is better than a university press?
What do you think of UC Press in L.A.?
Any advice you can give me would be greatly appreciated.

Do you ever come to New York? I'd love to see you again.

Best regards,

Anna Balakian

* In an age (now) totally involved in rationalism!

New York University
A private university in the public service

Graduate School of Arts and Science
Department of Comparative Literature

19 University Place, 4th Floor
New York, N.Y. 10003
Telephone: (212) 998-8790

January 11, 1990

Professor Robert Lima
Penn State U.
University Park, PA 16802

Dear Robert,

I got a letter of inquiry about your candidacy for a Chair
at Miami University and although professional ethics prefer
that copies not be send to the candidate, I can assure you
that I wrote a very strong letter of support.

What I do want to send to you, herewith enclosed, is the
first paragraph of my letter of recommendation because I want
to alert you to the fact that you are perhaps being used as
a "token" candidate.

I hope things are going well for you. But why are you no longer
listed in the PMLA Directory? You may be as disgusted with MLA
as I am but dropping out is not the way to change things.

My translation of Eva y la Fuga by Rosamel del Valle is
finally being published by the University of CA Press and
should appear sometime in the "late spring." I'll see that
a copy reaches you.

Best of success in getting this Chair, which would be very
deserved, and good luck in everything else you do in the
New Year.

Sincerely yours,

Anna Balakian

231

New York University
A private university in the public service

Graduate School of Arts and Science
Department of Comparative Literature

19 University Place, 4th Floor
New York, N.Y. 10003

Sept. 17, 1990

Dear Bob,

I am a few months late in acknowledging your thoughtful gift of copies of your articles on Lorca & Cuban theater but I hate perfunctory notes and I try to read before writing. The harvest of works colleagues sent me this summer filled me with joy—but also required a certain stretch of time to do my homework.

Your essays were very enlightening. I realized how ignorant I am of the Cuban literary vein and of course in the case of Lorca I have in my own studies probed the pale symbolist aspects rather than the powerful, earthy character of Yerma which you connect with the Greek.

You have been a great asset

to the profession. While
some of our colleagues protest
that we must shatter the
canon, they continue to earn
their livelihood with the
standard Norton readers,
while you, quietly, have been
opening up so many new
fields of explorable materials
which are indeed enriching your
whole notion of literature.
Through the years I have enjoyed
your writings and learned from
you. I have just published
a neglected Chilean writer,
Rosamel del Valle, & you will
be receiving your copy from
Univ. of CA Press (soon I hope —)
my copies were sitting on the
stoop of my house when I returned
from vacation! Eva is an earthy,
primeval character, and this
translation on which I worked
for years is my small effort
to step outside the canon.
Thank you again for thinking of me.
Warm regards, Anna

BARNSTONE

Jan 6. 66

Dear Bob –

Thanks so much for the
Valle-Inclán. Would you be in-
terested in doing translations for
Artes Hispánicas of unpublished
Spanish stories + poems?

Willis

234

INDIANA UNIVERSITY
BLOOMINGTON INDIANA

ARTES HISPANICAS
HISPANIC ARTS

May 31, 1967

Dear Robert:

I think I might have mentioned to you that in Hispanic Arts we will have some historical articles now and then, but the emphasis is on original unpublished creative material, like poems, short stories or an article about someone writing today.

What we are interested in are creative translations of contemporary writers and preferably of their unpublished works.

I am returning the works you sent me earlier.

Sincerely,

Willis Barnstone

INDIANA UNIVERSITY

Comparative Literature

BALLANTINE HALL 402

BLOOMINGTON, INDIANA 47401

TEL. NO. 812—337-7070

APril 26 77

Dear Robert,

Thanks very much for the book of poems. The poem Saudade is
very moving, good, and reminded me of a brief, terrible thing that
did not quite happen. Last year (now a year and a half) in Argentina,
on a subway, I was reading a book. The train was crowded. I started
to lean back, as we were going around a curve, to lean against the wall
or door when a lady said to me, Laa puerta esta abierta. If she hadn't seen
me leaning back, if I hadn't heard or understood immediately I would
have fallen out of the train between the close wall and the tracks
and surely been killed.

best and thanks

Willis

Robert Lima's statement is pure, untroubled by trends and isms.
His observations dart, like light on water, from image to
image, each with surprising allusions. So we read

> The fish
>
> looks for the sky
>
> with open mouth
>
> and frivolous tail
>
> splashing the lake

Here the "pure" apparently simple, observations have a whimsy and
a deep undertone. It is plain as Sappho's extraordinary "I could
not/ hold the sky/in my two arms."

Willis Barnstone

INDIANA UNIVERSITY | COMPARATIVE LITERATURE
Ballantine Hall 402
Bloomington, Indiana 47405
(812) 335-7070

March 4 8?

Dear Robert —

Thanks for the fascinating article on the Cameroons. You are in good company & deservedly. I also like the drawing of the figure at beginning of article. You deserve a place in Eliade's histories for the piece —

Will be coming from Boston. I got in touch with Massa + thanks for his address. I wish there were more Massa's around today. Yours —

Willi

INDIANA UNIVERSITY

COMPARATIVE
LITERATURE

Ballantine Hall 402
Bloomington, Indiana
47405-6601

812-855-7070
Fax 812-855-2688

Dec 1 93

Dear Robert —

I'll be glad to write letters for any request. Thanks so much for Valle. Don't know if you've seen my Borges memoir (with Borges on an Ordinary Evening in Buenos Aires (Yale?))

Six Masters of the
Spanish [...]
with [...] Plan[...]
my two Spanish
architects.

All is well.

best, with
nostalgia —

[signature]

BELL

May 13

Dear Robert:

I am returning two of your poems. The third,
"Chant," I am holding. I am fairly sure it will
contribute to our overall poetic and visual statement.

We are at work on issue no. 2. You will receive
that normal embarrassment of the small literary
magazine--the contributor's copy.

Best,

Marvin Bell
Ed., statements

new editorial offices: 5305 Blackstone Ave.
Chicago 15, Illinois

--a good clean design (and photog.) in the
anthology; congratulations.   Dec. 26, 1961

Dear Robert:

　　Well, see what you and Don Katzman think of these two
poems. Thankyou for sending along Seventh Street--it's always
good to see an anthology which neither shouts about itself,
nor limits itself to 'names' or a school.

　　I'm glad you liked statements 4; yes, I think the overall
content caught up with the visual materials and design with that
issue. No. 5 is at the printer's (has been for a while), and I'll
send it along when it is completed.

　　Time flies, but I've been pleased with what I've been able
to get done in photography in recent months. Poetry is a struggle
at the moment, as it is periodically. I think something challenges
me when one kind of poetry becomes a little too easy to be
meaningful as more than technique. It's not technique that is poetry,
as you well know. On the other hand, I think the continual changing
of pace that the form of "Motion, a Preoccupation" accomplishes
makes much of the poem. And even in the other, untitled poem,
the occasional rhymes don't hurt anything. (I can add a title,
if need be, to that poem--I've thought about one for a long time,
though I don't have it yet.) All this to nullify whatever it is
that I've said.

　　I'm much more concerned with honesty and perception in my
criticism than in consistency--whatever that is. And I've been
doing literary and photographic criticism lately for Trace,
Contemporary Photographer, Choice (Chicago), and Aperture, and
Midwest. Poetry recently in Epos, Choice (Chicago), The Outsider,
Targets, Descant, The Chat Noir Review, etc.

　　Good luck with the Review; call on me if I can help.

                                    Best--

STATE UNIVERSITY OF IOWA · IOWA CITY

THE COMMUNICATIONS SKILLS PROGRAM

*M*emo

Dec. 14

Dear Bob:

Well, it's taken me a long time to reply to your sending copies of the Seventh Street Review--a gift which let me know of the acceptance of the two poems, as well as of their publication. Anyway, thankyou. I enjoyed the issue; and seem to remember careful proofreading, which pleased me particularly. I've had a terrible time with misprints lately.

Well, there are many good poets, story-writers, translators, etc. around here. Are you still interested in receiving material for Seventh Street? For a revived Exodus? If so, let me know what's what and I'll post a notice at the writer's workshop hq. I'm interested myself in learning of your activities now. Did you receive statements no. 5? If not, yell, and I'll send one. And--assuming one or both of those magazines are going--do you care to make a regular exchange out of it? Give me an address, if so, so I'll be less confused than I seem to be presently.

This will probably be my last year here. Meanwhile, teaching keeps me busy, and I've had a little trouble finding the right moods and situations for writing and photographing. Looking back, more seems to have been done, however, than I would guess.

How are you; and what are you up to?

Best--
Marvin Bell

1017 fifth avenue
iowa city, iowa

STATE UNIVERSITY OF IOWA   IOWA CITY

THE RHETORIC PROGRAM

Memo

June 18, 1963

Dear Bob:

Greetings; and thanks for your letter and for sending
these poems. Sorry about my delay in responding--I've been
far removed from statements and such for the last few
months while other issues came to a head. You may know
that I've been teaching here, while liesurely adding
another degree. But I've owed the Army Infantry two
years since 1958, and will probably enter in Jan. There's
a good chance that I will enter as a first lt.--a feat
only the red tape of the Army could accomplish.

Good to hear of your writing activities. I'll be looking
for what is to come. I haven't had a chance to see your
Lorca book yet, but will have the chance this summer, I'm
sure. I've always responded well to Lorca, both as poet
and playwright playwright. I remember his Poet in N Y
in particular. That's not the place to start Lorca, I
suppose, but I did, by accident, and it had a beneficial
effect on my own start as a poet. Even though I've turned
toward a very grammatical, explicit kind of poetic
statement, eliminating images and metaphors, I still find
the book strangely exciting and inspiring.

Enough on that. I'll be looking for the first issue
of Judson Review--which is due, I guess? And statements
will come to you as always. I've sent the first issue you
requested, separately, in cardboard, in hopes.... It's
easy to see how the magazine got better as it rid itself of
editorial workers who published their own material, etc.
Its next issue should leave no. 5 in the dust, and reveal
a new bias perhaps. But its future is up in the air. I've
several choices of almagamation with a larger quarterly,
expansion through foreign publishing, abolition in favor of
a new small or large magazine or in favor of taking a poetry
editorship on a large quarterly, etc. Its next issue, which
might be its final one if my choice demands that, will
probably be devoted to Iowa workshop poets--perhaps co-

sponsored by <u>Midwest</u>, whose editor wanted to sponsor the
entire project, originally.

I'm sorry I did not get on the stick to obtain
short stories and/or essays for you. Is Judson Rvw
continuing, and what are you now looking for? Of course,
everything imaginable is obtainable here, because of
the presence of the Workshops--fiction, poetry, and
translation, and play-writing.

I've been writing and photographing a great deal--
mainly writing. I haven't had time, strangely enough,
to market the poetry, though I have sent a few things
around. A couple will appear in Poetry, another in
Elizabeth, one or two in Genesis West. A few others,
I guess. Generally, however, I've been leading an Iowa
City life--that kind of existence easily adopted by
writers who stay here for any length of time. Having the
society of so many good writers tempts one not to seek
a public.

--a break in continuity; it is now later that day:

Of these pieces, I liked I HAVE LOST MY PITY FOR
BONES best. There's something of the Poet in NY surrealism
in it. I'm less warm toward your dependence on
abstractions, mainly in the other pieces: confusion,
fear, mysticism, for ex.--such concepts pop up here and
there where I find myself wishing for much more concrete
definitions, operational definitions I suppose.

I can't remember, now that the day is ending, if there
was anything more I wished to say. Good luck with
everything, at any rate. Keep us in mind when you're
marketing translations. Generally, I steer clear of them,
so long as I'm bound by this thin format. But I'm anxious
to make exceptions for pieces previously untranslated.
The odder, the better. Let there be fresh breezes, eh?

                                    Best,

                                    Marvin Bell

THE UNIVERSITY OF IOWA

IOWA CITY, IOWA 52240

The Program in Creative Writing
Department of English

27 August 1968

Dear Robert,

Thanks for the copy of TOWN & GOWN containing your poems, for the inscription and for the letter. Completing your Ph D and working on readings for your Arts Festival sound like fine accomplishments, and I'm glad you've been writing too.

Statements, alas, went the way of all little magazines. Its last number was a chapbook of IOWA WORKSHOP POETS / 1963, published as no. 6 of Statements and as a special issue of Midwest--also now defunct. The chapbook appeared in two editions, libraries kept renewing, I collected some more poetry, but the magazine never appeared again. I suppose it had served its purposes, whatever they might have been.

Briefly, I returned to Iowa City to teach in the fall of 1965, and have recently bought a house here. This fall, there will be five teaching poets in the Workshop: Director George Starbuck, me, Anselm Hollo, Ted Berrigan, and Jon Silkin. Seven or eight fiction writers. The students, of course, are terrific.

As for my own writing, I try to do more and more of it. A pamphlet of two "long" poems, POEMS FOR NATHAN AND SAUL, appeared from The Hillside Press in 1966, and a first full-length volume of poems, THINGS WE DREAMT WE DIED FOR, appeared from The Stone Wall Press at the end of 1966--in limited edition, now out of print. A new collection, reprinting a few from that first book, will be published by Atheneum a year from now. Title presently is THE MUMMIES OF GUANAJUATO.

I edit and review as situations seem irresistible (sp.?), but have been trying, of late, to withdraw from whatever takes away writing time or energy. I admit I have had a horrible reputation as a non-correspondent--indeed, am writing now in the middle of the night because I couldn't sleep. No doubt I'll be unable to stay up tomorrow.

It's good to have poets at PSU. And I'm grateful for your greetings and good will. Good luck with your poems, with PSU, with the Festival, with infectious academia in general.

Sincerely,

Marvin Bell

BLY

THE SIXTIES

R. F. D., Madison, Minnesota

EDITORS: WILLIAM DUFFY, ROBERT BLY

Dec 7, '60

Dear Mr. Lima,

Thank you for these translations. The Lorca Translations <u>are</u> much more accurate than those commonly available. I like especially "The Poet Arrives in Havana", which Belitt simply massacres. We have already more Lorca than we can use, including 6 poems in the new issue, which will be out in a week or so. We may include more Lorca later, in special groups, such as poems to the moon, poems about death etc, so I would still like to see any more Lorca poems that you do in the future. The only fault I see in these is the occasional archaism of language or sentence structure, for instance in *Dance* "Coiled on her head a yellow snake"

something stilted about that — one would never hear, today, I think someone speaking that construction — also in *Flight from New York* a leaf <u>did</u> fall —

the moon

↗ within the grapefruit (sang)

↗ In *If My Hands*

"what other passion assaults me?"

I am returning the Lorca poems, but I would like to have the Spanish for the Manley poem, and to two Marti poems.

I would like to have a version without rhyme of the White Rose poem — or rather, — perhaps the half rhyme of "Tears" and "Bear" is accidental — with a less awkward next to last line —

the line

"Neither thistle nor weed do I bear"

seems to me archaic, and I am not sure about "tears / the heart"

Yours with best wishes,

Robert Bly

THE SIXTIES

Odin House, Madison, Minn.

EDITORS: WILLIAM DUFFY, ROBERT BLY

12 Feb. '61

Dear Mr. Lima,

Thank you for the letter, and the Spanish versions of these poems. I am returning here the poem by Mondoy, which I don't like too much.

I do like the Martí poems, and I think we will be able to find something satisfactory to us both.

In the "White Rose" poem — this is my problem — The word "cultivo" is used throughout, and I think we must have a single English word which can be used in all places. Neither "cultivate" nor "bring" will do, as you have noticed. Can you find a third word, something like "grow" perhaps?

I think the first stanza of "My Friend" is perfect. In the second stanza we have a similar problem "angelitos" comes down from "angelones". Perhaps "little angels." "Piously" doesn't seem quite right in meaning. Can flowers have "branches" in English?

Yours with best wishes, Robert Bly

Let me hear from you.

248

THE SIXTIES

Odin House, Madison, Minn.

EDITORS: WILLIAM DUFFY, ROBERT BLY

18 Apr, 61

Dear Mr. Lima,

I am well satisfied with the Martí "Painter" poem, as you know; I think "Timorous" is the best of the alternatives so far; as you mention, "bashful" makes the rhythm go a little flat. We can certainly use timorous if nothing astoundingly better turns up. It is a good poem, and a good translation.

I have finally given up on the White Rose poem — I think the problem of the single word (nurture, nourish, etc) is insurmountable. I have tried various ideas myself, none of which work.

Let us turn to other Martí poems, or to other Cuban poets: working toward a group of two or three Cuban poets

With best wishes,

Robert Bly

12 Feb, '62

Dear Mr. Lima,

Good heavens, I haven't answered your letter yet! I am waiting for either more Marti or more Cuban poets before I publish My Friend the Painter. If it is to be Marti, then he is good enough to have a larger selection. If the group is to be Cuban poets, then we should choose carefully & give Cuba a respectable representation. In that case the Marti poem could be the first.

I did receive the Deux Magots anthology, and enjoyed it, among them your poem Identities, especially the sudden "rain-soaked battlements".

I like your translation of Second Daughter — "endearing small clouds" is very good for "nubecillas". "Coltish" is very good also, perfectly in tone. I don't feel convinced of the greatness of the poem itself, however: though it is very interesting, it doesn't completely come together for me.

Let me see more. With all good wishes,

Robert Bly

THE SIXTIES

Odin House, Madison, Minn.

EDITORS: WILLIAM DUFFY, ROBERT BLY

20 Ap; 62

Dear Mr. Lima,

Thank you for these new translations! Forgive me for my spring slowness. I am going to jump on these for the use of weak language. For example, in the Marti: "caress" - that's terrible - "breeze" - "expires" "ire" - these are all words that died in the 19th century of exhaustion. No blood will go through a poem in which these words are.

One other note on "I know of Egypt" - I think "obscuro" here suggests "in obscurity - that is to say, without power - and the heart is not so much failing as exhausted after a lifetime of struggle - I think Marti is thinking of the old revolutionary's feelings, here. "gold" is also archaic.

"The valiant" is corny; "is cast" is weak, as is "heightened carmine". he means his poetry is pure green and wild scarlet - fiery red - "the wounded fawn" is too pastoral. You have modified & smoothed out the sharp images here, made them more misty and vague.

The Acosta too is translated too much word for word - for example "transparency" for "transparencia" - Yrs   Robert Bly

THE SIXTIES

Odin House, Madison, Minn.

EDITORS: WILLIAM DUFFY, ROBERT BLY

23 April, 62

Dear ~ G. Lima,

Thank you for the Hernandez poem. His work is very uneven, it seems to me; and this poem seems to me a little weak. Also I do feel that "rustic hermitage" "peals" with inverted syntax is ~~·~~ literary in the old sense.

Yours with good wishes,

Robert Bly

THE SIXTIES PRESS

Odin House
Madison, Minnesota

EDITOR: ROBERT BLY

6 May, '64

Dear Bob Lima,

I am interested in "I want to Depart This World"; I have a few comments I'll wait with till I can bore over the Spanish. Would you ask Mr. Massa to send me a copy of the Selected Marti poems (by ship mail) — which I think he published?

The two Marti poems of yours I've already accepted are My Friend the Painter and — by gum, I've checked up, and there *is* only one! No wonder you couldn't remember the other! Well, if we plan for a group of five, we'll be all right. Let me see a couple free verse poems also.

As you can see by the simpering Queen on the envelope, I'm in England — till July 20th, my address will be Hill End, 21, Thaxted, Essex, Eng.

Best wishes,

RB

THE SIXTIES PRESS

Odin House
Madison, Minnesota

EDITOR: ROBERT BLY

18 July. 64

Dear Robert Lima,

The Marti book arrived from Las Americas; many Thanks. I am enclosing "I Want to Desert This World" — There are a few minor points in it that seem to need work, a few places in which the language becomes slightly archaic.

For example "depart" — wouldn't "leave" be more natural? The close so crucial here — "as such", but I don't think, if shift the sentence to another context, that we would really use "as such" in speech in this way. Suppose a man were old and said.

> I'm an old man, and as such,
> I like to sit in the sun.

He wouldn't say that. He'd say something more like "I'm an old man, and being old, I like to sit in the sun": Perhaps there's a third poss. Safety.

"would" and "should" both sound too translated.

Let me hear from you again. By the way the Cuban Cultural Attaché here, Pablo Fernandez, is preparing, perhaps for Penguin, an anthology of Spanish American poetry in verse translation. I told him about your Marti and he was very interested. May I show him the Marti of yours I have here?

Best wishes

Robert Bly

Mill End 2,
Thaxted
Essex, Eng.

CODRESCU

English Department
University of Baltimore
Charles at Mt. Royal Avenue
Baltimore, Maryland 21201

April 23, 1983

Dear Robert Lima: I was delighted by
your wonderful present! I had a brief
correspondence with Zeller & Wald a
few years ago, and all my letters had
the Surrealist stamps until they ran
out -- and now here they are again. The
Corpse is delighted to have your contribution: We haven't had our editorial pow-
wow for May yet but we will let you know
what we will use. The April issue (due
back from the printer on Monday) has a
wonderful, big essay on Bataille -- I
hope you enjoy it. In May, there is work
by Nanos Valaoritis, Stefan Baciu -- and
I am hoping to get a drawing from Marcel
Janco from Izrael. I would also be very
much interested in your suggestions for
reviewers, essayists, artists -- And: I
seem to have misplaced Ludwig Zeller's/
Susana Wald's address in Canada: Could
you send it to me? I would like to ask
them for a collage.

Best, Yours

A. Codrescu

DELANY

23, South Park,
Blackrock.
March 12th 1964.

Dear Bob,
I was surprised and delighted
to hear from you this morning. Congratulations on setting the day! I'll
look forward to meeting you again when
you come to Dublin.

The Mont Clare Hotel, 14, Clare Street
Dublin is central, attractive, and not
expensive. You could arrange for
Bed and Breakfast, eating your lunch
and dinner out. However the meals
generally are good in the hotel.

Most of the first class hotels
have excellent restaurants; a four course
dinner would cost approximately £ 3, per person,
wine and drinks extra. Worth eating in
are the Dolphin (steaks), Russell (French cuisine),
Jmeshuam (Irish & American) and the Hibernian
and Shelbourne (International)

Other excellent restaurants are Jammets and Alfredos, both expensive but good. The Red Bank is good for fish meals, the Moira an excellent grill house. Inexpensive but good are the Windsor Hotel, the Anchor Hotel, and the Wicklow Hotel (where I normally eat out).

By the way I forgot to mention one other outstanding eatery, Delany's. Joan and I will enjoy showing you some Irish home cooking. You plan to arrive in Dublin on the 29th so if the 30th for dinner in our place would suit you would be very welcome. Incidentally I'm a proud Daddy of his a aged one year and Joan is expecting again in April. Anyway I'll be meeting you on arrival at Dublin Airport on June 29th.

There is much to see and do in Dublin; theatres to visit, museums, art galleries, georgian houses, Trinity College et al. C.I.E. also offers excellent scenic tours of the Dublin Mountains

and Wicklow. These towns are well
worth taking.

I hope the above info
is some little help. Let me know
if you have any other specific
enquiries.

I was glad to get the
news of the boys, especially to
learn Nick had fallen. I'm
sure we'll be in touch with
each other on and off before
June so I'll say cheerio for
now. Give my very best wishes
to Sally.

Sincerely,
Ronnie & Joan Delany.

Subject: Email from Ronnie Delany
Date: Fri, 29 Feb 2008 16:36:11 -0000
X-MS-Has-Attach:
X-MS-TNEF-Correlator:
Thread-Topic: Email from Ronnie Delany
thread-index: Ach68TG+9qjG/VzQTcCAM1ZH/kOKQw==
From: "Enquiries" <enquiries@laydenproperties.ie>
To: <rxl2@psu.edu>
X-Greylist: Default is to whitelist mail, not delayed by milter-greylist-3.1.8 (tr10n04.aset.psu.edu
[128.118.142.105]); Fri, 29 Feb 2008 11:36:16 -0500 (EST)
X-Virus-Scanned: amavisd-sophos
X-PSU-Spam-Flag: NO
X-PSU-Spam-Hits: 2.114
X-PSU-Spam-Level: **

Hi Bob and Sally,

Great to hear from you. Probably will go to re-union (with or without Joan). Will let you know later. Have you read my biography 'Ronnie Delany – Staying the Distance', publisher O'Brien Press. Let me know.

Kindest regards
Ronnie
25 Priory Hall
Stillorgan
Co. Dublin
Ireland
Tel: 00353 1 2836077
Fax: 00353 1 2836133

7 Cairnbrook Avenue
Carrickmines
Dublin 18

Tel: 01 2955942

22 April 2008

Hi Bob,

The enclosed article on García Lorca appeared in yesterday's Irish Times. Thought it might be of interest. Is it (the article) correct. Have you heard of the author or the Irish historian Ian Gibson

Best wishes,

Ronan

IGNATOW

DAVID IGNATOW
660 WEST 180TH STREET
NEW YORK 33, N. Y.

4/3/64

Dear Robert Lima:

Enclosed is a group of poems for consideration
by Stephen Mass of Columbus Publications, following
an invitation to submit poems for the projected
anthology of New York Poetry in conjunction with
the forthcoming World's Fair. I am indeed honored
by the invitation.

Sincerely,

David Ignatow

David Ignatow

August 18, 1965

Dear Robert: Here is our new address, in hopes of
of hearing from you, especially in reference to the
Mass anthology: 315 McDowell Rd, Lexington, Ky
40502.

    We are still deep in unpacking and arranging
our stuff, with little time to relax. I imagine
the same for you, but even more so. You took your
furniture along!

    First opportunity you get let me hear from you.

    We live in the Chevy Chase section of Lexington:
wide, shady, silent, empty streets. No traffic.
Huge gardens, birds in the morning, crickets at
night.   Best to both of you,

                    Dave

UNIVERSITY OF KENTUCKY   LEXINGTON, KENTUCKY 40506

CENTENNIAL 1865-1965

COLLEGE OF ARTS AND SCIENCES
DEPARTMENT OF ENGLISH, SPEECH,
AND DRAMATIC ARTS

Home: 315 McDowell Rd
      Lexington, Ky 40502

                                             October 16, 1965

Dear Bob:

        Of the material I read, assuming Mass had shown all, I didn't
think there were enough good poems spread among enough poets to
warrant even calling it a nucleus. Certainly there wasn't wide
enough representation of the scores of poets living in the
metropolitan area, assuming that the objective of this anthology
is to exhibit the work of New York poets. Charles Reznikoff,
George Oppen, Louis Zukofsky, Denise Levertov, Alan Dugan, A.R.
Ammons, Allen Ginsberg, to name a few, were not in this collection
shown to me by Mass. A serious anthology such as both of us
contemplate, if it's to be done in proportion XX and in quality
to correspond with the importance with which the city New York
is held throughout the world, not to mention U.S., would have to
begin from the beginning, with the most comprehensive list of
working poets within the metropolitan area, including such poets
who consider themselves influenced by New York one way or another.
This of course we could decide between ourselves. There is much
to talk about, if we can get together on the basic need for an
anthology of such comprehensive scope. I'm all for it, but let
me hear from you.

        In my discussion with Mass, this above was what I had to say
to him, at which point he recognized the inadequacy of his
material. Perhaps for that reason he is withholding decision, but
as you say we can proceed without him. Unquestionably, the
undertaking will require enormous expenditure of time, of energy
and correspondence between us, but I think it's worth it on every
count. We certainly could tux get together periodically, we're
not so far apart, a day's ride or so. But basic to the whole
project is the need for a publisher to underwrite the idea before
we go further than a token gesture. This we could show him or her
together with a prospectus whose central theme would be the
overriding centrality of New York poetry in the world today.

        Unquestionably, we could salvage material from the batch you
now have, assuming it is the same as shown to me by Mass. I did
see some lovely poems there, but the question of an anthology is
too wide to permit any immediate commitments. As you see, lots
remain to be discussed between us, if you should decide we have
hold of something good.

        Our love to your family.

                                             Dave

2/27/66

Dear Robert:

I thought I'd answer that part of your letter to Roe about us. That's fine that you're still keeping open the chance of an anthology of New York poets and of course I'll be glad to look at your poems for any help I can give. I too miss New York badly and wish I could return permanently, with a job there or in the area. Right now it seems I'M about to accept an offer from the University of Kansas at Lawrence, a very enterprising school on the lookout for writers. I've been there and have found it pleasant and busy, numerous programs in the works, an atmosphere that comes close to New York, but I hesitate to think I may have to spend a good many years there. I'll be reading up and down the New England coast this April, perhaps get an offer from one of the schools there.

We're delighted at your response to her book of drawings. The poem is charming. She will answer you soon, I believe. In the meanwhile, it's interesting that you should be organizing exhibitions of paintings. Your school seems wide open to new ideas, new approaches, especially surprising and suggestive that you have this opportunity to push another art than writing.

Please write when you are ready either with the poems or the search for poems for the anthology of New York poets. I was very glad to hear from you again, after the long pause.

As ever,

Dave

May 26, 1966

Dear Robert: I'll arrive at your house either June 2nd or June 3rd in the evening. However, will call the morning of the day I expect to arrive to confirm with you. Coming from New York.

How did the show go?
Have you heard from Wayne Williams (Broadside Lexington, Kentucky? He's interested in publishing at least one of your poems. Broadside is a new modest periodical meant to encourage modern Kentucky poets. Its first issue will be out in September. He found at least four of your poems very interesting. Regards to Sally and of course Mark!

Best, Dave

also those who care to contribute.

August 31, 1967

Dear Bob:

I'd like very much to ride your poetry circuit in late April-
May, but I can't be definite about it until later. I must find
out how Vassar College will like the idea. Already I'm booked
in November for the Michigan Circuit, two weeks. Additional time
off from Vassar might raise additional problems for them. But
please let me know the date on which John Haag must have an
answer, the latest possible. As for a one night stand, that is
conceivable either on a Wednesday or Thursday or Friday evening,
or Friday afternoon or Weekend. Does the fee $125 include
traveling expense? I hope not. Incidentally, the regular fee for
one night stands is $250, at least, but let us leave this problem
aside until the question concerning the circuit trip is answered.
It may also answer the question I've just raised concerning the
one night stand.

Allen Planz, your buddy, is looking for poetry to fill out
his social, political guest issue. I hear you sent him work that
he had to turn back. Please try him again with more stuff. He's
very short, as I see it.XXXXXXXXXI'm sure you must have work
that would meet with his ok. At least, several translations from
the Spanish? We're trying to cover the political and civil rights
issue from the point of view of other countries - as they see us.
Or prose x relevant, yours or Spanish.... We need prose badly also.

This last week or so has found me able to relax and get to my
own work - so near to the start of a new semester, damn it. After
which I'll be riding a merry go around between Poughkeepsie and
East Hampton each week. I'm stuck and have to go through with it.
I'll be teaching one course at Southampton College, with the
possibility of teaching full time permanently starting 1968 Fall.
It's much closer to home, about ten miles, but I don't know that
I'm going to like the school. It's academic reputation is low.
We'll see... And I have to I'll move again. I don't want to be
stuck with a low grade rebellious student body there only to keep
out of the draft. How are things with you? Not far from Philly?

I'll rush to meet my rural mail pickup, but let me hear from
you soon. Our very best to Sally and you. It's always good to hear
from you.

Dave

266

April 12, 1968

Dear Robert: I'm not getting much chance to correspond these days, but I'm taking time out to write that I like Love Poem for Cathay. It has everything that Tale should have: mystery, suspension, suggestive imagery, sensuous quality. I've noticed for a long time this dichotomy in your style and perhaps it's how you must learn to decide for yourself the more effective manner. To me, Love Poem is it, and I bet you must have dozens in your drawer.

It was my problem too for a long time and maybe I never did overcome it but I sure as hell try to avoid it. I'm not a preacher, I'm a reacher. How about you?

I've been in touch with John Haag about a circuit reading in Pennsylvania perhaps next Fall. In the meanwhile, still another circuit in Penn.,managed by Marcus Konick at Lockhaven College, has been inviting me to read at several schools. I'll be Franklin and Marshall College in Lancaster on the 18th this month, evening. Maybe you can make it? And we'll have a drink together. At Vassar, I met the Spanish poet German Bleiberg who teaches here. His name must be familiar to you among the contemporaries of Lorca, of whom German was one of his closest associates in the theatre. German writes a beautiful intllectualized emotional poem, with evident Rilke influences. Look him up in the original, if you can. Translations of his work have just been started by his colleage Inman Fox.

Ever the best to you,

Dave

June6,1968

Dear Bob: About my black raincoat, I feel sure John Haag spoke to you about it. He says he brought it into the house the night of the party and gave it to Sally along with my black bag. John and I returned after breakfast to look for it but you were not home. Could you drop me a line about it, just to say whether it is in your house? You can send it ahead collect, I believe. And thanks much.

I'm too depressed, as all of us are at this time, to comment on anything other than the Kennedy horror. We must try to keep living and win through to some peace, for ourselves, for the nation, for the world. There is no end to suffering but peace is in seeking to do right, by ourselves and by our children. Change America.

Dave

P.S. I have sent ms under separate cover.

June 13, 1968

Dear Robert:

You'll notice that I have divided the ms. into four sections.
First, love poems; second, poems personal, subjective, contemplative;
third, poems to do with poetry, art and related subjects; fourth,
poems of religious consequence and related subjects. The actual
order within each section I leave to you, should you find merit in
the arrangement I have found suitable to the ms. as a whole. I
imagine that within each section there may be a poem or two or three
that you would want transferred to another section. However, I
believe that the scheme into which I have put the poems is a very
sound one and is practised in virtually all published books of
poetry. The natural affinity for like poems and the cumulative
effect that one gets as a result, in addition to the insights that
go beyond the immediate aesthetic impact - all these are assets
not to be ignored in this kind of arrangement. Anyway, it's how
I arrange my material, so what else could I do but repeat myself
in you...? I have a one track mind, little me.

The poems that get to me strongest are the ones colloquial,
imagist and rhythmically strong or put another way in which the
rhythm is quite pronounced and often forceful. We've talked about
this before. A book made up of poems of that order should have no
trouble getting a publisher: Scorpio Rising,The Death of the Spanish
Cantante; I Have Lost My Pity for Bones and others which you yourself
can recognize from my choice of these sound, to me, the most
natural and free flowing and apparently come from deep within you
where you feel free and are released. They sway, they have hypnotic
language and rhythm. As the ms. stands now, I feel sure you will
get mixed reactions. I'd advise you to wait and write more. Now
that you have completed your Ph.D., the time is ready for intensive
writing and thinking. You should be encouraged by the fact that I
think you could write a book of exceptional power and truly unique
rhythms and sound and imagery in American poetry if you follow your
instincts to concentrate, at least for a time, on your marvelous
Spanish background. There would be nothing like it in American
poetry and it would coh tribute an entirely new dimension. When I
think of it, I realize we have few or no poets of Spanish descent
writing in America, with the exception of Frank Lima who I think
has something but not the depth and control of which you are easily
capable.

Anyway, think about it. I was glad to look this ms. through
and am convinced, affirmed in my instinct about you. I'll be very
interested to see what happens from here on.

Did you get my letter mailed to your school address? I wrote
of the possibility of my raincoat being left behind in your house.
John Haag is sure he brought it over the night of the party. Please
let me know what you can about this. My best to Sally and to you.

Dave

July 11, 1968

Dear Robert:

The raincoat came okay. Got my check too. A-okay.

You've got an interesting idea in the occult project. I
personally don't know of anything helpful and Rose has your message
and will look into it and probably contact you, if she comes across
anything of value for you, but there must be tremendous amounts.

About Broadside, that has been suspended indefinitely, I'm
sorry to say. At least until Wayne Williams manages to extricate
himself from the worst details of his job. But there's no telling
when. If he is holding any of your material I'd suggest having it
returned to you.

I'm on a Rockefeller grant as of August 1968 through August
1969, which means I've taken a leave from Vassar College but will
not return. It was only for two years, and so I'm faced with the
plaguey need to uncover another job. This time it has to be
permanent. I've got to stop moving around. If you should hear of
anything in or within commuting distance of New York, please think
of me in connection. I'd appreciate it. This Rockefeller grant
came as almost a complete surprise, though I had heard through
various sources that my name was being brought up, but I had little
hope and in some way I was apprehensive about getting it because
it would mean a hassle with Vassar College with whom I already had
signed a contract for the second year. However, as things are
working out now, Vassar has been persuaded to look at the brighter
side and apparently will go ahead with administering the grant
while finding someone to take my place. I just hope though that
I haven't prejudiced them against me for having had to break the
contract, but I hear it's nothing new in the academic world.
We may travel to Europe next summer, if all goes well.

Did I tell you I had a very good time reading and visiting
with you? The horrible accident I had on Rte 80 nearly
marred everything. I'm lucky to be alive. My car skidded into
a guard rail, bounced off and returned to bounce off again, the
whole rear smashed. Without my seat belt securely fastened around
me I would have been a dead man. If you recall, the weather was very
heavy during that period, rain, fog and wind. Anyway, that's over
with, though the accident itself is costing me at least 100 dollars
above the insurance payment.

Finally, my room is completed. Should you be in New York and
want to come out here give us a call. We could put you up.

Our fond regards to all of you,

Dave

July 14 68

Dear Bob:

Can you send me John Haag's home address? I have written to him at the University but haven't heard from him since nearly 3 weeks. It has to do with my fee which has not yet come, though it was due 2 weeks ago. I wonder whether it was mailed correctly.

Dave

September 1968

Dear Bob: The last stanza, Hawks decide incessantly
l..., says it. We're in real bad trouble. I got a
letter recently from Stephen Mooney, editor of the
Tennessee Poetry Journal, in which he predicts
fascism in the South, from all the evidence he has
been gathering in his travels and correspondence.
It certainly could spread to the North. Wallace is
coming on strong. First of the Roman Caligulas...
     That last stanza is an imaginative horror,
very real for that reason.

     Very busy with editorial technicalities of the
forthcoming Chelsea. Keep in touch....

                                        Ever the best,

                                        Dave

December 14, 1968

Dear Robert: Now that I'm coeditor at Chelsea, how about sending us tranëlations of prose and poetry? We're working on Chelsea #27 Fall 1969 and translations seem to be taking up a large part of issue. So?

We got your enclosure of Town and Gown and leaflet of new course. That is fascinating. Bly is in a new direction of the occult also. Seems to be in the air. Do you have occult poems of your own that we can look at, not excluding other work.

Are you interested in writing omnibus reviews of poetry, like informal but rounded. What did you say? Can't hear you. Louder.   Affectionately,

Dave

CHELSEA

February 8, 1969

Dear Robert:

You're knowledge of Spannish and Spanish-American poets is much more encyclopedic than mine. Why don't you make a few suggestions to us, particularly of poems interesting you at present of an occult nature or in the surrealist, dream mode?

Also, can you let us know what books of poems you'd like to review for us, in omnibus style. If we have these books on hand from the publishers we'll gladly let you have them for review and for keeps.

Let's hear from you soon.

C O N G R A T U L A T I O N S. You're doing the right thing, increasing your family. If more of the intellectuals had larger families we might eventually count for something in American. Really a delightful surprise. Rose and I send Sally and big, warm salute.

Affectionately,

Dave

CHELSEA

June 13, 1969

Dear Bob:

Answering late but affirmatively.
We can wait for your translations, since
we already have two issues filled. How
about translations from foreign occult
dramas also? That's going to be fascinating to read.

Incidentally, we are looking for prose
and poetry by talented black and Puerto
Rican writers coming up. If any are in
your school or class or among your friends,
won't you please ask them to let us see
their stuff?

What's with Haag? I wrote him long
ago but haven't heard from him. How is he
and give him my regards.

We're staying in East Hampton for the
summer. I wish it were possible to put
all of you up for a weekend. This is such
a small place we have. If you happen to
be in the area come for dinner and a swim.
The trip from Manhattan takes about three
hours by car. I'd suggest a motel for
overnight stay but they're so outrageously
expensive at this time that I'd shudder
to suggest staying at one overnight.
However, if you can stand the thought of
driving back and forth in one day (I've done
it over and over but not with kids) then
think of spending a very pleasant afternoon
and evening in some of the most beautiful
surroundings in New York.

Allons,

Dave

BOX 242, OLD CHELSEA STATION, NEW YORK 11, N.Y.

CHELSEA

November 10, 1969

Dear Bob: Sonia Giap Raiziss tells me that
your translation were mailed back to you quite
some time ago, with a note enclosed. It's
possible she's wrong and may have misplaced
them during her siege of moving from one apt
to another. Rose tells me that you do have
copies, so I feel believed about that, incase
the envelope has not shown up yet in your
mail. We turned the translations down but
I can't recall exactly why. I would have to
have the mss. in front of me again. I hope
though that the explanation for the rejection
was explicit which would make it that much
more helpful to you. You see, I don't handle
everything in detail. It would be impossible
to succeed in getting a fraction of the work
done that piles up here.

    You shouldn't feel discouraged. It's
very hard to turn down writers we know. It
depresses us. We continue to hope though that
the professional spirit in all of us will
keep us doing our particular thing, without
too much irritation.

    Incidentally, in all the years of my
writing I haven't succeeded in getting one poem
into the Hudson Review where I have received
some of the best reviews of my books'. Am I
pissed off at them? I sure am. Can I do
anything about it? Well, if ever they invite
me to submit or contribute I'll calmly do it.

    With warm regards to Sally and the kids,
                as ever,

                Dave

BOX 242, OLD CHELSEA STATION, NEW YORK 11, N.Y.

CHELSEA

November 9, 1970

Dear Robert: I wonder whether you could send us
a translation of "Nos Vemos'." for possible use
in the next issue of Chelsea? We are gathering
folk, primitive and ethnic prose and poetry and
the description of the poem in your essay sounds
like the thing we would want for the issue.
The essay was interesting. Of course, anything
else that might occur to you for translation
in the above categories would certainly be
welcomed here for study.

with best wishes,

Dave

KAUFFMANN

Stanley Kauffmann
Films and Theater
Penthouse E
10 West 15th Street
New York, N. Y. 10011

THE NEW REPUBLIC

Nov. 1, 1972

Professor Robert Lima
College of the Liberal Arts
Pennsylvania State University
University Park, Penn. 16802

Dear Mr. Lima:

Thank you so much for your full letter of October 26th and the copy of the McGraw-Hill letter. I'm glad to have confirmation of my opinion -- and suspicion -- from one who knows so well what he is talking about.

I'm grateful too for the monograph and will read it with pleasure.

Every good wish.

Yours sincerely,

1244 Nineteenth Street, NW • Washington, D.C. 20036 • 338-2494

KERRIGAN

47 Fitzwilliam Square West, Dublin 2, Ireland
Dos de Mayo 33, Palma de Mallorca, Spain

13 September 67

Dear Robert Lima:

It was very good to have your letter of July 12—at last.
Between the forwarding by Cela, and my own absence from
Dublin, it has taken some time to reach me.

I know and appreciate something of your work, and it is
good to have the description of some of your achievements,
for use as we get into the mainstream of the project.
At present the Board of Editors has not assigned any
work in the 8 volumes of Unamuno's prose to any translators other than myself and the wife of Federico de
Onís, who was on the Board before his death.

However, there is one area where I can offer you positive
encouragement, and that is in the poetry volume. If
you are interested in attempting any of the poetry, you
need only contact Sir Herbert Read, Stonegrave House,
Stonegrave, York, England, tell him I have recommended
you—unless you know him yourself already—and submit some
~~work~~ plan of your own. I don't know exactly how he ~~~~ intends
to divide up the poetry, but he is in complete charge
of this volume. You can contact him, in any case, and
make any suggestions you care to offer.

I hope this will be of some use to you at this time,
and meanwhile I will keep your letter and description
of your work, for the future.

Cordially,

Anthony Kerrigan

ANTHONY KERRIGAN · ELAINE KERRIGAN

47 Fitzwilliam Square
Dublin 2, Ireland

5 November 68

Dear Mr. Lima:

Sorry to be so late in answering your letter to
Dublin. We are not long back from a lenghty
stay in Spain.

The poetry volume is still up in the air. We
won't lose track of you, however, and will get
in touch as soon as any planning for it is
clear. We are all working away on the Tragic
Sense of Life volume. Everything is taking
a lot of time, but eventually we will get to
your interests.

It would probably help if we all could meet
in the U.S., as you suggest, and perhaps it
will come about sooner than we had previously
thought.

For the moment only,

best salutes,

Anthony Kerrigan

LEVERTOV

October 26, 1982

To All and Sundry:

I have made, year by year, an effort to keep up with the
mail, which amounts to an average of 15 letters, MSS., and
items of political or literary interest every day (after
the junk mail has been sorted and thrown out). Even with a
twice-a-week secretary to attend to business and simple
queries, I can never catch up. I love getting mail but this
backlog is a constant nagging problem. At this point, busy
with teaching and other work, and tired from the ongoing
worry over Nikolai's health (he is still suffering the
side effects of radiation, and the outcome is of course
still uncertain) I have had to decide to just let a majority
of letters go unanswered, much though I dislike doing so.
I try to keep in mind Oscar Wilde's advice to the young
Yeats never to develop the habit of correspondence. '...I
have known men come to London full of bright prospects and
seen them complete wrecks in a few months from a habit of
answering letters,' said he! So, please don't take offense!
and for my part I'll try to attend as usual to urgent mail,
and shall hope not to lose all my friends by my apparent
unresponsiveness.

Denise

Denise Levertov

January 10, 1983

Dear Robert Lima:

Denise asked me to add a note to you that Nik is better and is
back at work.
She, however, does not have the extra time to comment on Fathoms.
I am sure you can understand, with her two coastal jobs and Nik's illness,
that she has had to cut down on doing extra work. She wishes you best
of luck and sends her regards.

Sincerely,

Carlene Carrasco

Carlene Carrasco
Secretary

LLYWELYN

lyonesse ardgillan balbriggan co dublin

Dear Bob—

Too much work to do for letter-writing,
but thank you *so* much for "Skerries"!
I look forward to seeing you
and Sally in Ireland whenever!

Love,
Morgan

February 12th, 1985

Dear Bob,

Here is an uncorrected copy of the letter I sent to Eoin
McKiernan together with your Fulbright app. As I said on the
phone, I can't promise anything at all will come of it, but
it is certainly one avenue to pursue. Eoin himself is a truly
marvelous man, with enough energy and enthusiasm for six, and
if you ever have a chance to get to know him personally you'll
enjoy him.

Thank you so much for FATHOMS! I read it with the keenest
pleasure, savoring the resonances of both the Celt and the
Japanese, interestingly enough. There are similarities between
those two cultures that would bear close inspection some time,
if we all live long enough. At any rate, I like your poetry
very much and am delighted to add FATHOMS to my library.

And the poems in The Penn Stater really got to me. The stones
are my passion; the ancient stones, their faces eroded by time
but the power still humming in them. Have you ever laid your
naked palm on the Stone of Fál, for example?

Someday, when I am more matured as a writer and have a better
understanding of the many aspects of physics I feel necessary
for such a project, I hope to write The megalithic novel, as
other writers dream of writing The great American novel. But
that's still in the future, some years down the road.

In the meantime I hope I get to meet you personally, soon. We
are friends already with so many common interests. Let me know
how things go for you, and if you hear from Eoin. (Which might
take some time, he's always on the wing for somewhere.)

Best wishes always,

Morgan Llywelyn

March 18th, 1985

Dear Bob,

Thank you so much for your good letter. It caught up with me as
I was going through the agonies of moving, in order to have my
husband closer to the Dana Farber Cancer Center in Boston. Our
new address and phone number (unlisted) are below.

When you reach Massachusetts, at least give me a phone call. I
would love to see you in person if your schedule permits. I'm
nursing Charlie 'round the clock myself - his condition is very
serious - and keeping him with me at home for now, which is how
we both want it. So I'm not very mobile. But perhaps you could
plan a quick sidetrip to Weston?

At any rate, you are more than welcome to what little help I've
been able to offer - I certainly hope something productive develops
from it. Do keep in touch.

Always,

Morgan Llywelyn
751 Boston Post Road
Weston, Mass. 02193

(617) 647-0179

Dear Bob,

Thank you so much for your wonderful letter. You obviously understand how it is with Charlie and me.

Only the body dies, thank God. The spirit lives on, giving love and strength and growing ever more radiant.

Keep in touch, my friend.

Always,

Morgan

MORGAN LlYWELYN
29 ROCKWELL COURT • ANNAPOLIS, MARYLAND 21403

30 August 1986

Dear Bob,

Congratulations on being appointed an Institute
Fellow for the Insitute for the Arts and Humanistic
Studies! That's exactly what you deserve for being
a true Renaissance Man.

Thank you so much for inviting me to the reception.
I regret that I won't be able to attend, but the days
are "dwindling down to a precious few" right now,
and I am trying to run in six directions at once in
order to get everything ready for my move to Ireland.

You read right . . . my move to Ireland. I'm going
to follow my heart at last and go home. I'll be on
the Aer Lingus magic carpet winging east at the end
of October. It occurred to me when I was there this
summer that I was always dreaming about doing it, so
why not quit dreaming and get on with my life? It's
about time!

As of this minute, I don't have a permanent mailing
address to give you. There are several very attractive
possibilities and I'm going over the last two weeks in
September to make a choice among them. Then, when I
go back, it will be for good, with my lares and penates
(and all those books!) following me by sea container.

It's harder for us lit'r'y folk to move than for others
who need only put a toothbrush and a can opener in a
carton to consider themselves portable.

Anyway, when I have an address I'll send it to you.
In the meantime, please accept my congratulations and
very best wishes. I'm so happy for you, and proud to
know you.

Always,

5 May 1988

Dear Bob,

Your letter arrived this morning. I'm delighted to hear that
you're on your way, and of course I'm counting on us having
some time together.

I don't know if - given the incredible laxity of modern postal
authorities - this letter will even reach you before your May
20 departure, but am sending it just in case. (And wasting all
that typing to tell you that.) But be certain you have my
phone number - 065-20125 - with you, as it is unlisted.

Then ring me whenever you arrive and let me know your plans.
Early June is ideal for me, and of course you can stay here
when you're in the west of Ireland, as I have a guest room
and can make you comfortable. We'll have, as we say in Erin,
a grand auld natter. I'm really looking forward to seeing you
and catching up on all the news.

Eamonn arrived here, stayed a couple of days, decided (again)
that he couldn't hack it, and took off for England. I haven't
heard from him since he arrived there, but I left him with
firm instructions to telephone me if he got himself into any
difficulties he couldn't get out of. Which, knowing him,
seemed a distinct possibility. Just between us I'm very worried
about him, his mental state isn't good at all. Perhaps by the
time I see you something good will have happened for him. I
do hope so.

Your poetry excited me, as it usually does. The imagery, the
passion, the flow of it . . . some new things for you, new
ways of expressing the inmost roil of emotion. You have a
gift, my friend; you definitely have a gift.

See you soon! (And if your plans result in dates other than
you originally thought, that's all right, too - you're welcome
here any time. Just be certain to keep ringing me until you
get me, as I'm in and out a lot. Generally here early in the
morning or late at night, though.)

In haste and with love,

Morgan

Dear Bob,

In the chaos of moving to Ireland I didn't get any Christmas cards — but was delighted to receive yours.

My address until May is GARRANBOY, KILLALOE, Co. CLARE, phone 061-76496.

Then I'll be looking for new digs here, no time only able to get this house for six months. But I'll be staying in Clare, which I love and I know.

Do let me know when you're coming more —

plans on getting together!

I've not heard a word from Myra & Kevin since I married, nor from Eamonn. I'm of course worried about all of them. Have you seen them? Of Eamonn living now?

Do write when you have time, and I'll be waiting —

Always,

[signature]

"The Bungalow"
Limerick Rd.
Ennis
Co. Clare
IRELAND
Tel. # 065-20125

Dear Bob,

How lovely to hear from you! Lost in finishing a big
book under deadline, I have, as usual, been a hopeless
correspondent, so I'm delighted you wrote.

And what a treasure you sent! I hardly know where to
begin. I sat right down with THE LAMP OF MARVELS and
was promptly lost in it. Every page is overflowing
with so much food for thought it has to be digested in
tiny nibbles. I am reduced to keeping it beside my
chair and picking it up at random, just opening to any
page and finding there enough to occupy me for an
afternoon. Thank you so much, dear friend!

Your poems, as ever, I found both moving and exciting.
HELIX spoke to me, very strongly indeed. Also RIAS,
with its fresh vision of the creative interchange
between land and sea. Written on site in Galicia, I
would guess?

The odyssey of a Celt in Africa was great fun to read,
stirring up all my own wanderlust. Cameroon seems as
exotic, and certainly as distant, as Mars - yet as you
write of it it sounds eminently enjoyable. I deplore
the 20th century's increasingly successful attempts
at homogenizing Man. What sort of a world would this
be without the bright spice of Otherness? We are in
great danger of having that happening - a threat I am
keenly aware of here in Ireland, where "American
Enterprise" is seen as the answer to Irish problems.
Unfortunately, no culture seems capable of taking one
good aspect of another without also absorbing and
imitating all that is undesirable as well.

Having said that, I am throughly enjoying living in
Ireland. I don't know if I'll spend my entire life
here or not - I have certainly learned not to predict
the future, even as far ahead as Thursday. But the
land and the people nourish me, mind and soul, and

- 2 -

I can honestly say I have never been as happy anywhere
as I am here. Moving over when I did was the best
thing I could have done.

My house is a very Irish bungalow (not a thatched
cottage!) between Ennis and Clarecastle, about seventeen
miles north of Limerick. I have all sorts of little
walled gardens, replete with plum trees and cherry
trees, and I share digs with a marmalade cat of literary
pretensions.

If you can come over in '88 please do, and plan on
spending some time here. I have a lovely guest room
and even (I have learned to point this out to Americans)
good central heat. As I am so close to Shannon this
makes a nice first stop.

I've spent considerable time visiting archaeological
sites here myself, as you can imagine. The novel I'm
just finishing is based on Cuchulain and the Ulster
Cycle, so I've practically memorized every path and
bramble for miles around Emain Macha. Have you ever
seen Emain? The Tara of the North? It is simply
hackle-raising.

And being on site does make all the difference.

Now that I'm at the end of the writing and RED BRANCH
will go off to my editor this week, I do promise to be
better about answering letters. So do write again
and keep in touch - and I hope to see you here in
1988!

My love always,

Morgan

28 LAURLEEN
STILLORGAN
Co. DUBLIN
IRELAND

Dear Bob,

Thank you so much for the poem. I read it aloud — I hope you don't mind — in the Arts Club at the annual dinner. It received a thunderous ovation!

So stop being an admirer from afar and come visit me in Ireland.

Love always,

Megan

3 Sept. 1992

Dear Bob,

My heartiest congratulations!
Your election to the Academia Norteamericana
de la Lengua Española is a milestone
achievement. In such ways we measure
our progress through life, looking back
to observe the footprints leading to this
place, and looking forward to survey
the untracked distance to the horizon.

Your work as both linguist and poet sets
the standard for us all. The gorgeous, sinuous
subversion of human language can unite
or sever, deceive or illuminate. Your career
is an example of illumination.

With my love always,

Morgan Llywelyn

lyonesse ardgillan balbriggan co dublin

Dear Bob,

Thank you so much for sending me notice of your EYE OF THE BEHOLDER exhibit. It sounds wonderful! I wish I could have been there.

As it happens, that was the time when I was busy moving house. As you see from the above, I have a new address. I've bought a cottage on the north side of Dublin, between Balbriggan and Skerries, with views of the sea. And I love it.

The last few months have been taken up with getting settled in, writing, and all the attendant busyness of life. I didn't even get around to sending out my usual Christmas cards, for which I apologise. But I'm trying to make up for it now by writing the friends I care about most and sending them my new address.

I hope things are going well for you, and that you'll be coming this way in the not too distant future. I'm due for a trip to the States myself. TOR Books plans to bring me over for the entire month of March, for one of those marathon nationwide author tours to promote my upcoming FINN MAC COOL, due out in March.

Alas, given the nature of book tours, I won't have a minute to myself to go out and visit friends. The schedule already is packed beyond belief. I am supposed to be in Philadelphia once, briefly, but I don't yet know where I'll be appearing or exactly when. I could turn up on your telly any time!

With love always,

Morgan Llywelyn

MILER

7009 Rainier Av. So.
Apt. 4
Seattle, Wash. 98118

Dear Bob,

Howdy! Did you get the card I sent you during the summer?
I daresay you've moved from Riverside Drive, particularly if you
got spliced (to put it delicately). Well, I'll take a chance
& write you again, in hopes that the letter'll be forwarded.

Whatever happened to the "New York" anthology? Some of the
pomes, which haven't been returned, were unique copies, i.e. I
had no copies at hand; if they're lost, that's the end of that.
I haven't done a thing about my poultry since making ze contribution
to the anthology.

How goes it in the academic world? And in double harness?

Yrs.

Fred

Fred R. Miller

356 W. 34th St.
New York 1, N.Y.
9 April 1963

Dear Bob,

Give me enough time---say 47 years---and I'll always get around to doing the letters I yam under obligation to write. This screed frixample should've been writ a good, ah, months ago; but here it is, only, ah, months late. Things work out after all.

I finely sent the copy of "Gutbucket and Gossamer." But I meant to say when I mailed it, ah, mos. ago, that you air certny under no obligation to print same in the Judson Review. Fact is I'd rather have you used a long story called "The Painter," which ain't never seen print---but that's stashed away in Palm Beach with my friend Bert Hunt & besides it needs to be rewritten from 1st word to last; & God knows when I'll have "time" (ho, ho) to do the rewrite job. The "Gutbucket" I spose has historical innarest. It was writ before, out in Sanfran Cisco, Rexroth began putting on poetry & jazz evgs. at that there night club.

I still ain't seed a copy of Judson Review, Vol I, no. 1. Nor of yr. book on Lorca. But Diane located her copy of the "anthology," & I have read that, & wd. comment as follows (so who assed me to comment?):

I do not like Howard Ant. That's my privilege, no? Denise Levertov wrote you a much more graceful foreword than I'd been capable of pounding out---the correck construction is "than I would've been"--- Some time the true story of why I dinT do the foreword will out, & poor old Diane will get it in the neck. By & large the anthol is impressive. Did you write the prose note "Les Deux Megots"? Very good. "Drunks Have No Reality for Thirst" is a pome I remember without skimming again through the book; Jackson MacLow I can do without; the lady poets are as always lady poets;. Bob Nichols I guess is the poet with whom I feel most at home.

Now then, R. Lima, what're we to say abt. yr. poultry?

       Barren ashes on a tinted soil
         earth of disappearances and howls

And howls is right. The howls're not real howls, that's the trouble. Your howls are not the HOWL of Ginsberg. They, your howls, remind me of Doc Williams' exercises "Kora in Hell," imitations of Rimbaud which got nowhere. For the poyet the moral is, Don't pretend to be crazy if you're not crazy; don't pretend to be a Rimbaud if you're a good old Doc Williams; in short, don't pretend.

You'll get there, man, under your own power!

Fred

PLANZ

145 2nd Ave
New York 10003
28 November

Dear Bob,

a quick note:

on the Borges reading, the surest way is to have <u>him</u> recommend you, & follow it up.

Miss Galen Williams at the Y is the person to contact. On the Neruda reading I think she had Bly organize the translators, tho Belitt got in I'm sure on someone else's insistence.

Next best thing is to get Borges' approval (Dear Misss Williams, Luis asked me to introduce myself...or some such jazz..P

Next best, is introduce yourself to Miss Williams, with credentials, trans, copies, etc.

I will press Dave to mention it to her, & if I run into her I will sound her out---I see her couple times a year....

She couldn't resist a combo of these things--unless some establishment has it wrapped up.

about the translation issue....any number of mags will do, since just anybody who applies--with a good come-on---can get a modest grant--tho a lot are refusing on account of the war...I'll sound Chelsea out...but the grant's the thing & a anthology of spanish/latin american poetry should go over grand.
                                                    it might be prestigious to suggest your school's mag, or make one up, draw up a list of willing translators, cite history & present it to the national council......

editing stinks..I literally hate it & myself....

all this can be talked over better in person....

all best,

allen

137B Taliwa Ct.
15 March 61

Dear Bob:

It was very good of you to write as you did when you and jayzuz
if you can accept the excuse that I was so damn busy, so damn damn busy
adjusting to this life with a minimum of booze, you'd better, for it's the
only one you'll get,
Fungus life of Academica,huh? Boy, I hope it gets you. Wow.
I like teaching and my kids like me, but the gungho scholarship is a stick
up the old poop. It is enervating, it is levelling, it is the end.
If you conceive of literature as something to believe passionately
in, if you have lived poetry and cannot foreseee any other life than a
life in poetry, boother stay as far away as possible. This is a ratrace
far more deadly, perhaps, than any in the literary circles of N.Y. Here
no enthusiasm is tolerated, creative literature is suspect, and reputation
is based upon publications in scholarly journals. I know you may know this,
but it is absolutely true. How good a teacher you are doesn't count.
Now, if you have anything remotely resembling a prospect for a
xxxxgx career in the theatre, however irregular, take my advice and stick
to it. The university is no place for the creative writer. The people who
are interested in writing are without ideas or passion; they do not know
anything about life; they are very much afraid and that is why they teach
and talk writing. Talk writing! You see that shit in the coffeehouses.
Yap yap yap and no poetry, no feelings, no idea of and no belief in beauty.
Listen: without the outdoors around here I would have gone
abzie nuts, nuts, nuts. Fortunately for me, tho, fishing is superb and
I go three times or more a week. That way I preserve my sanity.
Aside from Venture, about who which I think you heard, only Arbor
has accepted my poems lately: the fact is, I only got around to sedding them
out again recently; the further fact is that I've written but one poem
since I got here, well maybe two. Now that my first quarter is over, however,
I shall be writing more.
The only people around here with whom I have established any
rapport, aside from a few university men interested in the outdoors but
otherwise without any conception of Balls, are the natives, who are deeply
alive, sensitive and dont give a goodgodamn for anything but hunting and
fishing and keeping the negroes in their place. Unbeknownst to them,
however, I have contacted some antisegregationist groups----and these
consist of people without depth who have but one passion. So it witx
is with the natives, mostly bred in the smoky mountains, I feel any
kinship; and it has been through an intimate daily contact with nature,
a relaarning of its mysteries, that Doris and I have been reborn into
a more sensuous existence---I am an expert fishermen and a skilled woods-
man, an ap aspiration I yearned for throughout all my citified life.
Moonshine helps too. Bootleg Seagrams sells for 650 a fifth,
and the bootleggers have been raided recently, so I drink mountain dew
and beer. Some I got hold of is like congac. Aside from movies and
drinking and the library there's nothing else to do around here. The
university theatrical productions are unbelivably primitive: Carousel
etc. Oak Ridge, tho , is putting on your boy Durenmatt? this weekend
and I'll see---The Visit?
I cannot possibly say all that I wish nor in my frazzled state
think very well, having graded 50 finals today. I propose that you
send me extra copies of your latest poems---I know no better way of
getting to know a man---and I shall send you mine, although I have none
at hand right now...and send some of Katzmans if you can....Watch that
Diane: she's no poetess, but she is ugly enough to want more than most
woman and sly enough to get it---I may be cruel but I found something
in her downright inhuman.

Good luck with Williams.....and with the stage managing--though that's
probably...and for christsake finish that thesis

Doris tenders her love and asks how you are making out with the douchebags
---the ladies

Give everybody affectionate thrusts.

Allen

Dear Robert Francis Lima:

If all I had to do was to sit on my fat ass and dawdle over a lousy thesis
and then cat all round town and read and write poems and not put up a
front and not correct papers and write term papers and kissass and watch
my lip, well by jaysuz I could write back as quick as you. But seeing as
how I love teaching, hate the scholarly horeshit that keeps my balls in
an uproar, fish no matter what the weather, try to write verses, keep
correspondence, keep sane, refrain from killing, then bb jaysuz its a
blooming wonder I am not gaga, paunched, witless, conservative, halfassed,
gungho, and etc.

Fortunately I am not. Fortunately you are not. And this period in which
you are roaming about the city meeting people, seeing things, taking it all
um, this period should be most instrumental in tempering your work. you
watch and see if it isn't.

I enjoyed the poems very much. aAsideFROMxENJOYMEXXX Aside from enjoyment
I believe that all are sucessful, in varying degrees. I should like to
see you extend yourself a little, not necessarily like Katzman's early
stuff, but retaining the same compression and intensity, the music perhaps,
only vastly more ambitious. Much more memmorably than any of these
was the poem about the night you showed me---I can still remember the
cadence of that repeated line, perhaps the heavy regular accent...
anyway I remember that, and do not see it in these.....you mentioned
in an earlier letter the possibility of see WCWilliams...have you
been reading him preparatory to these....o what a fucking academic
question!....o, o, o, shove all that wot as far as it can go and write
write write...that's the only way.

Send me Dan Klok's address. He is a guy with spirit, but he permits all
sorts of shit to cloud that spirit, and for me it was sometimes hard to
break it down. When I did wexwere great.

That reminds me; George Dargo ought to be back from the Holy Land, beard
and all. Whey dontcha look him up........and you poor bastards, dig this,
the Army put me in a control group and I dont have to attend meetings
just annual training in Georgia ha eat shit my hearties

But I get mine, right in the end, a long academic pole.

Dave Johnson knows Bly fairly intemately, but so hates the regular
literary world that it is hard to get him to do anything. I showed Bly
some of my earlier work and talked to him about Johnson. Since we all
know each other maybe we can do something. you're the idea men: save
us.

you

I'll bet such a deep immersion in Lorca will permit to get out of the
American bog eventually. Not that youre in it now, but you will be.
Boy, I am, I mean poetically.

There's so much to sayand so little time to say it in, and this being said
is waste, so reserve a couple of nights this summer for booze and talek
between us, and keep your notes coming, and I'll get mine off, when I
can, believe me they are wonderul fo receiver.

Allen

RR# 9 Deaderick Rd
Knoxville, Tenn

Dear Bob:

Well, I did lose your lousy list anyway. So what I now send
is of my own choosing, but a couple are of those you checked.

I did not write sooner because I was waiting for the list to
turn up and because I'm very busy with this here book I'm writing, called
American Wilderness---a tentative title---which formally is a socio-histor-
ical survey of the present outdoor surge. Informally, it is the architecture
of my rebellion to and from nature. While neither scholarly in conception
nor execution, it is so structured that someday I might turn it into a
ph.d thesis, inasmuchas it has a lot to say about American nature writing.
What I like about it is that I have been able to pour everything, literally
everything, into it---fishing, hunting, physcial and symbolic activities,
regional planning, sociology and anthropology, history debunking, nature
study, symbolic interpretation....enough! Well hell I8ve never written
abook like this before....much more difficult, and satisfying than, say,
fiction or subjection to regular scholarly discipline. By summer it should
be half done, and i shall have you read it.

I have no ggssip, no adventures to relate. I could sing you this
isolation, and nature....but nothing would do. I miss the city terribly.
But I'd rather get sentimental over it than debauched in it.

But tell me of your book; give me details, and I shall have the
library order at least two copies. I would like to see some of your
Lorca translations, sometime---I gues you saw the ones the sixties featured
a while back--they looked competent.

I am going to the reserve, not much, but will make summer camp this
year, and then I shall be outoutout.

As for the rest of the summer, I don't know what I will do.
I want to get to the city, but it is too expensive. Last summer we camped
all over the northeast, staying with many people, fishing and drinking.
This year Doris will be pregnant. I'd like to get into some sort of
community where people are not frozen by money or academica. Perhaps
you know something. Anyway, what are you going to do? Work? Why not
come down to his mindless haven? Probably you'll remain where you are.
And when I do come up, we will get a chance to talk, not that crazed
scene.

Write me if you find time, and tell all about yourself. You make
me happily jealous with your success, and rather proud.

Allen

Dear Bob:

I got your letter while I was preparing a few poems which I
wanted to send with the others and didn't. Some letter.

There is an article in Commentary this year sometime about the
graduate student in Liberal Arts. Everything it says my experience affirms;
you get yourself into an increasingly difficult position. Read it before
you decide upon entering academica. From what you say, I take it, you are
now eclectic and creative; you would have to submit to a foreign discipline
that might squash both---i.e. you will simply not have time to do all that
your own work dictates. Let me add two observations: most graduate students
have sought refuge from themselves and the world in their studies; they do
not necessarily like literature; in fact they hate it. the job offers them
prestige and security and pretense. I say most, but not all; there are
genuine scholars. But rare. Secondly, since you are successfully working
at your own stuff now, you need not capitulate fully--if you must associate
yourself with graduate studies, take a little bit at a time. For if you
start teaching freshman and start taking courses, you will be busy for at
least a year. Being a teaching assistant means, at least down here, a
harrowing process of proving yourself to your superiors. Proving yourself.
Love of literature, scholarship, integrity are diminished in direct ratio
as you proveyourself the image of what they want. Now, as for me, I feel
I do not want to prove myself to anybody; and having proved yourself to
yourself, how badly to you want to do it for others? A number of schools
around New York would present other opportunities. A friend of mine with
a MA from NYU walked last fall into the General Education dept of Queens
College and landed a 750 hour job of teaching the modern novel and modern
drama. I know that I could get a similar position. It is immensely easier
than teaching freshmen, which demand much work. I mirror my own discontents,
true. But since christmass I have deliberately avoided workand the result ing
freedom has permitted me to get a lot down, be healthier, eliminate my
neurotic clashes, and stop hating myself. I am on better relations with
the professors inashmch as I don't dislike them anymore......

I prove myself full of wind! One does what one must. Hell, I've
confidence in you, and I'm sure your grasp of the situation is at least as
good as mine, if not better.

I predict an upsurge in interest in Latin American Poetry in the
next few years. I guess since Fitts' anthology nothing has been done in
scale, and even with my slim reading I found Fitts' remarkably defieient.
I cannot account for the lack of interest in the S.A, literary world, but
I know I'd rather go there than Europe.....I found more kinship with
latin poets than with French or German, and certainly the homage due to
Spain for literature has shifted since the 30's to SA. The poets have
an experience that parallels ours in many ways, but the rich chafe where
they diverge is what I like. Two things stand in the way: the academieising
of those few SA poets who are affiliated with conservatiwiis and institutions,
by American institutions,and lack of adquate translation and review. US literay
journals ignore SA poetry entirely; why? I know why they ignore the more
controversial poets,who don't like the U.S. for simple reasons.

....Again, Wind!

These new poems you've sent are, I take it, newer. Some poems.
you can certainly sustain a piece in spite of words which I would
think otherwise inadmissable;+ something I can't do. and sustain
tone and style. I like the reality of which you write, infintely
plastic, infinitely referential. But I bet, having opened it up,
sometimes you feel yourself lost...yet I sense a fabric of experience
unbroken....in other words, dont stop.

Here's a couple more of mine, one a takeoff on highfalutin titles
written some time ago. Game I'm glad I can send you, it has an
interesting history of four acceptances and no publications, beginning four years ago when Mainstream accepted it and I pulled
out when I found myself being investigated, and ending with
Venture this spring, who had taken it once before but couldn't
publish it for a couple of years, and who now return it a second
time, though it was already at the printers, because their finances
are insoluble and they are quitting.

I am arranging an order for your book as well as deux magots and
the quarterly. The library usually does its ordering semiannully
but I think --I'm sure--I can get them to place an order now. And
the local bookstore.

You got me in a talky mood, tough shit. Whassamatta? you dean like
Rhee? Do you sense something strange there? I knew her four years
ago and joined some of her readings...I guess she something like
Wakoski, and I'll bet they dont like each other a damn. THERE is
is fellowship somewhere, and It's vital: I found it with Dave
Johnson, and nothing helped me more. I am suspicsious of people
who are poets and not human beings and who write poems about other
poets.....Someday we shall all be in New York together and then O
                                                              me
i have been terribly impressed with Bly ever since he wrote a very
kind letter years ago. But only now am I seeing the value of the
downtoned short lyric --unrhymed, syllabic, etc. I got a few which
are pretty good, and I'll send them along--not the stuff I now send.
I do not see any point in syllabics, unlessim is in repetitive
counterpoint: Gymnosophist is syllabic. So what?

You may not realize it, but you sound healthy.

Doris is not pregnant--we hadda buy insurance first: this month
we go under the guns: the feelings involved ought to make a good
story, but I dont feel literaryish.

If you ever see Jim Boyd, say hello. He's making his way thru poetry
groups and at present is very enthusiastic about them (Now, who wasn't)
But he's a nice guy and has a natural talent and real courage.

As long as you're producing the amount and quality you're doing now,
I trust you will get along damn well: you thrive on adversity.

Write only when you get a chance   *anyway good luck*
                                                    to you!

                                    Allen

Yes I'm interested in the publishing

Dear Bob

I will be in New York in two weeks and you and I will go out

and find some neon armpits to turn on (you really like that lousy poem?)
                be
I will in town a couple days and then alternately while staying at a

Abandoned Coast Guard Station 60 miles down the Jersey Coast where you

'll come and maybe stay with us a while.

I got a new teaching job at a little rinky dink college in

the Carolina mts where I'll make lotsaxxx lotsa money and my isolation

and exile complete.

I have placed an order for your book of Lorca with the University

library, which wont be able to send for it till after August when they
        be
will allocated more funds. I will also see that Carolina gets it.

Okay I won a poetry contest down here--50 bucks--and this

summer Beloit journal will publish three lousy poems of mine.

Well you sit tight till we come but if you aint around leave

word at your home and I'll get in touch wherever

                        ALLEN

oh yeah and The Massachussets Review is gonna do one or two too

Deaderick Rd, RR#9
Knoxville, Tenn
16 Oct

Dear Bob:

To have missed seeing you again lastsummer remains a deep regret. Chaos
and circumstance just would not permit it. Although I wanted to stay
around NY,my home is in the last stages of disintegration and I disin-
tegrate every time I get near it. Doubt and guilt and revulsion mastered
me.
Okay. Now back to Academica. Well this time I have it better; and bett
er yet I found in myself a greater will to work, a greater surety of purpose, a clearer vision. I am writing more than ever.
We have a house and a ridge behind it and behind that there are fields and
forest---the rural bit, but it serves this purpose: that while NY is
most stimulating it is in the end incestuous---I dont think I can work
there and remain true to myself. Too many phonies. There is still too
much that is phoney in me, and I gotta burn it out. I dig sophistication,
playin the lit game, etc, but this too is a fact: that every guy I know
is crippled by it one way or other.
Okay agin. Galway Kinnel and James Wright of recent poets have come to
mean more to me than any others, Kinnel for his vision and Wright for his
honesty. Purely partisan opinions. But I am in such a fantastic, inclusives
revolt against academic form and academic feeling in poetry that I have come
to dismiss 99% of recent stuff....I cant ignore my backgrounds and exalt
pure ideality divorced from the bloodymeat we walk on, and I cannot ignore
erudition, sophistication,and tradition, like the beats do. This may
mean a running fight with schizophrenia, but a good fight is better
than acquiesence.
And you you sophisticated bastard, what makes you tick? You're a marvel,
arising mysteriously from New York City, but holy hell I'll bet your screwed
here and there. Maybe you're best suited for a 100% adoption of the city,
instantly conveting its chaos into order....Maybe.
Let's see your recent poems....Let's see Katzman's recent stuff. I got a
shot note foom Doe Liddell crying about don's "goody"....O, you guys,
I think youtre equipped with overcoming the literary racket.
Last time I saw you, you mentioned some new magazines that have come out.
I'd appreciate it if you would sened me some addresses, along with a word
indicatedg whether they are rags, academic, nonpartisan, or beat. Iam
running out of markets; I have had alot of recent stuff accepted, but more
and more of the places I'm sending to are either going out of business or
are getting more academic
The reserves scared me shitless a while back, being in a Contraol group.
Down here they'fe taking guys not attached to any unit. And Im joining one.
3½ yrs more!

Sweet jeuses I'd like to talk to you! Write as soon as you can, even if
it short.

                                        Allen

Rte 1, Allen's Branch
Sylva, North Carolina
2 March

Dear Bob:

Well hell Robert we missed again-----again so much happened during
Christmass mostly drunkeness, but also a marriage (my sister's second),
eating of chaos, Etc/ Literally I blow up on vacations, this here ise-
lation gets me schizoid.

Right now we're marking time for a baby, due two days ago. Doris's.
Mine. Any minute the fun starts happening. And God knows when I'll
get another chance to say hello to you..... so how the hell are you?
We aren't decided on the name yet; I wanted Harold Hart but Doris didn't
dig Harry Planz, none of these literary names, Percy Byshhe, shit.
Maybe something cleancut, like Dana Brooks, or Lawrence Loring, or
Laurel Vale/......how dya like this junk, huh? Some of my cornball
students sport appelations like Almond, Seabright, and, I swear, a
girl called Queen Elizabeth Lowery.....in any event I'll drop
you a birth announcement with the name on it.

The academy gets us all. How do you like teaching? Yes, it keeps one
busy, gives a semblance of activity not altggether unworthwhile. A
nice safe place to hide in.

Me, I'd rather write. My capacity for work has grown, and swiftly is
approaching the time when I shall have to devote my major energies to
writing. I should like to return to NY, for a year or two, to get the
books out of the way, one on the wilderness, and one for poetry, which
I got so goddamn much of it swamps me. I'm sure I could pick up a
teaching job, and Doris wants to return to graduate work with a
scholarship. How do poets get along? Do you know where I can get a
writing fellowship, a grant, x art colony, or some such shit? O
I get so jealous sometimes, envy eats me up, it corrupts my responses
and fills me full of wind. Excuse me.

I hope you got your book out, Songs for an Apocalypse, wasn't it? Send
me a copy. If it isn't out, why not? How's Lorca doing? I dont know
whether University of Tenn ordered it. They want the price and publisher
down here at Western Carolina, so send me that.

I'm sending along some poems for yr perusal, stuff I got copies of.
I got many others but I can't get them to you, now. Please feel no
pressure to reply, you are up to yr ears in work I know.

The kid's gonna start flying any moment now, so excuse this mess and my
haste.

                                        Allen

Rte 1, Sylva, N.C.
may

Dear Bob:

Some book.

Just finished it, all of it. Nice, very nice writing, even, concise, versatile, solid. Damn pleasant to read. Nothing hack about it, ine sustained leap, look's easy but I know how long & hard you sweated it, geezuz it's an achievement..

What's best about it, for me, is how it makes Lorca all of a piece, I mean brings the poetry in, into perspective, even Nueva York—the images, the feeling. I doubt from now on I'll miss an opportunity to see any the plays, now. And I want to read them too.

Well, we'll be in NY end of may, thereabouts, maybe earlier. I'll call soon as we get in. Don't bother to answer this unless you are going out of NY.

Some letter, too. As for my work, it's goming along but my poetry has a long way to go—maybe. I haven't done some things I want to do—it takes courage, really courage, and I must build it up. Sure I get published, this year pretty hot, the Nation, Poetry, Yugen, among others. But much has been lucky accident....maybe next year. American Wilderness, when I get to it, moves, but not yet finished.

Hang on to Everson and Gilbert, they sound great. Ane thanks again
'm
for the book. I rather proud of it.

This summer we gonna try to stay in NY and see a lot of you, fur sure.

Allen

Summer address:

General Delivery
Sag Harbor, new York
July

Dear Bob,

your generous letter came just as I was plunging into summer, &
though still plunging I have recovered enough. Here we live, I take
it, much like you, with a jeep, a runabout, a shack, equipt. all
over, & each dawn I fish, then work unless—as up to a week ago—
I get some chore to do—eat, drink & go fishing again; on weekends,
this being near east hampton, there's an active social life, with
artists like de kooning & writers—mostly the New Yorker type, though
Armand Schwerner, Blackburn & si perchik & others are about—having
cookouts & parties etc. In Sag Steinbeck works in the morning & gets
drunk on a yacht in the afternoon; I've talked fishing with him, though
if I see him this week I will put Yestuvenche's demand as reported in
last Sunday's Times that he speak out againsthe war—He's a grouch, a
tough, incredibly stupid giant of a man.

As for my own work I am chiefly integrating, experimenting. This
past year I finished a long poem which pretty much did what I had been
wanting to do for ten years & which, though for a while left me exhausted,
has given me more to work with. I work out some prose, but have great
difficulty with it because I can't work from myself in it, and adopting
a posture, an attitude is impossible because transient.

I have given all thoughts up of editing for the summer, just don't want to
but probably by Fall will be full of ambitions, & am projecting venture
involving publishing some books of poetry, putting a mag devoted substantially
to socially oriented poetry, & pushing my weight around in the NY reading
scenze —which I did a deal of last winter, it was easy, fun, I like the
working association of poets such as NY offers, but for a while I've just
had enough of it, & scarcely see anyone.

Specifically, The Chelsea R asked me to edit a civil rights insue, Mondadori
& Einaudi sent their NY agent to see me about a east european edition of the
anthology (vague; i didnut push, but could), have a guy in europe who can for
200 put out proofread & all 500-1000 copies of book of poetry, Dersky Gallery
wants me to edit luxurious edition of prints & poems, people in Queens C
want to start poetry circuit—have three, four other colleges, each with
appropriations, probably help run St Mark's readings—we had everybody
there this winter & spring, from Ginsburg to Auden. But right now, jack,
I dont want to follow thru any. If you have any ideas running along these
lines let me hear from you. I've operated as a good PR man & organizer,
but I'm not, now a good editor, & am after all interested finally mostly
in my art, the rest is escape, fun, & for the moment I'm fishing.—your
address indicates the Brodhead, a great trout stream, whacha go try.
    I'll happily send you the book whenever it comes out—sometime in the
fall or winter—no hurry. I urge you to settle, when you get the Ph.D.,
in the NY or Berkeley area—there's so many more opportunities—& do lets get
together—regards & love from laurie & deries & me to all

CHELSEA

4 / 21

Dear Bob,

good to hear from you, good to hear that so much is
underway.

Alan Swallow died two weeks before my book was
to come out, &he had the anthology with all materials
too, over which we were then coming to terms....the
estate isn't settled, the whole bloody mess is, as far
as I can make out, up in the air. Balls.

I look forward to seeing a book of your xown
work, & to those others, especially the latin american
anthology--which I think I told you is much needed----
& the fascinating thing about Spain's celtic backgrounds,
of which mueh of the recent archeology should lend light.

I'll have a small book out bext month by
frank murphy, of what I call dirty poems, entitled
Studs Song, subtitled fuckaround poems; he wants to
test the censorship &obscenity forces, but it's
unlikely he been called out. I hope to get your
a copy, but we've yet to confront the mails.

Otherwise, since I last saw you, it's been
the roughest time of my life: misfortune, deaths,
poverty, all that, had me down constantly....better
not, hopefully, & thankfully Doris & Laurie have been
& are well.

& I trust your family is fine.

Best

CHELSEA

General Delivery
Sag Harbor, New York
5 / 30

Dear Bob,

Thanks for the poems: I liked them...but I can't see how I could any one of them for this rather specialized project. they are, simply, not concrete enough in the context as I have built it up —meaning that the poems I seek must be extremely concrete & specific & avoid nearly altogether the general & the abstract.

Yes, the Ammons' issue will come out eventaally & is probably being published right now.

Sorry to be so dogmatic, but that's the way I'm forced to see it.

My best to the family & I look forward to seeing your poems in Ahhanor.

best,
Allen

BOX 242, OLD CHELSEA STATION, NEW YORK 11, N.Y.

RABASSA

36 Red Creek Road
Hampton Bays, N. Y. 11946
January 20x, 1975

Dear Bob:

I have waited too long to write you and thank you and
everyone else for such a good time at Penn State. In recompense
I enclose something that may seem familiar since a great many
of the ideas were batted around there during my stay. I have
also written Stanley Weintraub and Martin Stabb concerning the
possibilities of Clarice Lispector's coming to lecture. She
wrote me sometime back and is interested in coming up for a
visit and some talks and I have been trying to round some things
up for her.

Things go on with all their pressure. Right now I am
working on Cortázar's LIBRO DE MANUEL and waiting for García
Márquez' new novel to surface finally. Also, next semester I
shall be teaching nothing but translation, with a course for
undergrads at Queens and another at the Graduate School, both
under the aegis of Comp Lit. We might be able to get something
started, especially since PEN is dissatisfied with the way
Columbia has been handling their joint translation center.

I hope we come together again sometime soon and meanwhile
may the new year be prosperous for you and yours.

Abrazos,

Gregory Rabassa

READ

STONEGRAVE HOUSE, Stonegrave, York.
England.

11th October, 1967.

Dear Professor Lima,

I was very glad to receive your letter of
October 4. The position about the volume in the
Bollingen Series to be devoted to Unamuno's poetry
is that I have been asked to collect specimen
translations from several sources and to decide on
their merits as English verse (for I am no Spanish
scholar). I should therefore be very glad if you
would be willing to submit some examples of your
translations of verse to me - they need not
necessarily be of Unamuno's works but it would make
the comparison easier if they were.

When I have reviewed the whole field of
possible translators I hope I might then be able to
invite you to take a more specific part in the
enterprise.

Yours sincerely,

Herbert Read.

Professor R. Lima,
College of the Liberal Arts,
THE PENNSYLVANIA STATE UNIVERSITY,
211 Sparks Building,
University Park,
Pennsylvania 16802.
U.S.A.

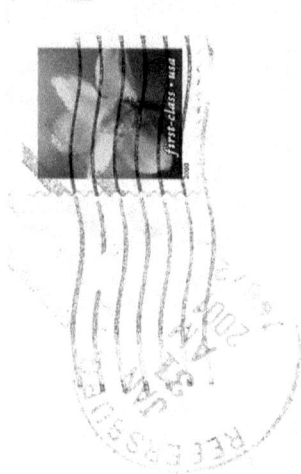

Robert Lima
Spanish / Portuguese
352 N. Burrowes
University PK
PA 16802

Do not write below this line

FIRST CLASS MAIL

Elegant beauty and shopping on Royal Poinciana Way.
Photo © Warren Flagler

24 Jan '01

Dear Bob,
Fascinating offprint, so congratulations! I'm basking here while finishing my big novel set in Ancient Egypt (Cheops, Giza, et al.). It may be your cup of hemlock. Weather's divine: highly recommended. I trust PSU's treating you well. We are bunkmates, I see, in Who's Who in the World. All best regards

Dan

309

THE PENNSYLVANIA STATE UNIVERSITY
246 SPARKS BUILDING
UNIVERSITY PARK, PENNSYLVANIA 16802

College of the Liberal Arts
Department of English

Area Code 814
865-6381

9 May 1967

Dear Mr. Lima:

I have asked our secretaries to run off a xerox of
my Greene chapter (its appearance in my collection was its
first). They are busy just now, so this will take a little
time; but it will come, and I wish your friend the best of
luck with his dissertation. I hope the chapter will be of
use to him.

Yours sincerely,

Paul West

THE PENNSYLVANIA STATE UNIVERSITY
Department of English

From: Paul West

To: Robert Lima

Bob:

I gather that Diane Ackerman has now
sent you a formal application concerning
a position in Comp. Lit. I have just
heard that she has just won the prestigious
Cornell Corson French Prize ("for the
most distinguished scholarly essay on
a French author"). Her topic was André
Gide. She'll probably send you a bit
of paper to add to her <u>vita</u>, but I
thought I'd let you know anyway. I know
of no PSU student who has collected so
many honors at an Ivy League campus --
indeed, she looks like sweeping the
board. Maybe the French Dept. might
be interested in her too -- she's
certainly broad in scope!

                              Best,

                              Paul

THE PENNSYLVANIA STATE UNIVERSITY
Department of English

Bob:

Here is Diane Ackerman's

vita, a copy of which I've also

passed to Leonard Rubinstein.

I do hope we can work something

out. And I enjoyed our chat

the other day (thanks again for

serving on the committee!).

Best,

Paul West

Paul West

20 Hill Top Avenue
Wilmslow, Cheshire
England

25 November 1970

Dear Bob,

I seem to recall you now administer
Comp. Lit. and I've just realised it may
be time to submit my list for CL 570 (Spring
Term). So would you please hand on the
following to the Comp. Lit. secretary?

André Breton, NADJA, Grove Press

Abram Tertz, THE TRIAL BEGINS, Vintage

Jakov Lind, LANDSCAPE IN CONCRETE, Crest

Jean Genet, MIRACLE OF THE ROSE, Grove

Julio Cortázar, BLOW-UP, Collier

Italo Calvino, COSMICOMICS, Collier

Witold Gombrowicz, FERYDURKE, Grove

Alain Robbe-Grillet, MAISON DE RENDEZVOUS, Grove

Samuel Beckett, STORIES AND TEXTS FOR NOTHING,
Grove.

All paperback. I'll add one more in January,
probably something by Solzhenitsyn, which
I'm sure I've mis-spelled! I've just finished
a new novel and am feeling rather pleased
with it so far. I hope you thrive. See
you in the new year.

Yours,

Paul West

THE PENNSYLVANIA STATE UNIVERSITY
Department of English

Bob:

Help! The following appears in Beckett's
MORE PRICKS THAN KICKS; is it as obscene
as it seems?

No me jodas en el suelo

Como si fuera una perra,

Que con esos cojonazos

Me echas en el coño tierra.

Many thanks.

Paul West

Bob,

I'm giving a Colloquium
Tuesday night, 8 p.m. Kern:
a reading of 3 fictions.
There's a party afterwards at
Charley Mann's, 416 South
Allen. Do come if you can.

Bob:

10 Feb.

Thank you from us both for the voluptuous
poems, which we'll be looking at closely at
the end of term. I hope you enjoy the purple
patch this ribbon makes!
That was a lovely evening, and many thanks
to you both. All best,

Paul West

126 Texas Lane
Ithaca, N. Y. 14850
607-257-3166

15 March 1985

Dear Bob,

How very good to hear from you today; I miss my friends
there, few as they may be. And it is hard to sit around,
hour after hour, doing the right thing, knowing that it
will make you well if you keep fairly still for another
month. Agh. Anyway, West is trying.

I looked at The Snow Leopard, wincing a bit, not least
because some of the poems seemed written a century ago, and
thought that one of the following might do: Theory of
Flight (26), Peter's Dream (39), Ball-Park in Winter (59).
Please choose, and by all means Americanize the spelling.

Did you know that I'm to receive a prize from the American
Academy and Institute of Arts and Letters in May? Out of the
blue. All being well, I fly in ad receive it from their
president, John Kenneth Galbraith, on the 15th. Just what
a convalescent needs! The money is good too.

Again, many thanks for calling. I enjoyed our chat and I
promise to keep in touch. See you soon, the gods willing.

Regards,

Institute for the Arts & Humanistic Studies
Ihlseng Cottage   (814) 865-0495

126 Texas Lane, Ithaca, NY 14850
28 June 1985
Dear Bob,

Belated but heartfelt thanks for
your note about the Academy award.
I went in for it, and had a wonderful
day being fussed. Ran into Carlos
Fuentes there too, who was also
getting something. Jacki-O was at
the next luncheon table, looking
(Diane says) a bit worn. Then I got
applause the next day when I went in
to Doubleday (who ran an ad in the
Times). It was fun, and the weeks
after it have been a bit anti-climactic
and I must learn that every day is
not Xmas. I'm getting my new novel
ready for the printer at the same
time as trying to start a new book.

THE PENNSYLVANIA STATE UNIVERSITY, UNIVERSITY PARK, PA 16802

Diane's <u>On Extended Wings</u> is due out
on Aug. 1, I think -- a lovely
rhapsody to flying.

As for health, I guess you know I had
that ❧ TIA back in last August and
then, this March, had a pacemaker put
in as the ticker was down to 30 a min.
Am feeling great now, though the scare
was gigantic.

All health to <u>you</u>, and I hope you are
having a productive summer.

If you are there!

I hear a poem is to be bussed, but I
don't know which one.

      Best,

      Dave

      Paul West

Institute for the Arts & Humanistic Studies

Ihlseng Cottage   (814) 865-0495

Bob:

Many thanks for The Lamp of Marvels,
into which I have already dipped,
with enthusiasm. It's full of
sly riches. They've made a pretty
book of it too. I'll be
reciprocating (like an engine) in
a few weeks, with a copy of
Sheer Fiction.

All best,

Paul West

126 Texas Lane

Ithaca, N.Y. 14850

607-257-3166

4 January 1990

Dear Bob,

Good to hear from you, with poems too; I still like
"Sheet Metal" best, I think (is "screwd" deliberate?),
but your snow geese spoke to me, and now I've put the
florilegium on Diane's desk. She came back from
Albatrossing in Japan with three broken ribs; that was
weeks ago and now she seems okay again. Imagine. Her
long book on the Senses will be out in May, from Random,
who are now my own publishers as well and will be doing
my Ripper novel late this year. I'd had it with Doubleday, though I liked the junior folk there.

Hey, that's great about your article on PW -- there is
a delay, I gather, so you'll have time to hone if you wish.
They publish books too and I gather they just had too much
on their hands. Never mind: I look forward, and I thank
you heartily. Yes: lunch. I'll be there next semester,
though to kick it off I have an IRS audit, which means I
have been an abacus for several weeks. What a year it was:
good creatively, but full of disasters -- my mother died
in her sleep at 94, which cut me keenly as she and I
were very close. Nothing wrong with her; the engine just
wore out. I am trying to write about her, having already
put her into print a lot. Nothing helps: it's awful.
Maria Thomas, our own student who published 2 books of
fiction, was killed in that Ethiopian air crash, and May
Swenson, D.'s mentor, died of asthma. Thank God for 1990.

You sound chipper, but I can't believe you are ready for
the fray. I confess I find my mind wandering to the book
in progress when I should be holding forth. 570 will always
be fun, but I fear I become reclusive, letting literature
talk to me in its eerie way. Diane says thank you for your
kind remarks on her inspiration squib. They chopped it up,
of course, but the original will be in the Senses book.
Oh, I have a new Stauffenberg for you. Will send or bring.
I'll be in touch.

Love from us both,

2 October 1995
Dear Bob, Thank you so much for your new book, which I look forward to reading in the sun as the season wanes. Maybe now they'll give you a Pugh. I'll reciprocate with a novel soon, one some reviewers call obscene! Just imagine. All is well here, tho' D. broke her foot this summer. She's ok now. With best regards, Dave

FENIMORE HOUSE MUSEUM
Cooperstown, New York

Tsimshian Rattle c. 1850

Rattles such as this are said to have a calming effect on the unseen spirits and are used by the Tsimshian shamans of the Northwest coast to invoke spiritual assistance. Eugene and Clare Thaw Collection, photo by John Bigelow Taylor. T173.

Published by C/Harrison Conroy Co., 800, Graham Ave., Charlotte, NC 28203

Printed in U.S.A.

An aerial view of the Royal Poinciana Plaza, an

Palm Beach

18 Aprie 2000

Dear Bob,

I know nothing of academic agents, but you should call Mark Seinfelt, former student of mine, and tell him I asked him to tell you the name + no. of his agent, who may know something. Mark's at 814 342 0312.

Lovely here, where I have productively been since December. Go back to Ithaca. Friday to I hope a warmer Ithaca. Good luck. Yours aye,

Dave

BIOGRAPHICAL DATA
ON THE CORRESPONDENTS

Harold ALTMAN
(1924-2003)

The New York-born printmaker studied at the Art Students League, The Cooper Union and L'Academie de la Grande Chaumiere in Paris. He served in Europe in a camouflage unit during WWII. He had over 300 solo exhibitions and his work is in the collections of New York's Museum of Modern Art, the Whitney Museum and the Brooklyn Museum, as well as in major museums and corporate collections throughout the world. He was the recipient of two Guggenheims, a Fulbright, a National Institute of Arts and Letters Award, and a grant from the National Endowment for the Arts.

A.R. AMMONS
(1926-2001)

The North Carolinian poet served on a destroyer escort in the Pacific during WWII and it was on that ship that he wrote his first poems. After attending graduate school he worked as an educator and as a sales executive but ultimately became poet-in-residence at Cornell University. He won the first of two National Book Awards in 1973 for his *Collected Poems 1951-1971*, the Bollingen Prize and a MacArthur Fellowship.

John BALABAN
(1943-)

The Philadelphia-born poet is the author of twelve books of poetry and prose. He has won the Lamont Prize of the Academy of American

Poets, the National Poetry Series Selection, the William Carlos Williams Award, a Guggenheim Fellowship and the National Artist Award of Phi Kappa Phi. His works have twice been nominated for the National Book Award.

Anna BALAKIAN
(1915-1997)

Born of Armenian parents in Constantinople (now Istanbul), she came to the U.S. at 11 and received the M.A. and Ph.D. from Columbia University. Her career was in French and Comparative Literature, mainly at New York University, chairing the latter discipline for eight years. She did much to promote that discipline through works on Symbolism and Surrealism, books that set the standard for scholarship in those fields.

Willis BARNSTONE
(1927-)

A Maine Yankee, he studied at Bowdoin, Columbia and Yale, taught in Greece after its civil war, went to China during the Cultural Revolution, and taught in Buenos Aires during the "Dirty War." Four times a nominee for the Pulitzer Prize, he has published extensively in poetry, religion, children's books, songs, and memoirs, along with translations from the Hebrew, Spanish, Chinese, French, Latin and Greek. He has received Guggenheim, NEA and NEH grants.

Marvin BELL
(1937-)

Born in Brooklyn, NY, he is a poet and university professor, long affiliated with the Iowa Writers Workshop. His second book of poetry earned the Lamont Poetry Selection of the Academy of American

Poets. He is the author of nineteen books of poetry. In 2000 he was appointed the first poet laureate of Iowa.

Robert BLY
(1926-)

A Minnesotan of Norwegian extraction, he served in the U.S. Navy during WWII, went to Harvard and lived precariously in New York City. After two years at the Iowa Writers Workshop, he held a Fulbright to Norway, discovering there the works of the Chileans Neruda and Vallejo. He founded the journal *The Fifties* and its sequels to promote translations of poets unknown in the U.S. His book *The Light Around the Body* won the National Book award and *Iron John. A Book About Men* is the cornerstone of the international Mythopoetic Men's Movement. In 2008 he was named Minnesota's first poet laureate.

Andrei CODRESCU
(1946-)

The Romanian poet, novelist, filmmaker, and editor, has lived in the U.S. since 1966, earning citizenship in 1981. After teaching in Baltimore at Johns Hopkins, he taught at Louisiana State University, from which he retired in 2009. He edits the journal *Exquisite Corpse* and is a commentator on NPR's program "All Things Considered."

Ronald (Ronnie) DELANY
(1935-)

The renowned Irish athlete attained international fame when he set an Olympic record in the 1500 meters in Melbourne and was featured on the cover of *Sports Illustrated Magazine*. He was the first Irishman to win an Olympic title since 1932 and became a national hero. He continued his winning ways at Villanova University, attaining four AAU titles in the mile, and three NCAA titles. In the process of winning forty consecutive indoor races, he broke the World Indoor Record for the Mile three times. He was granted the Freedom of Dublin City in 2006.

Paul ENGLE
(1908-1991)

The long-time director of the Iowa Writers Workshop and co-founder, with Hua-ling Nieh, of the International Writing Program, he was a noted poet, editor and novelist. His first poetry collection appeared in the Yale Series of Younger Poets and he went on to become a Rhodes Scholar. For his indefatigable devotion to bringing international writers to the University of Iowa, he was nominated for the 1976 Nobel Peace Prize.

David IGNATOW
(1914-1997)

A Brooklyn-born poet of great range and humor, he was also an important editor of name literary journals, among them, *American Poetry Review, Beloit Poetry Journal, Chelsea Magazine, and The Nation.* He was president of the Poetry Society of America for four years. Among his awards are the Bollingen Prize, two Guggenheims, the John Steinbeck Award, the Shelley Memorial Award, the Frost Medal, and the William Carlos Williams Award. For a lifetime of creative writing, he was awarded the National Institute of Arts and Letters Award.

Stanley KAUFFMANN
(1916-2013)

The noted New York film and theatre critic wrote for *The New Republic* since 1958 and published numerous books in these areas. He was for many years an actor and stage manager with the Washington Square Players, wrote plays, and published seven novels. He has also written for *The New York Times*, and *Saturday Review*, as well as for academic journals. He has won the George Jean Nathan Award, two Ford Foundation fellowships, an Emmy Award, a Rockeffer Fellowship, and a Guggenheim.

Anthony KERRIGAN
(1918-1991)

Noted as a poet and translator of major works by Spanish and Latin American writers, he won a 1973 National Book Award for translating Unamuno's *The Tragic Sense of Life*. He also brought to readers of English numerous works by Jorge Luis Borges, José Ortega y Gasset, Pablo Neruda, and Camilo José Cela. The National Endowment for the Arts awarded him a $40,000 grant for his lifetime contributions to American culture.

Denise LEVERTOV
(1923-1997)

A prominent poet, she emigrated to the United States from her native England in 1948 and taught poetry at numerous American universities, including Stanford. She was a stalwart at many Greenwich Village poetry venues in the 1960s. She published fifteen volumes of poetry and penned the introduction to *Seventh Street. Poems of "Les Deux Megots,"* the only anthology of the 1960s New York poetry scene.

Morgan LLYWELYN
(1937-)

An American writer who lives in Ireland, she has devoted a great deal of her writing to the Celtic traditions in such novels as *The Horse Goddess, Bard: The Odyssey of the Irish,* and *Brian Boru: Emperor of the Irish.* She has written over 34 novels and other historical works on Ireland. She has served as Chair of the Irish Writer's Union. In 1999 she was named Exceptional Celtic Woman of the Year by Celtic Woman International.

Fred R. MILLER
(1903-1967)

He was the editor of the proletarian story magazine *Blast,* which, although short-lived, published such writers as William Carlos Williams. in 1950, he published *Gutbucket and Gossamer. A Short Story* with The Alicat Bookshop Press's Outcast Chapbooks, a series which published Henry Miller, Anais Nin, D.H. Lawrence, and William Carlos Williams, who recommended it to the press.

Allen PLANZ
(1937-2010)

Having served in the U.S. Army Reserves at Ft. Dix, NJ, he returned to New York's Greenwich Village poetry scene. He taught at various universities and became the first Poet-in-Residence at the Walt Whitman Birthplace. From 1969 through 1973, he was Poetry Editor of *The Nation.* He was a Coast Guard licensed captain on Long Island but continued to be active as a presenter of his poetry in person and in videos.

Gregory RABASSA
(1922-)

Born into a Cuban-emigré family in Yonkers, New York, he served during WWII as a cryptographer for the OSS and thereafter earned a doctorate at Columbia University, where he taught for twenty-years before taking a position at Queens College. He is the renowned translator of Julio Cortazar's *Hopscotch* (for which he received the National Book Award for Translation), Mario Vargas Llosa, José Lezama Lima, and Gabriel García Márquez's *One Hundred Years of Solitude*, among many other Latin American and Spanish authors. He was awarded the National Medal of Arts in 2006 by President George W. Bush.

Sir Herbert READ
(1893-1968)

British-born, he was a poet, literary critic, essayist, and a proponent of modern art. A decorated hero in WWI, he went on to write of his war experiences. But his interests were broad, as his varied publications attest, including works on anarchy, politics, art and artists, literature, and education. He was knighted in 1953.

Mother TERESA
(1910-1997)

Born in Macedonia, she early-on felt the call to be a missionary and after training in Dublin was sent to India to teach. In time, she received permission to work among the poor in the slums of Calcutta, her commitment extending from 1948 until her death. Her selfless work made it possible for her to found her own order, the Missionaries of Charity, which has become a worldwide congregation of dedicated women and men. In 1979 she was awarded the Nobel Peace Prize. The Catholic Church has raised her to the level of Blessed.

Paul WEST
(1930-)

British-born, he made the U.S. his home and taught until his retirement here. He is the author of numerous novels, poetry, memoirs and criticism, publishing with major houses and in the world's leading literary journals. Among his honors are the American Academy of Arts and Letters Award, the Lannon Prize for Fiction, the Grand Prix Halperine-Kaminsky Award, the Aga Khan Prize, and being named a Literary Lion of The New York Public Library.

INDEX OF PROPER NAMES

ABOUT THE AUTHOR

ROBERT LIMA, poet, critic, bibliographer, playwright and translator, is Professor Emeritus of Spanish and Comparative Literatures at The Pennsylvania State University, as well as Fellow Emeritus of the Institute for the Arts and Humanistic Studies. He is an Academician of the Academia Norteamericana de la Lengua Española and a Corresponding Member of the Real Academia Española. He has been honored as a Distinguished Alumnus by Villanova University, inducted into the Enxebre Orden da Vieira in Spain and named Knight Commander in the Order of Queen Isabel of Spain by His Majesty King Juan Carlos I.

Among his books are *The Theatre of García Lorca* (Las Américas, 1963), *Ramón del Valle-Inclán* (Columbia UP, 1972), *An Annotated Bibliography of Valle-Inclán* (Penn State U. Libraries, 1972), *Dos ensayos sobre teatro español de los veinte* (U. de Murcia, 1984), and *Valle-Inclán. The Theatre of His Life* (Missouri UP, 1988). He has translated Valle-Inclán's aesthetico-mystical treatise *The Lamp of Marvels* (Lindisfarne Press, 1986) and his selection of short dramas *Savage Acts: Four Plays* (Estreno, 1993). His most recent books are *Dark Prisms. Occultism in Hispanic Drama* (UP of Kentucky, 1995; also in paperback, 2009) and *Valle-Inclán. El teatro de su vida* (Editorial Nigra, Spain, 1995), *Ramón del Valle-Inclán: An Annotated Bibliography* (Grant & Cutler, 1999), *The Dramatic World of Valle-Inclán* (Boydell & Brewer, 2003), *Stages of Evil. Occultism in Western Theatre and Drama* (UP of Kentucky), published in December 2005, and *The International Bibliography of Studies on the Life and Works*

336

of Ramón del Valle-Inclán (2008). The Spanish version of *Dark Prisms* has been published in 2010 in Madrid by Editorial Fundamentos.

He selected for publication, edited, and translated Barrenechea's *Borges the Labyrinth Maker* (NYU Press, 1965), the first critical study on Borges in English, as well as edited and contributed to *Borges and the Esoteric*, a special issue of *Crítica Hispánica* (Duquesne UP, 1993). He has published well over one hundred fifty articles in a variety of fields.

In 1974 he created "Surrealism–A Celebration," a multi-faceted event in honor of the 50th anniversary of the Surrealist Movement. Included were theatre productions, music concerts, films, displays of rare publications, paintings, sculpture, jewelry and other objects, presentations by leading art historians, artists, and literary critics. And a Surrealist banquet. Elements of these events appeared in a special 1975 issue of *Journal of General Education*, which he edited.

Over four hundred of his poems have appeared throughout the U.S. and abroad in periodicals, anthologies, and in his poetry collections *Fathoms* (1981), *The Olde Ground* (1985), *Mayaland* (1992), *Sardinia / Sardegna* (2000), *Tracking the Minotaur* (2003), *The Pointing Bone* (2008), *The Rites of Stone* (2010), *Self* (2012), and *Por caminos errantes* (2014). *Poems of Exile and Alienation* (with Teresinka Pereira, 1976) and *Corporal Works* (1985) are two of his chapbooks.

He has been elected to membership in PEN International and the Poetry Society of America. From March through August 2004, Penn State University Libraries exhibited "The Poetic World of Robert Lima," a retrospective of his poetry career from 1955 to the present. The first poetry competition by Phi Kappa Phi was won by his poem "Astrals," which appears in the honor society's journal *Forum*.

His biography appears in *Who's Who in the World, Who's Who in America, Who's Who in the East, World Who's of Authors,* and other creative writing directories in the U.S. and abroad.

Homepage: http://www.personal.psu.edu/RXL2

www.ingramcontent.com/pod-product-compliance
Lightning Source LLC
Chambersburg PA
CBHW060326100426
42812CB00003B/891